DATE DUE

AP 19 '99			
NO 4 '99			
NO 30 '99			
DE 1 9			
DE 17 '05			

DATE DUE

AP 4 01			
JUN 1 1 2001			
FE 7 02			
JE 9 '03			

DEMCO 38-296

ADULT PROTECTIVE SERVICES
Research and Practice

ADULT PROTECTIVE SERVICES
Research and Practice

Edited by

BRYAN BYERS, PH.D.

Sociology
Valparaiso University
Valparaiso, Indiana

and

JAMES E. HENDRICKS, PH.D.

Criminal Justice and Criminology
Ball State University
Muncie, Indiana

CHARLES C THOMAS • PUBLISHER
Springfield • Illinois • U.S.A.

Published and Distributed Throughout the World by

CHARLES C THOMAS • PUBLISHER

2600 South First Street

Springfield, Illinois 62794-9265

With THOMAS BOOKS *careful attention is given to all details of manufacturing
and design. It is the Publisher's desire to present books that are satisfactory as to
their physical qualities and artistic possibilities and appropriate for their particular
use.* THOMAS BOOKS *will be true to those laws of quality that assure a good
name and good will.*

Printed in the United States of America
SC-R-3

Library of Congress Cataloging-in-Publication Data

Adult protective services : research and practice / edited by Bryan
   Byers and James E. Hendricks.
      p.   cm.
   Includes bibliographical references and index.
   ISBN 0-398-05873-3
   1. Abused aged — Services for — United States.   2. Aged — United
States — Abuse of.   I. Byers, Bryan.   II. Hendricks, James E. (James
Earnest)
   HV6626.3.A4   1993
   362.6 — dc20   93-4492
                                                                        CIP

CONTRIBUTORS

Bryan Byers, Ph.D.
Steven Chermak, Ph.D.
Beverly Favre, Ph.D.
Lawrence H. Gerstein, Ph.D.
James E. Hendricks, Ph.D.
Richard A. Lamanna, Ph.D.
Jerome McKean, Ph.D.
M. Steven Meagher, Ph.D.
Janet Mickish, Ph.D.
Shirley Salem, Ph.D.
Dena Wiese, B.A.
David Wilson, M.S.W.
Timothy F. Wynkoop, M.A.

A brief biographical sketch of each author may help one understand the author's perspective. It also helps establish their area of expertise and the reasons for their work being included in the book.

Bryan Byers is a faculty member at Valparaiso University in the Sociology Department. His previous academic experience include faculty positions at the University of Notre Dame and St. Mary's College. His previous field experiences include positions as an adult protective service investigator. His publications include numerous articles and a book.

James E. Hendricks is a professor of criminal justice and criminology at Ball State University. Previously, he was a member of the University of Tennessee and the Southern Illinois University faculties. His field experience includes the following positions: police officer, chief deputy sheriff, director of a victim advocate program, correctional counselor, and mental health worker. In addition, Dr. Hendricks served as a combat marine corpsman in the Vietnam conflict. His publications (2 books, 30 articles) focus on crisis intervention, law enforcement, and victim advocacy. Dr. Hendricks is a diplomate and certified crisis intervener of the American Board of Examiners in Crisis Intervention. He is also a member of the Education and Training Committee of the International Association of Chiefs of Police.

Dena Wiese is a graduate of the Criminal Justice Department at Ball State University. She serves as a victim advocate in Indiana.

Janet Mickish is executive director of the Colorado Coalition on Domestic Violence. Her twenty years of field experience includes work in domestic violence and rape/sexual assault crisis intervention. Prior to her service on the coalition she was employed as a criminal justice faculty member at Ball State University, Muncie, Indiana. As a result of her teaching, research, and consulting work, Dr. Mickish has enjoyed national recognition.

Richard Lamanna is a professor of sociology at the University of Notre Dame, where he has been for 27 years. During the past four years, Dr. Byers and Dr. Lamanna have conducted extensive research in the area of adult protective services.

M. Steven Meagher is a faculty member in criminal justice at Ball State University. His previous field experience includes being a police officer and later as deputy director of public safety in Louisville (Jefferson County) as well as director of a correctional half-way house in Louisville. Dr. Meagher also served as a full time consultant to criminal justice/social service agencies (on a national level) for years.

Steven Chermak is a faculty member in criminal justice at Indiana University. Dr. Chermak received his Ph.D. from SUNY–Albany and his knowledge of the criminal justice/social service system makes him well suited for chapter five.

Jerome B. McKean is a faculty member in criminal justice at Ball State University. His previous academic experience includes a faculty position at Florida Atlantic University. Dr. McKean's previous field experience includes work as a resident manager in a half-way house.

David L. Wilson is Assistant Professor of Social Work at Florida Atlantic University. Dr. Wilson is a social worker by training and has a keen understanding of social services systems.

Shirley Salem and Beverly Favre are faculty members at Southern University, New Orleans in criminal justice and social work respectively. Their combined expertise in criminal justice and social work make for their unique contribution.

Timothy F. Wynkoop is completing his doctorate in Counseling Psychology at Ball State University. His previous field experience includes work in community mental health and as a psychologist (six years) with the Texas Department of Corrections. His coauthor, **Lawrence H. Gerstein** is a professor of counseling psychology at Ball State University. He has held numerous counseling psychology positions (family and clinical). Dr. Gerstein's publications (45) are in various aspects of psycho-social behavior.

To Peggy and Nancy
and
To the practitioners and academicians
in the field of Adult Protective Services.

INTRODUCTION

Adult protective service (APS) laws have proliferated throughout the United States over the last ten years in an effort to combat elder and adult abuse and neglect. With these legal changes has come the need to examine research and practice issues pertinent to this area. Adult Protective Services refers to interventive efforts focused on the abused and neglected elderly and special adult populations. Often, this area combines social service with law enforcement. Other important areas which APS draws from include medicine, psychology, psychiatry, social work, crisis intervention, criminal justice, and sociology. Therefore, the field is vast and multidisciplinary.

In addition to its multidisciplinary focus, the area of adult protective services has recently been one which has combined practitioner related issues and scholarly examination.

In its very short existence, adult protective services had been primarily an area of concern for practitioners. However, in recent years there has been a proliferation of research articles featured in many well known journals. Much of the research which has been conducted in this area has been applied and relevant to the practitioner. This volume keeps with that tradition.

This edited volume adds to this body of knowledge. There are specific contributions the book makes. First, it is the first book available which specifically focuses on the topic of adult protective services or "APS." Second, it amasses experts from the field in order to share their expertise. The general purpose of *Adult Protective Services: Research and Practice* is to focus on the topic of protective services, to provide a comprehensive compilation of research, and to provide a forum for the identification and analysis of practice issues. It is our hope that this volume will serve as a key resource to both academicians and practitioners which sheds light on important issues and influential trends in protective services. This is all accomplished by providing a multidisciplinary approach to the provision and delivery of adult protective services within contemporary American society.

Each chapter addresses important and significant areas of interest and concern within American adult protective services. The authors address the topic of adult protective services from both a research and practice levels. With each being of equal importance, chapters within this anthology reflect the interrelated nature of scholarly research and the special issues pertinent to the practitioner.

The anthology chapters follow the book's thematic approach. The first three chapters introduce the reader to the areas of primary concern here: adult protective services and elder/adult abuse and neglect. In Chapter 1, "Introducing Adult Protective Services," Dena Wiese and the Editors outline the field of adult protective services. In so doing, this substantive area, which combines many aspects of social services and criminal justice, is discussed and disseminated. As the reader will see, the field of adult protective services is vast and an essential societal response to the problem of elder/adult abuse and neglect. Chapter 2, "Abuse and Neglect: The Adult and Elder," also dealing with a primary substantive area, introduces the reader to the problem of elder/adult abuse and neglect. As the author, Dr. Janet Mickish, indicates abuse against special populations and vulnerable adults fits appropriately within the broader area of family violence as an area of professional and legal concern. While Chapter 2 primarily addresses the issue of adult/elder abuse and neglect in cases involving external perpetrators, Chapter 3 by Drs. Richard Lamanna and Bryan Byers discuss self-endangering behavior. "Adult Protective Services and Elder Self-Endangering Behavior," Chapter 3, addresses the complexity of elder self-neglect and other forms of self-destructive behavior, legal definitions and case examples.

"Legal and Legislative Dimensions," Chapter 4, Dr. M. Steven Meagher outlines the specific legal aspects of adult protective services. With rapid proliferation of adult protective services laws in the 1980s, there have been many changes to the systems which deliver services to the elder and disabled adult. The presence of the adult protective services laws, and continued legislative changes, creates the need for special attention given to this most important dimension due to the impact on both social service and criminal justice systems.

Chapters 5 and 6 address the system level interaction, integration, and response in the field of adult protective services. Chapter 5, "Adult Protective Services and the Criminal Justice System," by Dr. Steven

Chermak addresses an often neglected area of concern for the practitioner in the field of adult protective services: the important interface between the adult protective services unit and worker and the criminal justice system. Chermak outlines thoroughly the importance of this relationship. Chapter 6 also addresses an important system level area. Drs. Jerome McKean and David Wilson in "Adult Protective Services and the Social Service System" address the critical role the social service network plays in the new field of adult protective services. As the authors point out, adult protective services is an important and integral component to the social service network and the adult protective services practitioner relies on this system immensely. Both chapters deal with the important system levels issues pertinent to the field of adult protective services.

The next chapter ventures away from the macro orientation to the field of the adult protective services and into the micro realm of intervention. In Chapter 7, Drs. Shirley Salem and Beverly Favre in "Providing Protective Services to Special Populations" address additional issues and concerns paramount in the actual delivery of protective services to special populations of elders and disabled adults. This chapter makes a significant contribution to the field of adult protective services.

Chapter 8, "Staff Burnout and Adult Protective Services Work," by Timothy Wynkoop and Dr. Lawrence Gerstein shifts the orientation of the anthology from the victim/survivor to the practitioner. An important, and often neglected, area within adult protective services is stress and the subsequent burnout some adult protective services investigators may experience. The adult protective services investigator is a very unique social services and criminal justice practitioner. Their unique role, and the special demands placed on them by society, service systems, and crisis situations, underscores the need to address practitioner needs.

Taken together, this anthology introduces the reader to the field of adult protective services, outlines important research and practice issues, covers the primary substantive areas in the field, and we hope the anthology provides the field with important resources which combine the complementary nature of research and practice.

Bryan Byers
James E. Hendricks

CONTENTS

ADULT PROTECTIVE SERVICES
Research and Practice

Chapter One

AN OVERVIEW OF ADULT PROTECTIVE SERVICES

Bryan Byers, James E. Hendricks, and Dena Wiese

INTRODUCTION

Adult protective services (APS) programs have proliferated through-out the United States over the last two decades. In response to what was defined as the growing social problem of elder abuse and neglect, legislators and influential special interest groups in society have helped to bring this issue to the national forefront. The benign neglect which has surrounded the issue of abuse of the elderly, mentally ill, and developmentally disabled led to a hue and cry in the 1980's which ultimately brought the problem into the national consciousness. As a result, state laws protecting vulnerable adults and the elderly have been passed in all states and federal initiatives are underway.

While celebrated cases of extreme instances of elder neglect and abuse are the ones of which most citizenry will be aware, the national prevalence and response has all but gone untouched. Each day hundreds of cases of elder and adult abuse and neglect are reported to local adult protective investigators nation-wide, all in an attempt to put an end to the victimization. Adult protective services, being a reactive mechanism to this problem, relies heavily on citizen involvement and cooperative relations with social service and criminal justice personnel in each given adult protective services jurisdiction. Adult protective services, being an entity which often has components of both social service and criminal justice, rests between these two systems. Therefore, local APS efforts, with the assistance of community members and other professionals, has led to a response to the call for protection.

Further research is sorely needed in order to address the myriad of protection issues which surround abuse and neglect of the elderly and other dependent adult populations. The following discussion addresses this need by presenting an historical overview of adult protective services, a definition of adult protective services, operation of adult protective services and issues surrounding adult protective services practice, and the need for future research.

AN HISTORICAL OVERVIEW OF ADULT PROTECTIVE SERVICES

Several authors have commented on the brief history of adult protective services (Regan, 1978; Burr, 1982; Dunkle, et al., 1983; Quinn and Tomita, 1986; Leiber, 1988) and the recognition of adult abuse as a social problem (Pratt, et al., 1983; Bookin and Dunkle, 1985). However, most of the literature has been quite recent as a result of society and scholars "discovering" the problem. Part of the reason for this historic absence is that the problem " . . . only recently received attention in professional literature . . . " and " . . . has largely been ignored by state legislatures . . . " (Pratt et al., 1983, p. 147). Bookin and Dunkle (1985) suggest that "because both government and the general public have been slow to recognize the significance of the problem, legal tools and support of community-based services appropriate to meet the needs of this population (such as protective services, respite, day care, and the like) have remained limited in many communities" (p. 3). Therefore, recognition of the problem of adult abuse, and the response to this problem, are both recent historical developments.

Like many other social service initiatives, adult protective service programs emerged historically due to several factors. First, such programs have proliferated as a result of a recognition of the changing demographics and social practices of society. In terms of demographics, American society is graying and will continue to do so into the next century. Consequently, there are more mature adults in society who may need protective services. In terms of changing social practices, there has been a decrease in the institutionalization of the mentally ill and mentally retarded for extended periods of time. As a result, more mentally ill and mentally ill adults are living in the community either independently or with some community-based assistance. Although this is clearly an improvement over many types of institutionalization, the unintended consequence of placing many vulnerable people back into society has been the possibility of victimization.

Second, there has been an increasing recognition that the elderly and other potentially vulnerable adult populations may require special legislation and protective measures in order to keep them free from harm. Due in part to the natural consequences of aging and the vulnerability which may occur as a result of diminished mental capacity, it has been recognized that special protective measures may sometimes be warranted which would be based on statute and provided by specialized personnel. Third, there has been an increasing effort to unify interventive steps based on the two aforementioned criteria. Historically, protective services have been a hodgepodge of interventive steps, some quite paternalistic, designed to enable the person to be free from harm. This desire to form a concerted effort to respond to the special needs of the abused or neglected elder/adult has had an important impact on the proliferation of state adult protective services programs nation-wide and has also provided the main impetus for continuing efforts on the federal level.

During the 1930's protective services for vulnerable adults became an issue of importance within the federal government. As Quinn and Tomita write, "The notion of protective services grew out of government concern for adults who had difficulty managing their own affairs. It was recognized, then, that certain groups in society may suffer from a special vulnerability due to abuse and/or neglect. The passage of the Social Security Act in 1935 most likely marked the beginning of protective services when state departments of public welfare and several private agencies began providing assistance to the aged, blind, and disabled" (Quinn and Tomita, 1986, p. 236), and these initiatives have a contemporary legacy in well established "representative payee" programs orchestrated by the Social Security and Veteran Administrations. It was, then, during the Great Depression that protective services took the first step toward becoming an institutionalized aspect of American social welfare policy and practice.

It was not, however, until over a decade and a half later that "protective services for older people became a social welfare issue in the United States" (Dunkle, 1984, p. 357). It appears that protective services may have had a somewhat gradual and modest beginning. This was due mainly to limitations in services and a lack of clarity of desired case outcomes. In other words, the goals of intervention were not always clear and the means of intervention were often limited. Moreover, as society and social welfare professionals formulated the most effective manner to respond to cases calling for protective services, civil liberties were not always considered. In fact, some have suggested that early protective services were quite paternalistic and modeled after the principle of *parens patriae* (Quinn and Tomita, 1986; Leiber, 1988, 1992). It was not long until the idea of protective services for adults began to take shape.

Staudt (1985) claims that in the late 1950's "a number of national agencies and organizations had expressed an interest in adult protective services. Among these were the Social Security Administration, the National Council on Aging and the American Public Welfare Association" (p. 204). With the interest and involvement of such agencies in the needs of vulnerable adults, the movement became more institutionalized. This new awareness grew primarily from an increased visibility of older Americans who were able to live independently within the community while receiving support through such sources as social security and veteran benefits (Dunkle, 1984, p. 357). By the 1960's, protective services were being offered to people who could not manage their own affairs or protect themselves from external harm (Quinn and Tomita, 1986, p. 237). What was to follow would be additional attention given to elder populations which was a natural byproduct of an aging society.

According to Burr (1982) and Leiber (1988), the 1950's and 1960's gave birth to a number of national conferences centered on the problems of mentally impaired mature adults. These meetings were held by various organizations and focused on the special needs of such populations. The objective of these efforts was to "establish preventative and supportive services" for the aged and other adult groups in need of protective services (Leiber, 1988, p. 44). As cited by Leiber (1988), these efforts led to many "legislative enactments" which provided funds for protective service programs. Some of the more noteworthy federal initiatives were amendments to the Social Security Act which were passed in 1962 and 1965; the 1965 Older Americans Act; Title XX amendments to the Social Security Act which were completed in 1974 (Regan, 1978); and amendments to the Older Americans Act in 1978 (Burr, 1982; Leiber, 1988). As Quinn and Tomita (1986) note, the 1970's were an important time in the development of adult protective services programs based on Title XX:

> In 1975, Title 20 of the Social Security Act mandated and funded protective services for all adults 18 years of age or older with no regard to income. Additionally, emphasis was placed on clients who were found in situations indicating abuse, neglect, or exploitation. With this federal mandate, most states created adult protective services (APS) units in their social service agencies (p. 238).

While most protective service steps prior to these efforts were some what unified in purpose or focus, the 1960's and 1970's ushered in a time in which program goals and intervention strategies began to be examined. In particular, with the advent of funded demonstration programs by the U.S. Department of Social and Rehabilitation Services designed to spur the National Protective Services Project, and to identify APS clients and intervention techniques, many important questions could be answered with regard to protective services (Quinn and Tomita, 1986).

Although this era ushered in several model demonstration and research projects which addressed the "issue of the effectiveness of protective services for older people" (Dunkle et al., 1983, p. 195), one particular project deserves special mention. The research conducted by The Benjamin Rose Institute (BRI) is probably the most noted by practitioners (Staudt, 1985, p. 204). Margaret Blenkner and her associates at BRI in Cleveland, Ohio constructed a research project consisting of both a control group and an experimental group (Dunkle et al., 1983, pp. 195–196). The experimental group was "provided a wide range of services: medical, legal, homemaker-home aide, psychiatric, financial assistance, placement in a protective setting if the need arose, and casework services from specially trained social workers who played a central role in coordination and planning" (Dunkle et al., 1983, p. 196). The control group received only that assistance which was normally available in the community in an effort to evaluate protective services on quality of life.

Dunkle (1984) maintains that "the study demonstrated that specially designed intervention with this group of elderly was no more effective than customary social services. In fact, Blenkner et al. found that special services may have a deleterious impact on the lives of protective clients they studied" (p. 357). Consequently, it was not long after these findings were made public, and available to social service agencies, that interest in issues surrounding protective services for adults seemed to slow to a trickle (Dunkle, 1984, p. 357). On subsequent reanalysis in the 1970's, however, the conclusions of the original BRI study were called into question on methodological and substantive grounds. In particular, the groups compared on service outcome and the assumption that certain outcomes were accurate measures of service benefit created more questions than answers. This study, and other similar research designed to measure and evaluate the effectiveness of adult protective services, merely emphasizes the need for additional research.

The 1970's brought on a renewed interest in protective services for adults. Additional services were provided through a "Comprehensive

Service amendment to the Older American Act of 1973, which broadened the definition of client eligibility for services provided" (Dunkle, 1984, p. 358). During this decade of reform, the Supplemental Security Income Program (SSI) was also initiated as an additional service focusing on the elderly. Coleman and Karp (1989) state that "with the passage of the Supplemental Security Income Program, a minimum federal amount of income was made available to all older people" (pp. 51–52). However, as stated earlier, the piece of legislation that may have made the most impact on protective services came in 1975 in the form Title XX of the Social Security Act.

The 1980's may be remembered historically as the decade in which the problem of elder abuse and neglect truly became a national issue (Pedrick-Cornell and Gelles, 1982, p. 457; Pillemer and Wolf, 1986). It's recognition as a problem of national importance came primarily from lawmakers and special interest groups. Most notably, Congressman Claude Pepper, who is often credited with coining the term "elder abuse" pushed the problem into the national consciousness in the early 1980's with the national momentum being sustained by such organizations as the National Committee for the Prevention of Elder Abuse. The Committee includes within its mandate the protection of both elder victims and other vulnerable adults such as the developmentally disabled. Moreover, since 1983 the National Committee for the Prevention of Elder Abuse has worked in concert with the Texas Department of Human Services and together have held the Annual APS Conference. Although these efforts have had a profound impact on the formation of a successful social movement during the 1980's, many states had already taken on the cause of adult protective services and elder abuse and neglect. By 1980, twenty-five states had implemented "adult protection laws, with laws pending in fourteen others" (Dunkle, 1984, p. 358). Moreover, Dolon and Hendricks (1989) claim that " . . . by 1988, all fifty states had established reporting requirements, with forty-three of them operating mandatory statewide systems" (p. 75).

The 1990's ushered in the topic of elder abuse and neglect with the congressional report, "Elder Abuse and Neglect: A Decade of Shame and Inaction" (U.S. Congress, 1990). This report, a follow up to its predecessor a decade earlier, chronicles how much is yet to be done in the area of elder abuse and neglect. The decade of the 90's and the next century will undoubtedly be a turning point for the field of adult protective services. It will likely be a time of additional program evaluation, a reassessment of need, and a time of innovation in adult protective services. Given that many states are either in their second decade of providing protective services, or nearing the end of their first, such review is undoubtedly on the horizon.

DEFINITION AND FUNCTION OF ADULT PROTECTIVE SERVICES

Definitions of Adult Protective Services

Quinn and Tomita (1986) define Adult Protective Services as a "multitude of services" that "draws on nearly every resource available to elders in any given community" (p. 235). They describe a protective services program as "a unique mixture of legal, medical, and social services that permit the broadest array of interventions" (p. 235). Such definitions have evolved from the nearly 60 years of practice in protective services rather than any concerted effort to define the field. As Quinn and Tomita further note, with the passage of mandatory reporting laws in most states, that adult protective services (APS) units " . . . have become synonymous with the reporting and investigation of elder abuse and neglect." (p. 237).

It must be noted, however, that many states also include other vulnerable population groups as clientele in possible need of adult protective services assistance. Partly due to legislative enactments on the federal level, influence from advocacy and special interest groups on behalf of the mentally retarded and mentally ill, and subsequent state legislation, a state's adult protective services program may address the protective needs of the elderly *and* other vulnerable adult populations. Herein one can find the primary distinction between the terms "Elder Abuse" and "Adult Abuse." While the former is common nomenclature for describing the case involving and elder victim, the latter refers to the victim suffering from mental illness or mental retardation/developmental disability. While these two client groups will require different treatment in practice, the definition of adult protective services for each group will generally be the same.

Adult protective services may further be defined through the characteristics of such programs and the traits which effective service systems should possess. Bergman (1989) mentions three essential elements of protective services programs necessary if they are to be successful in their purpose of adequately assisting the elderly and protecting them against abuse and neglect. The three required traits of an effective service network are:

(1) a coordinated, interdisciplinary service system to respond to both chronic and emergency cases.
(2) a set of core services (social, health, housing, mental health, and legal services) available to utilize in these cases.
(3) a set of preplanned individual case responses or protocols to guide service providers in responding to emergency and chronic cases (p. 97).

Regan (1978) adds to the list two more features that would facilitate the needs of older and dependent adults in the community. Regan suggests that APS programs consist of two elements. First, they consist of a "coordinated delivery of services to adults at risk" (Regan, 1978, p. 251). That is, adult protective services programs ideally provide the "myriad" of services of which Quinn and Tomita (1986) also discuss. Second, such programs also may have "the actual or potential authority to provide substitute decision-making" to those at risk of harm (Regan, 1978, p. 251). Taken together, the adult protective services program is one which provides services through coordinated efforts with other community-based agencies and sometimes has the authority to initiate the imposition of services on clientele when such services may be warranted, the client is incompetent, and the client does not wish to be in receipt of these. These characteristics or features have generally become standards in the field of adult protective services in terms of defining the role of APS and accompanying responsibilities. Quinn and Tomita (1986) attempt to clarify further the definition of adult protective services through a description of APS clientele. Protective Services cater to "a unique mixture of people. They fall into several categories: voluntary or involuntary, neglected or self-neglectful, abusive or abused, compliant or noncompliant with their medical care, and consenting or not consenting to intervention" (p. 236).

These definitions provide a somewhat overgeneralized view of adult protection services. This may, however, not seem very unusual to an adult protective services investigator/worker reading this chapter. The reason for this has to do with Quinn and Tomita's definition provided above and the idea of an "array of services" provided to clientele. Perhaps more than any other helping profession, which relies heavily on a social casework model, the definition of adult protective services is often dictated by the activities performed. That is, the role defines the service. As one investigator we interviewed reported:

> I would never know from one day to the next what I was going to encounter. Sometimes my services involved just being a friend to someone who was not really in need of my services (yet), other times the job could involve confronting an angry abuser, and then again, it could involve working with delicate family systems. There were times when it was really hard to do interventions because of the refusal from the client and apparent incompetence. Sometimes I would be viewed as the client's friend, sometimes an enemy. It would just depend on the day.

The myriad of roles and responsibilities which confront the adult protective services investigator are endless as this investigator aptly points out. In the delivery of protective services, there are many issues which correspond to the definitions and subsequent roles found within this profession. In order to better understand the purpose and place of adult protection services in human services, it is important to examine the functions of APS.

Functions of Adult Protective Services

An important function which accompanies the role of the adult protective services investigator is making critical decisions regarding social, legal, psychiatric or medical intervention. Such programs have been described as those which attempt to fill the gaps between medical, social, and law enforcement services. As Quinn and Tomita (1986) have stated, the role of adult protective services is indeed broad and multifaceted.

All APS tasks involve decisions, discretion, and social judgments. The decision to intervene on behalf of a client is never an easy one, because there are many important factors to consider such as autonomy, beliefs in self-reliance, and the right to privacy. These are ever present aspects of daily APS practice. Also a common companion to the investigator is the crisis situation. The APS investigator is often a crisis intervenor who must often respond to life-threatening crisis situations involving elder/ adult abuse and neglect. Crisis responses often involve potential intervention and, as such, may be on either a voluntary or involuntary basis.

Before any intervention may take place, the APS investigator must make field decisions, using personal discretion much like other social service and criminal justice professionals (e.g., caseworkers, social workers, police, prosecutors, judges, parole boards). In the investigative process involving APS cases, there are several "decision points" which call for investigator discretion and judgment. Often, there is a high degree of decisional autonomy, but there are often influences external to the investigator which will guide decision making. For instance, the APS investigator will likely be influenced by the APS organizational structure (i.e., program mandates, preferences of supervisors, practices of other investigators in adjoining jurisdictions). In addition, important value, moral and ethical considerations will also likely come into play in case judgments.

Although part of the same organizational structure, state programs and local units have somewhat different functions when carrying out the objectives of adult protective services law. Depending on the organizational structure of adult protective services in the respective state, these different levels may dictate varying roles and responsibilities. If the state has an administrative office for adult protective service programs/units within a particular state, the functions of the state administrative office may include the following: (1) legislative advocacy, (2) continuing education, (3) consultation, and (4) state level data collection and dissemination.

Each of these organizational functions are important to the operation of the state program and to local unit functioning. The first, legislative advocacy, pertains to the role the State has in lobbying legislators in an attempt to keep programs funded and operating. In addition, the state office may be involved in legislative advocacy designed to make changes and additions to existing APS law. Second, state offices may be responsible for identifying training needs for the investigators and other support personnel in administering the law. This could include disseminating the latest research, knowledge gleaned from such studies, and practical implications of such research. Third, the state office may be available for consultation on legal matters not resolvable on the local level. In addition, some states operate 24-hour toll-free crisis hotlines to receive abuse complaints to be referred to unit offices. Normally, in states where there is a central APS program office it is a valuable resource to the field investigator. Finally, central state offices may control the data bank for reported and investigated cases of adult abuse, tabulate statistics from this data, and provide summary statistics to APS investigators and others. This will undoubtedly continue to be an important role as efforts move forward to create unified definitions of mistreatment and national statistical profiles. Herein are the primary functions of state APS administrative offices.

The local unit offices (APS units) are normally designed to have a different set of functions. These may be summarized as: (1) investigation, (2) client protection, (3) unit level data collection, and (4) community education. The first, investigation, refers to the primary role of the worker. Adult protective service programs are mandated by law to investigate (or in some states to "cause" the complaint to be investigated which means another appropriate agency may investigate the case) reports of elder and/or adult mistreatment. APS may not always be the most appropriate agency to investigate a case. An example could be the case of a homicide of an elderly person since there are other legal and bureaucratic mechanisms for such matters such as the police, a coroner's office, or a medical examiner. In some cases, it may be more effective to refer the case to another, more appropriate, agency. However, many of the reports and referrals received by APS units due to mandatory reporting laws will be appropriate for the unit to investigate especially if the referral comes from another community agency familiar with the jurisdiction of APS units.

Important outcomes of investigation are judgment and decision making. Before any action or intervention can take place on behalf of an abused/neglected adult, however, a full investigation takes place in which the information and evidence in the case is used to either substantiate or unsubstantiate the case. When a case is substantiated the investigator has judged the evidence to be strong enough to support the original allegation of abuse and/or neglect. If substantiated, investigators are required to judge and assess the case further and make a determination regarding the best possible outcome, or alternative, for the client. This point relates to the second unit level function. That is, the investigator, as a decision maker, must recommend the most appropriate option regarding client protection. Above all, the investigator is "ideally" supposed to provide the necessary level of assistance to the client which is the "least restrictive" (and possibly the least paternalistic) and most effective (Regan, 1978; Quinn and Tomita, 1986). This is to be done while trying to reach the ultimate goal of protecting the client from further incidents of abuse or neglect. Depending on the severity of the abuse or neglect and available resources, an outcome or case disposition may be as lesser restrictive as informal case monitoring by the unit to the more restrictive steps of guardianship, civil commitment, or adult protective services protective order. Whatever the dispositional outcome, the level of restrictiveness will normally mirror the seriousness of the case (i.e., highly serious will likely lead to highly restrictive steps). We must add that the provision of protective services (providing protective services) may very well be one of the most demanding and stressful functions an investigator will carry out.

Third, units may be required to maintain data on the frequency, type, and outcome of abuse and neglect cases investigated. Such data help to evaluate program investigations and outcomes. The data compiled from each unit normally would make up the state level adult abuse case data. Although one might view data as nonpolitical for APS units, it is doubtful that this is the case. Local data can be quite important to each unit because it is a symbol of performance. Although it is highly unlikely that APS units create cases in order to justify need, there may be statistical reasons (i.e., a desire to reflect a consistent number of cases per unit, to maintain current levels of funding, etc.) which lead to various responses to cases. The tabulation of statistics, then, can be an important characteristic of the unit level function.

Fourth, local units often serve a community education function through public speeches concerning the topic of elder abuse and neglect to area groups and organizations. Some groups which APS may address include local hospitals, nursing associations, social service agencies, police departments, and government agencies such as the Social Security Administration. This is a vital unit level function because it allows the unit to create a bridge between APS and potential service agencies to fulfill the adult protective services mandate.

ADULT PROTECTIVE SERVICES: OPERATION AND ISSUES FOR THE PRACTITIONER

The primary purpose of the adult protective services programs is to provide, or arrange, "protective services." These may include services necessary to protect the client's health or safety and could include medical, psychiatric, residential, and social services. Further, the service is intended to be the "least restrictive" possible. That is, the option which places the least amount of control over the client's life and liberty. In many instances, however, the adult protective services worker can possess much more power over limiting individual liberties than any police agency (Quinn and Tomita, 1986). They are not always bound by the same due process and procedural regulations as police agencies, so their task and role must be taken seriously. This has been determined to be an important aspect of protective services (Regan, 1978; Bookin and Dunkle, 1985; Quinn and Tomita, 1986; Leiber, 1988, 1992).

APS: Interfacing Social Services and Criminal Justice

Adult protective service programs seem to carry both a social service and criminal justice function. That is, there seems to be a social welfare as well as an investigative emphasis, with particular significance placed on the former. Adult protective services rests somewhere between the social service and criminal justice systems. While not occupying full membership in either system, the APS investigator may, at times, seem like a marginal practitioner. Depending on the case, the investigator may need to use a soft touch or a more authoritative approach. As one APS investigator, also a sworn law enforcement officer, noted for us this was clearly a possibility in practice:

> The type of case would often dictate how I would present myself. Sometimes I would be more like a social worker and other times I would be more law enforcement oriented. I was fortunate enough to have the option of putting on either hat, because I carried a badge and had full arrest power. There were many times when my business card was the most appropriate manner of introducing myself because I did not want to scare the client or the family. In those instances, I was more like a social worker. On the other hand, there were those times when the badge and the law enforcement role came in handy due to severe abuse, the dangerousness of the situation, and/or resistant family. There were times that I would even ask a uniformed police officer to come with me on a case. Other times, this was not at all warranted and could have done more harm than good.

There are times, then, that the APS investigator may be either an advocate or an adversary and these two roles may emerge several times during the course of an ordinary day. However, the dilemma goes beyond this illustration of the client-investigator level of interaction and to the level of interaction between the investigator and various social service and law enforcement agencies.

Normally, the APS investigator will spend most of his or her time working with such agencies as county health departments, county and state departments of social service (in the event that the APS unit is not part of this entity), local hospital social service departments, older adult case management agencies, mental health agencies, and advocacy groups for the elderly, mentally ill, and/or developmentally disabled. The social service agencies and agents which APS may come into contact with may even extend beyond this brief list depending on the jurisdiction.

As Quinn and Tomita (1986) note, the adult protective services investigator is often viewed as an option of last resort where social service and criminal justice agencies may make a referral of an abused or neglected elder/adult. Sometimes, representatives within the social service system may become frustrated with the lack of action taken by the adult protective services unit or investigator in terms of the delivery of necessary and appropriate services. Part of this frustration, and potential conflict, between social service agents and the APS investigator rests in a lack of understanding of the role of APS, the dependency the investigator has on local social service providers, and limitations of the law. The "do something" mentality which often accompanies a referral from the social service system can be a tremendous source of frustration and stress for the APS investigator as well.

There are several ways to reduce this type of problem, all of which deal with APS actively interfacing more with the social service system. In particular, APS units have been known to serve on Adult Protective Services Advisory Boards along side social service personnel within a given community. In an effort to understand the issues and dilemmas which confront each player, such boards occupy an important role in the delivery of protective services. Often, these bodies are modeled after child protection advisory boards found in various communities. While the clientele are different than their counterpart, the APS Advisory Board can provide a constructive environment for the discussion of difficult cases, limited resources, and effective intervention strategies based on consensus of program goals and desired outcomes. In this way, the APS unit and investigator may interface effectively with the social service system.

The investigator may also find the need to interface with the criminal justice system as well. While many of the cases presented to APS are likely to be resolvable through the coordination of protective services within the social service system, there are times when the investigator will likely find him/herself interfacing with the criminal justice system. Within the criminal justice system the investigator may come into contact with three entities. These would be the police, the prosecutor's office/district attorney's office, and the courts. The investigator may need the services of the police in making home visits in which there may be serious instances of abuse or neglect. Since few APS investigators are trained in law enforcement techniques, while they are sometimes expected to have a law enforcement function, a trained police officer can be a highly valued co-investigator. Moreover, and since the police address a myriad of social service and law enforcement calls within the community, police departments may serve as an important referral source for cases of adult endangerment. The district attorney also plays an important role in APS practice. The prosecutor, being the elected or appointed official responsible for criminal charging decisions for a given jurisdiction, will be needed in order to file criminal charges against an abuser provided the APS unit believes such action is warranted. The APS investigator, either alone or with the assistance of a law enforcement officer, may need to present an investigation to a district attorney for possible criminal charges. This is yet another example of the interface between APS and the criminal justice system. A final illustration of the interface between criminal justice and APS rests with the relationship with the courts. In severe cases of adult endangerment, the APS investigator may find it is necessary to seek the assistance of the courts in securing civil commitments, guardianships, or protective orders for clients in need. In this way, the investigator will interface with the courts by providing petitions and accompanying testimony in order for a judge or magistrate to make a determination of the need for protective services. Moreover, the APS investigator may also come into contact with the courts if an APS case is criminally charged and that case results in a trial.

There are many ways in which the APS unit or investigator may come into contact and interface with social service and criminal justice systems. We have just mentioned a few we believe to be important, but there may very well be others depending on region-specific differences in APS programs. Further, there may be additional variation from unit to unit and state to state regarding the functions of state programs and local units described herein. We now turn to a discussion of discretion within APS practice.

Adult Protective Services and Discretion

Due to the nature of their investigative task and role, adult protective services investigators are essentially decision makers. They make judgments concerning cases which can lead to decisions of intervention on behalf of a client in need of protective services. Investigators make important judgments and decisions concerning the welfare of clientele.

These are sometimes in response to serious crises while other times the case may be somewhat routine. Decisions may involve living arrangements, health care, nutrition, or financial management (Quinn and Tomita, 1986; Byers and Hendricks, 1990). Whatever the case, however, investigators must necessarily make numerous social judgments. A concomitant component to this discretionary authority are various special issues which confront the practitioner.

Investigators are continually faced with the prospect of making judgments concerning the nature of abuse or neglect, who is responsible for the abuse, and opting for the least restrictive and the most suitable outcome. Most of these decisions rest with the personal discretion of the individual unit based on an interpretation of the adult protective services law. Adult protective services programs operate from state law, but much of the law is open to interpretation in the case of investigation and legal intervention. Adult protective service laws, like any law, are subject to interpretation based on discretion. Investigators, it may seem, are often left to their own devices for individual case judgment and intervention as long as there is a sense that the law has been followed and the least restrictive steps taken. There have been a few instances of judicial challenge/appeal in recent years. However, for the most part, the decisions and subsequent interventions made by APS units have gone uncontested. Therefore, social judgment discretion is very prevalent, and lasting, when coming from APS programs.

Since adult protective service programs do not exist within a social vacuum, the influences and exchanges from other agencies and their representatives can shape the nature of discretion in many ways. These include the "assessment activity" (a determination of the case which might involve some evaluation of the nature of the problem), and the "outcome" (type of service to the client, which could also be called "ends" or the intervention plan decision). Since APS emphasizes "results," in the form of clients served and problems solved, there tends to be an emphasis on the "outcome" or "ends" of the case. The "means" of getting there are of equal importance because the judgments made of cases will determine the "outcome," or the assistance provided.

Quinn and Tomita (1986, p. 241), drawing from Burr (1982), have suggested that an investigator's interpretation of a case depends on several factors or variables. These include: (1) the adult's functioning, (2) the circumstances or situation in relationship to the adult's behavior, (3) action by a third party detrimental to the adult (this is of lesser importance to the self-neglect case), and (4) the problem that brings the adult to the agency's attention. Taken together, the APS investigator will likely bear these in mind. However, as one may see from these four criteria, much is still left to investigator discretion.

Legal and Social Intervention

The value of intervention, or the act of providing necessary services or appropriate steps to alleviate client suffering, has been debated in social service practice (Dunkle, et al., 1983; Abramson, 1985; Bookin and Dunkle, 1985). The dilemma of intervention strikes to the core of social welfare practice concerning the influence of attitude and practice toward paternalism, client autonomy and self-determination.

Adult protective services units are normally required to conduct several tasks when a case is "made" (the informal term sometimes used to describe a unit level judgment that the matter warrants investigation) at the onset of a report of alleged abuse or neglect. Units are required to collect all pertinent information regarding the situation, conduct (or have conducted) an investigation, make a determination regarding the facts, and arrange for an appropriate solution if the case is "substantiated" (a determination that abuse or neglect is present).

Case disposition sometimes involves legal intervention. In the case of abuse or neglect from an external perpetrator, the investigator may attempt to intervene legally. Legal intervention usually involves an involvement of the law enforcement or judicial branches of the criminal justice system in APS cases. Social intervention always takes place with legal intervention, because the unit becomes involved in the lives of those being investigated. Therefore, social intervention involves any intervention not taking on a legal character. Some options of legal intervention may include, but are not limited to: criminal charges, contesting a guardianship, filing a petition for a Protective Order to require protective services, or sometimes requiring the abuser to "enjoin" from the delivery of protective services (a legal term used to forbid third party interference in a court ordered protective services plan).

Formal intervention normally occurs when a person is determined by a protective services investigator to be in danger (either due to some external threat or a threat to the self) and it is determined that steps need to be taken to provide safety. Often, intervention depends on the seriousness of the situation and the client's level of cooperation. In the final analysis, however, the perceived need to protect the vulnerable adult may outweigh any freedom of choice. However, the investigator, ideally, is to weigh the harm observed against the potential obtrusiveness of intervention. This is a value dilemma, if not a conflict, in practice which places the caseworker/investigator in a difficult position. The difficulty here is not only with regard to the client and his/her needs but also the emotional health of the investigator. Dilemmas of this nature can produce a tremendous amount of investigator stress. Determinations about the desired outcome of a case are normally made through a formal investigation of the allegation(s). The investigation normally involves a visit to the alleged victim's home in an attempt to assess the severity of abuse or neglect. This activity is referred to as a "home visit" and is a valuable APS tool and normally constitutes the first substantive step of intervention.

Intervention: Issues of Self-Determination and Paternalism

Potential situations for social intervention probably arise more often than the protective service worker would like. These are difficult and present serious ethical and moral dilemmas concerning responsibility, freedom of choice, self-reliance, and self-sufficiency. Quinn and Tomita (1986, pp. 237–239) present guidelines from Havemeyer (1982) which are intended to provide the worker with direction in instances of moral and ethical uncertainty:

1. When interests compete [between protective services and the client], the practitioner is charged with serving the client.
2. When interests compete, the adult client is in charge of decision making until he delegates responsibility voluntarily to another or the court grants responsibility to another.
3. When interests compete, freedom is more important than safety.
4. In the ideal case, protection of adults seeks to achieve, simultaneously and in order of importance, freedom, safety, least disruption of life style, and least restrictive care alternative.

These guidelines are not a mandate for protective services workers. They are, instead, recommendations based on norms regarding how to proceed in cases of endangerment and potential intervention. They suggest that intervention should not occur until it is absolutely necessary and only by respecting the rights of the APS client. Unfortunately, the dilemma of intervention is not resolved by these recommendations, because each protective services client and case is different and each protective services worker has a unique investigative approach. However, it is important for the investigator to avoid possible value conflicts between client and program needs which have been noted in APS practice (Quinn and Tomita, 1986; Coleman and Karp, 1989).

In severe cases of adult endangerment, legal interventions in the form of a Protective Order, guardianship, or civil mental health commitment are sometimes attempted. There is no guarantee that any of these options may be used since they depend on a court ruling and a judge's approval; however, the adult protective services investigator may often initiate any of these legal interventions. This is an ominous responsibility which has many potential consequences. Some have suggested that involuntary interventions present the investigator with an ethical dilemma (Quinn and Tomita, 1986; Coleman and Karp, 1989). Involuntary interventions are very difficult to process. They represent the dilemma between the assumed ability of every citizen to make decisions and the power of the State to take that ability away. Unfortunately, steps to preserve self-determination, decision making and freedom are not always possible.

Since "self-determination" refers to, " . . . that condition in which personal behavior emanates from a person's own wishes, choices, and decisions." (Abramson, 1985, p. 387), this notion presents a critical dilemma for the worker. If society expects people to be "self-determined," this implies that individuals are in control of their own destiny and responsible for the behavior. The following points by Ferguson (1978) illustrate this issue and the value conflicts which may emerge for the protective services worker:

1. Each individual has rights including self-determination and privacy.
2. Everyone should do productive work and be self-sufficient (except the old, the ill, and the very young).
3. Youth and vigor are, therefore, highly valued (the elderly are often stereotyped as being resistant to change, dependent, and unproductive) (p. 41).

These points state that the societal norm is self-sufficiency and self-determination, but it also outlines what might be considered exceptions to these standards (the "old" for example). To be self-determined and self-sufficient is to take responsibility for behavior. Unfortunately, cases of abuse or neglect are different and many are very complex. Disentangling these issues can be quite a task. In addition, one may not be able to account for all of the reasonable exceptions encountered in such instances, or the conditions which might elicit views that the adult should be more self-determined or self-sufficient. Ferguson (1978), however, attempts to resolve such issues and value conflicts by stating that intervention should protect the client and allow the most client decision making input.

As stated in the NASW Code of Ethics, " . . . the social worker should make every effort to foster maximum self-determination on the part of clients." Although adult protective services investigators are not always certified social workers, and as a result may not be ethically bound to this notion of "self-determination," they are, however, influenced by this tenet of practice. It has become an accepted practice that the APS worker find the "least restrictive" intervention alternative and this is often included in state APS law. This principle maintains that the investigator is supposed to find the interventive alternative which alleviates client suffering, while simultaneously allowing the client the most personal freedom and choice. That is, self-determination. This is not an easy task, because of the paternalistic nature of the state, the notion of *parens patriae,* and the pressure to find immediate solutions to complex problems. Some of this pressure to find solutions is due to the burgeoning caseload of APS workers due to mandatory reporting and inadequate staffing (Quinn and Tomita, 1986).

Some responses to the condition of elder/adult abuse and neglect may be characterized as "paternalistic." What may arise for the APS worker is the dilemma of *parens patriae* and the individual's right to privacy (Quinn and Tomita, 1986). The conflict or dilemma arises out of the tension between the client's inalienable right to privacy and the state's obligation to act as a "parent" to those who are vulnerable and in need of protection. This is a serious dilemma because of the worker's oft stated dual role of being a client advocate and someone who may have to intervene legally without the client's consent (Coleman and Karp, 1989). Some examples of paternalistic action may include mandatory nursing home placement, removal of control of one's finances, or guardianship when these steps contradict client/alleged victim wishes or self-determination (Abramson, 1985).

Unfortunately, efficiency and lack of appropriate alternatives can rule over effectiveness and assurances of least restrictiveness and self-determination. With a mounting caseload (due in part to more awareness and mandatory reporting), it may be much more efficient and labor saving to make paternalistic decisions toward the alleged victim and to limit self-determination in order to expedite case disposition. This could, however, violate the principle of least restrictiveness in the delivery of protective services and give rise to other moral and ethical judgment dilemmas as well.

Such a dilemma seems to be particularly acute in cases of self-neglect. Paternalism, a key issue here, is important because the worker acting in a paternalistic fashion could be operating under the assumption that the elder does not have the wherewithal to engage in adequate self-care, the desire to alleviate one's own suffering, or that the client has made some choice to live in squalor. Regardless of the reason for the behavior, the client, under these circumstances, is often expected to be a passive recipient to the protective care or services offered since it may be assumed that the APS worker, without question, knows what is in the best interests of the client. In particular, the tendency for some workers to view the client as someone who has failed to live up to social standards of day-to-day functioning, " . . . places clients in a role in which they are required to defer to the judgments of human services workers and to accept the programs those workers suggest." (Russo and Willis, 1986, p. 36). In another related treatment of this issue, Sengstock, Hwalek, and Petrone (1989) suggest that there is quite a difference between physical abuse cases and cases of self-neglect in relation to APS worker input and control:

> Many persons who engage in self-neglect present little competition to professionals for control of their lives. Workers are able to assume control, alter the elder's life situation, and feel a sense of accomplishment that the client has been moved to a safe situation. Physical abuse cases, on the other hand, . . . are cases in which an abuser, caretaker, or other family member may compete [against the worker] for control . . . (pp. 54–55).

One might expect that a controlling, paternalistic stance toward a self-neglectful elder would suggest there is a lack of responsibility for the behavior. This would be expected since the justifications for paternalistic action are often based in the inability of the client to make informed choices, mental incompetence, behavior which is far-reaching, or has irreversible consequences for the client (Abramson, 1985). It seems, however, that issues of client autonomy and self-determination are particularly important in cases of self-neglect due to the lack of competition over control and the subsequent likelihood that such cases will result in paternalistic intervention.

ADDITIONAL ISSUES IN ADULT PROTECTIVE SERVICES

While we have discussed a number of issues of importance to the organization and operation of adult protective services, there are additional issues which have yet to be discussed. There are two additional focal issues found within protective services which have importance to not only the client but also the investigator. These include guardianship and client refusal of services. Each of these issues is addressed in turn.

Guardianship/Conservatorship

"Guardianship is perhaps the most common, best known, and most studied of all legal protective services used to aide older adults (Iris, 1990, p. 58). Hull et al. (1990) describes guardianship and conservatorship as "methods our society uses to protect people who lack the capacity to protect themselves" (p. 145). While some have called such efforts paternalistic, and perhaps even the last bastion of paternalism in America, such interventions remain commonplace today for those who are judged to be in need of this level of protection. The concept of guardianship is not new. It closely resembles how ancient kings viewed their kingdoms and how the kings, themselves, were seen by the people within the kingdoms. These feelings of reciprocity fall "under the concept of parens patriae" in which the king was seen as a protector (Hull et al., 1990, p. 147). In the case of a person who is unable to make personal decisions or to manage his/her own affairs due to mental incompetence, a person may be appointed to make such decisions for the respondent or ward.

A guardianship and conservatorship, though similar, are not one in the same. Guardianships provide for the "personal needs of the proposed ward, including health care, personal safety, shelter, food, clothing, and education. The conservatorship, on the other hand, must contend with the administration of real and personal property, and other benefits" (Hull et al., 1990, p. 147–148). They may "be held in conjunction" with each other and both "must safeguard against exploitation" (Hull et al., 1990, p. 148). In some jurisdictions, the two terms are not necessarily used, however. Sometimes a simple distinction is made between a guardianship over the "person" (which would be liken to "guardianship" above) and guardianship over the "estate" (which would be synonymous with "conservatorship" above).

Adult protective services units may come into contact with guardians under a number of different circumstances. An adult, normally 18 years old or older, who has been judged incompetent in a court of law could be eligible for a guardianship or conservatorship. In the case of an elder/adult abuse or neglect investigation which involves a guardian as an alleged abuser, the APS worker may be placed in a position to confront the guardian concerning adequacy of care and/or appropriateness of decisions made on behalf of the adult. In such instances, the APS worker may need to contest a guardianship and petition to have a person removed as a guardian if it is determined that the person has not operated in the best interests of the ward or if abuse has occurred. On the other hand, guardians are sometimes used by protective services workers, on occasion as part of organized public guardianship programs, to provide ongoing protection for adult or elder abuse victims. Guardianships have, however, traditionally been overused as a protective service option. There are often less restrictive approaches that one may opt for such as durable powers of attorney or even representative payee programs (Byers and Hendricks, 1990) which can often solve a problem without undue limits to freedom and self-determination. Guardianships are, without exception, perhaps the most restrictive protective serve option available.

Although most discussions of guardianship pertain to private guardianships carried out under court order by individuals on behalf of a ward, there is another type of guardianship as well. This would be corporate guardianships. Seelig and Chestnut (1986) claim that this type of guardianship has "had a profound effect on the advocacy and provision of protective services to developmentally disabled persons..." (p. 221). Seelig and Chestnut (1986) define corporate legal guardianship as a "non-profit corporation that utilizes centralized resources and an interdisciplinary policy-making board of trustees to exercise the constitutionally protected rights of persons unable to do so for themselves..." (p. 221). The use of guardianships and conservatorships are necessary protective tools for people of any age who do not have the ability to make decisions for themselves. Such corporate approaches may be a viable way of using a very restrictive step in an effort to assure client civil liberties.

In order to further assure that guardianships are not overly restrictive, some jurisdictions allot for various types of guardianship which fall short of being permanent arrangements between the guardian and the ward. While a full or plenary guardianship encompasses "all matters of an individual's life" and "may create a loss of most constitutional rights..." (Hull et al., 1990, p. 148) an APS client may also be placed under a "limited guardianship" or a "temporary guardianship." Given that different cases and clients will require different levels of protection, a complete and all encompassing guardianship over the person or estate is not always necessary. Instead, one may opt for a limited guardianship which specifies that the guardian shall make decisions in only one aspect of a ward's life which "allows the court to match protection with the appropriate level of need for each individual" (Hull et al., 1990, p. 148). For example, this could involve decisions of health care only. Another lesser restrictive guardianship option is the temporary variety. In this type, the guardianship is only to last for a specified period of time. For example, a guardian may be appointed to see a person through a medical emergency in which decision making needs to be placed elsewhere but upon recovery the person may be capable of making his/her own decisions again. Both of these options reduce the paternalistic and restrictive nature that can characterize guardianships. Yet another type of guardianship, which could come in either of the aforementioned varieties, is a "guardian ad litem." A guardian ad litem is a person who agrees to serve as a person's guardian at the pleasure of the court. The unique feature of the 'ad litem' is the advocacy role which the guardian is to adopt in the role. The primary responsibility of the ad litem is to act as an advocate for the ward. Having different forms of guardianship available affords the APS unit and the courts to match the most appropriate type with client needs.

Refusal of Services

Refusal of services by the mistreated and self-neglectful is a critical issue faced by APS workers. Vinton (1991) relates the danger of this problem in the claim that "older persons who refuse services are at greater risk of future harm than elders who accept help" (p. 89). In a study conducted by Vinton (1991) on the factors surrounding the refusal of treatment, findings supported the assumption that abusers do not want their victims to receive interventions. Part of such resistance has to do with control over the abused while another aspect can be the financial benefit the abuser reaps as a result of control. This could result from a situation in which "perpetrators are emotionally and/or economically dependent on their victims" (Vinton, 1991, p. 99). The victim is also usually dependent on the caregiver/perpetrator for their care and personal needs. At times, such mutual dependency, and fear felt by the abused if s/he reports mistreatment, can lead to a refusal of services. In yet other instances, the abused may refuse intervention or assistance because the APS worker is judged by the victim to be a greater evil than the abuser.

Victims generally grow more vulnerable and dependent on the abuser rather than growing more strong and independent. Sadly, the longer a victim refuses assistance, the more severe the abuse may become and the less likely s/he may report the circumstances surrounding the abuse. Vinton (1991) identified two highly influential factors that are related to the decision of maltreated adults to refuse treatment and services. These factors are the sex of the perpetrator and the relationship of the perpetrator to the victim. It was concluded that "significantly more victims with male perpetrators refused service offers than victims with female perpetrators" and "the rates of accepting services for victims of spouse abuse or neglect were relatively high..." (Vinton, 1991, p. 98). One might expect higher rates of refusal with male perpetrators given the nature of control which is characteristic of traditional male gender roles. One might also expect higher rates of service acceptance in cases of spouse abuse given that services for victims of this form of domestic violence have become legitimized in society and are readily available in most communities.

The Vinton study described above was designed to examine the characteristics surrounding why elderly victims of abuse and neglect refuse services. However, that study did not account for the "victims" of self-neglect that refuse services. Cases of self-neglect are highly sensitive situations for both the practitioner and potential client and more than likely account for the vast majority of service refusals. Practitioners may find themselves in a struggle between two opposing principles: "parens patriae" and the principle of the "right to privacy" (Quinn and Tomita, 1986, p. 239). Coleman and Karp (1989) convey the concern that involuntary interventions could "impose different values and conditions on an individual's freedom" (p. 54) and Mixson (1991) reminds practitioners that a refusing client may very well understand the consequences of the refusal (p. 36). Too often, the self-neglect victim who refuses may be considered incompetent while the acquiescent victim may be judged as competent. The client's right to decide needs to be first and foremost in the mind of the practitioner and refusal should not be automatically equated with competency.

As stated earlier, Sengstock et al. (1989) propose that those who engage in self-neglect "present little competition to professionals for control of their lives. Workers are able to assume control, alter the elder's life situation and feel a sense of accomplishment . . . " (p. 54–55). However, this can lead to unnecessary changes for the elderly person. The practitioner should not get so involved with their own sense of purpose that they forget what could be the best option for the client. In the end, the practitioner's "good intentions" can be more harmful than helpful. It is essential for the client to retain a sense of self-determination and for decisions affecting life course to be his or her own. A practitioner, working toward a productive relationship, must gain the client's trust before any interventions are attempted. " . . . The practitioner who attempts intervention without first having established this basis of trust and rapport is sabotaging the potential for success" (Mixson, 1991, p. 40).

As mentioned earlier, self-neglect cases can be very frustrating for practitioners of protective services when clients refuse available services. Mixson (1991) describes the handling of self-neglect cases as "one of the most challenging and rewarding exercises undertaken by practitioners" (p. 40). Challenging, on one hand, if the client refuses available services designed to help and rewarding if a bond of trust is formed through encouraging the client to allow the practitioner to provide beneficial and necessary services. The refusal of services is a serious dilemma faced by the APS caseworker. Conflicts arise out of the need for services and the client's right to refuse. The practitioner must remember to abide by the client's wishes if he or she is capable of understanding the magnitude of the decision. This can be a difficult task, and a harsh realization, for those APS workers who are aware of the benefits of the services offered when these offers are met with resistance.

ADULT PROTECTIVE SERVICES: RESEARCH AND PRACTICE

The purpose of this chapter, and the chapters that follow, is to emphasize the vital relationship between research and practice in adult protective services. Continued research in the area of elder and adult abuse/neglect, and the services that are designed as applicable solutions, is essential. Attempts to "close the gaps" in service provisions and meet higher standards are only possible through research, which encourages new ideas, program designs, and innovative interventions which preserve client autonomy.

Dolon and Blakely (1989) claim that "practitioner-oriented research can provide enlightenment . . . and help in shaping future policies and practices regarding the discovery and treatment of elder abuse and neglect" (p. 48). Because of the rather new interest in providing protective services for the elderly and dependent adults, research is somewhat limited. Practical research in this area also is quite new, only spanning back three or four decades. Much is left to be done. As Dolon and Blakely (1989) state, "In spite of the reported prevalence of elder abuse and neglect, it is not known how effective we are in combatting these problems, what intervention methods and services are favored by practitioners, or which community resources are most helpful to practitioners" (p. 32). It is crucial that consistent reevaluation and assessment of adult protective services and the circumstances surrounding elder abuse/neglect be done through research. Blakely and Dolon (1991) suggest that "additional research is needed on the scope, quality, and outcomes of programs which are designed to prevent elder abuse . . . " (p. 39). We concur.

Research is vitally important to adult protective services practice. It is through such a connection between research and practice that the field of adult protective services will continue to improve in service delivery. However, there is also another benefit as well. Such research can increase public awareness of elder abuse and neglect and the state and local programs designed to combat this social problem. It has been widely stated that public awareness of the needs of adult and elder abuse victims will assist the field in providing services to those in need (Quinn and Tomita, 1986). As Blakely and Dolon (1991) maintain in their study of adult protective services workers, practitioners "identified the task of increasing public awareness as the most prevalent need within planning and service areas" (p. 38) for elder abuse and neglect victims.

Elder abuse/neglect "incorporates a wide range of phenomena, including the infliction of physical injury and pain, mental trauma, anguish, and isolation, withholding basic necessities of life—such as food, shelter, and medical and personal care—and financial exploitation" (Bookin and Dunkle, 1985, p. 3). It can also occur in a variety of family settings such as intergenerational household and spousal units as well as institutional setting such as nursing homes; and it may interchange the role of victim and abuser" (Stein, 1991, p. 92). Stein (1991) proposes "that all elders in family situations are potential victims by virtue of the presumed weaknesses, impairments, and/or dependencies brought about by advancing age" (p. 92). This speaks to the possible consequences if adequate programs are not established to protect dependent members of society.

Abuses inflicted upon the elderly and dependent adults is a growing concern. Adult protective services programs were designed and implemented as a response to the problem of adult and elder abuse/neglect. Research in this area is still in its infancy and programs intended to assist the elderly have only recently become a priority for states, the public, and the federal government.

Many issues surround the practitioners of adult protective services. Many of the issues merely touched on in this first chapter will be addressed in the pages that follow. It is our hope that this volume will assist those interested in furthering the relationship between research and practice in adult protective services. Research is a crucial element for improving existing programs, designing new and more innovative approaches, and to serve the needs of dependent adults within the community.

REFERENCES

Abramson, M. (1985). The autonomy-paternalism dilemma in social work practice. *Social Casework,* September, 387–393.

Bergman, J.A. (1989). Responding to abuse and neglect cases: Protective services versus crisis intervention. In R. Filinson and S. R. Ingman (Eds.), *Elder abuse: Practice and policy.* New York: Human Services Press.

Blakely, B.E. & Dolon, R. (1991). Area agencies on aging and the prevention of elder abuse: The results of a national study. *Journal of Elder Abuse & Neglect, 3,* 21–40.

Bookin, D. & Dunkle, R.E. (1985). Elder abuse: Issues for the practitioner. *Social Casework,* January, 3–12.

Burr, J.J. (1982). *Protective services for adults.* U.S. Department of Health and Human Services [Pub. No. (OHDS) 82-20505], Washington, DC.

Byers, B. & Hendricks, J.E. (1990). Elder financial self-neglect and exploitation: An adult protective services response. *Journal of Free Inquiry and Creative Sociology, 18,* 205–211.

Coleman, N. & Karp, N. (1989). Recent state and federal developments in protective services and elder abuse. *Journal of Elder Abuse & Neglect, 1,* 51–63.

Dolon, R. & Blakely, B.E. (1989). Elder abuse and neglect: A study of adult protective service workers in the United States. *Journal of Elder Abuse & Neglect, 1,* 31–49.

Dolon, R. & Hendricks, J.E. (1989). An exploratory study comparing attitudes and practices of police officers and social service providers in elder abuse and neglect cases. *Journal of Elder Abuse & Neglect, 1,* 75–90.

Dunkle, R.E. (1984). Protective services: Where do we go from here? *Social Casework,* June, 357–363.

Dunkle, R.E., Poulshock, S.W., Silverstone, B. & Deimling, G.T. (1983). Protective services reanalyzed: Does casework help or harm? *Social Casework,* April, 195–199.

Filinson, R. & Ingman, S.R. (Eds.). (1989). *Elder abuse: Practice and policy.* New York: Human Services Press.

Ferguson, E.J. (1978). *Protecting the vulnerable adult.* Ann Arbor, MI: Institute of Gerontology.

Havemeyer, H. (1982). *Legal and social work values in adult protection.* Lakewood, CO: Jefferson County Department of Social Services.

Hull, L., Holmes, G.E., & Karst, R.H. (1990). Managing guardianships of the elderly: Protection and advocacy as public policy. *Journal of Elder Abuse & Neglect, 3/4,* 145–162.

Iris, M.A. (1990). Uses of guardianship as a protective intervention for frail, older adults. *Journal of Elder Abuse & Neglect, 3/4,* 57–71.

Leiber, M.J. (1988). Interaction between civil commitment and protective services: A case study. *New England Journal on Criminal and Civil Confinement, 14,* 41–65.

Leiber, M.J. (1992). Interactions between civil commitment and protective placement: An empirical assessment. *International Journal of Law and Psychiatry, 15,* 265–281.

Mixson, P.M. (1991). Self-neglect: A practitioner's perspective. *Journal of Elder Abuse & Neglect, 3,* 35–42.

Pedrick-Cornell, C. & Gelles, R.J. (1982). Elder abuse: The status of current knowledge. *Family Relations, 31,* 457–465.

Pillemer, K.A., & Wolf, R.S. (Eds.). (1986). *Elder abuse: Conflict in the family.* Dover, MA: Auburn House.

Pratt, C.C., Koval, J. & Lloyd, S. (1983). Service workers' responses to abuse of the elderly. *Social Casework, 64,* 147–153.

Quinn, M.J. & Tomita, S.K. (1986). *Elder abuse and neglect: Causes, diagnosis, and intervention strategies.* New York: Springer.

Regan, J.J. (1978). Intervention through adult protective services programs. *The Gerontologist, 18,* 250–254.

Russo, F.X. & Willis, G. (1986). *Human services in America.* Englewood Cliffs, NJ: Prentice-Hall.

Seelig, J.M. & Chesnut, S.R. (1986). Corporate legal guardianship: An innovative concept in advocacy and protective services. *Social Work, 31,* 221–223.

Sengstock, M.C., Hwalek, M., & Petrone, S. (1989). Services for aged abuse victims: Service types and related factors. *Journal of Elder Abuse & Neglect, 1,* 37–56.

Staudt, M. (1985). The social worker as an advocate in adult protective services. *Social Work, 30,* 204–208.

Stein, K.F. (1991). A national agenda for elder abuse and neglect research: Issues and recommendations. *Journal of Elder Abuse & Neglect, 3,* 91–108.

U.S. Congress. (1990). *Elder abuse: A decade of shame and inaction.* Select Committee on Aging, U.S. House of Representatives. Washington, DC.

Vinton, L. (1991). Factors associated with refusing services among maltreated elderly. *Journal of Elder Abuse & Neglect, 3,* 89–103.

Chapter Two

ABUSE AND NEGLECT:
THE ADULT AND ELDER

JANET E. MICKISH

INTRODUCTION

In Wisconsin, a 79-year-old woman was physically and psychologically abused by her husband of 42 years. Although her husband had always been a controlling man who had threatened and emotionally abused her throughout their relationship, the physical abuse did not begin until her debilitating stroke 6 years ago. Besides being knocked around by her spouse, she is also being denied assistance in such tasks as preparing herself for bed. To punish her, her husband ignores her pleas for help (U.S. House Select Committee on Aging, 1990, p. 4).

An elderly North Dakota man lives in a house without indoor plumbing or adequate heating. He could upgrade his home except every month his son takes his Social Security check and cashes it for his own use. He provides the father with only minimal groceries (U.S. House Select Committee on Aging, 1990, p. 14).

A 40-year-old woman in Colorado who has progressive multiple sclerosis and who supports herself and her husband on her Social Security Disability income was repeatedly beaten by her husband. He would beat her and tell her that she could not live without him. He would also tell her that no one would believe her accusations of abuse and that if she did tell, he would kill her. After the beatings, he would kindly massage her and work with her so that she could improve her mobility. She believes that no one will help her and that he will eventually kill her (Hickman, 1992).

No panaceas for family violence are in sight. But it is the Task Force's firm belief that we as a nation are in a position to do much more in coping with and understanding the problem of family violence than we have in the past. With dedicated effort from individuals and volunteers, much progress has been made. We must continue to develop a strong, coordinated response to family violence. The criminal justice system, social services agencies and the entire community must work together to provide comprehensive services to family members.

—U.S. Attorney General's Task Force Report on Family Violence, 1984, p. 2

As these anecdotes illustrate, the United States can be a violent society. Violence is reflected in every level of our social system, from development of global war machines to family violence. Those who use violence or who abuse and neglect others act out of a belief that such behaviors are appropriate, necessary or legitimate in particular situations and that certain populations are appropriate targets.

This chapter discusses the dominant issues related to abuse of elders and adults with disabilities while focusing on spouse abuse as a form of elder abuse. It is not surprising that these two populations are in need of protective services since these groups are isolated, lack social power and experience social and physical disadvantages that make them vulnerable, and their abuse is minimized by nearly everyone (Finkelhor and Pillemer, 1989; Hickman, 1992).

Elderly people and people with disabilities consist of a cross section of the U.S. population. Most people with disabilities and elderly people live and work in the community. They may be in excellent health, fully functioning and lead active, vibrant lives. At the other end of the continuum, are those who are in poor health and need constant attendant care. The degree to which an elderly person or person with a disability is able to function in society is generally more a function of societal attitudes, the internalization of those attitudes, physical barriers and available resources than it is a function of their health or physical status.

Research concerning people with disabilities has centered on children with little reliable research focused on adults (Groce, 1988). Research on elder abuse has undergone an evolutionary process similar to research on child and spouse abuse. Initially attempting to demonstrate the nature and extent of elder abuse (Block and Sinnott, 1979; Lau and Kosberg, 1979; O'Malley, et al., 1979; Rathbone-McCuan, 1980), researchers more recently have focused their attention on the psychological and situational "causes" (Phillips, 1983).

Although commonly thought of as hitting, shoving, kicking, stabbing, and other serious physical attacks, family violence may also be sexual or psychological. Abuse also includes the infliction or threat of infliction of any bodily injury or unwanted physical contact or the destruction of property or threat thereof as a method of coercion, control, revenge, or punishment. Threats made by the perpetrator before, during and after he has used violence are emotionally abusive and reinforce the victim's belief that he will act on his threats again. The survivor is usually right. Not only does he repeat his behavior, he generally escalates his abusive behavior over time (Walker, 1979). Like threats and physical violence to a person, destruction of property or violence toward pets reinforce the survivor's fear of the perpetrator, for these acts symbolize the perpetrator's power to control and destroy.

This chapter focuses on the family context of violence, abuse and neglect as well as mistreatment (violence, abuse, active neglect and passive neglect) because:

95 percent of the elderly (Hudson, 1986) and 94 percent of people with disabilities (Kutza, 1985) live at home;

Physical abuse by a male social partner (husband, ex-husband, boyfriend, etc.) is the single more common cause of injury for women in the United States; in 75 percent of the reported elder abuse cases the victim lived with the abuser, in over 80 percent of the reports, the abuser was a relative (O'Malley, 1980) and 58 percent of the perpetrators of physical abuse were spouses while 24 percent were adult children (Pillemer and Finkelhor, 1986);

Children with disabilities experience very high rates of abuse—these children grow into adulthood and continue to experience high rates of abuse at the hands of their families of origin as well as in new primary relationships (Coalition of Provincial Organizations of the Handicapped, 1987).

We do not know as much about domestic violence in same-sex relationships as we do about its occurrence in heterosexual relationships. There is increasing evidence that it does exist between some same-sex couples and can be as lethal as in heterosexual relationships (Lobel, 1986; Renzetti, 1988; Island & Latellier, 1991). We do know that 98 percent of all currently documented domestic assaults are committed by men against women (FBI, 1989), that the majority of physical sexual and non-sexual assaults on the elderly and people with disabilities are committed by men (Anetzberger, 1989; Wolf, 1989; Ramsey-Klawsnik, 1991; Hickman, 1992); therefore, the perpetrator will be referred to as "he" and the victim/survivor as "she" in this chapter, even though some domestic violence is initiated by the woman (often in the care giver role) and some cases involve people of the same sex.

There is some disagreement about who is most likely to abuse an elderly family member. Because researchers use a variety of definitions of "mistreatment" (i.e., people who were abused prior to becoming elderly), as well as a variety of research techniques, we rely on various research which includes abuse that has existed over time as well as that which began after the person became elderly.

Mistreatment of people with disabilities and the elderly is not just a family matter. People are seriously injured and may die at the hands of their perpetrators. Most mistreatment of the elderly and people with disabilities constitutes criminal behavior and would be prosecuted as such if committed by a stranger. People who mistreat the elderly and people with disabilities should be dealt with on the basis of their harmful behavior, not on the basis of their relationship to the victim.

WHAT'S GOING ON BEHIND CLOSED DOORS

The American family and the American home are perhaps as or more violent than any other single American institution or setting with the exception of the military . . . in time of war (Straus, et al., 1981, p. 4).

Domestic violence against an adult intimate partner occurs in many families (Walker, 1979) and claims more than 4,000 lives annually in the United States (FBI, 1989). Estimates of abuse and neglect of the elderly range from a low of 4 percent to a high of 17 percent (U.S. House Select Committee on Aging, 1990, p. ix–x). Abuse of adult females with disabilities is estimated to be as high as 85 percent and for women with developmental disabilities as high as 95 percent (Hickman, 1992). According to Aiello and Capkin (1984) abuse is most widespread among elderly women with multiple physical and mental disabilities.

The cost of battering to the survivor, the batterer and society at large is staggering. Women who are abused have a much higher rate of substance abuse, depression, suicide, anxiety, psychological disorders and miscarriages. Abused elders and people with disabilities display similar reactions to mistreatment (Lau and Kosberg, 1978; Phillips, 1983; Hickman, 1992; Abrams, 1992). The cost to children who witness violence toward abused and neglected family members is cumulative, ranging from emotional disturbance in childhood to reenactment of violence and victimization in childhood, adolescence and adulthood (Straus, et al., 1981).

The cost to the batterer is also significant and mirrors costs to the survivor: employment problems, substance abuse, depression, suicide, homicide, anxiety and other psychiatric disorders, arrest, fines and imprisonment (Ewing, et al., 1984; Anetzberger, 1989). The costs are not just financial. With the increased media coverage of family violence comes the melting away of denial. The public's increasing awareness that perpetrators of family mistreatment may strike any where or any time has a detrimental effect on a sense of security within families, communities, and society.

MISTREATMENT: VIOLENCE, ABUSE AND NEGLECT

Since the early 1960s when Henry Kempe (Kempe, et al., 1962) first began to expose the horrors of child abuse and neglect, researchers and practitioners have suggested different ways to classify mistreatment. Such classifications have generally been based on whether the actor possessed the *motivation to cause harm,* and whether the mistreatment was *active* or *passive* (accidental).

Types of Abuse

A 25-year-old woman who has cerebral palsy was the director of a moderate size organization in a large city. She married a man who was loving and kind at first, but who later would beat, then sexually assault her while telling her that she was lucky to have any man at all and that she could not live in the "real world" without him.

Her husband would often tell her in detail how, if she tried to leave him, he would stalk and slowly kill her after he killed her parents and sister.

On one occasion, in a fit of rage, her husband picked up their small dog and threw it against the wall, killing it. On other occasions he would destroy pictures of her family.

He continually opened her mail even though she asked him not to. He also insisted that she turn over her pay check to him each month. He gave her a monthly "allowance."

When she had a baby, she wanted a divorce but was afraid that he would get custody of the child because of society's prejudice against people with a disability (Hickman, 1992).

A 75-year-old Ohio woman was confined in the basement of her son's home against her will. She was bedridden and mentally incapacitated. She was found to have been lying in her own feces for some time. There were no windows in the basement, therefore no sunlight. The woman was given food but only minimal care and personal contact. The son's family said they had to leave her down there because she was incontinent and would "dirty" the house. The family would not agree to pursue nursing home placement because the elderly woman owned the home in which they lived and they did not want to lose their home or any inheritance, as she had a sizable savings account (U.S. House Select Committee on Aging, 1990, p. 13–14).

Abusive behavior is typically *intentional* and *is of long duration.* There are five types of abuse: physical, non-sexual abuse; sexual abuse; psychological/emotional abuse; financial abuse; and violation of rights. Typically, a perpetrator will employ all five forms of abuse in addition to both types of neglect. Battered persons and batterers come from all socioeconomic and educational levels, age, racial, cultural and religious groups, and sexual orientations. It is important to consider domestic violence in the context of other social disadvantages its victims may suffer: gender discrimination, racism, homophobia, bias against the aging and disabled. Intimate violence is one deadly part of a broad pattern of social oppression.

Physical, Non-Sexual Abuse

Physical, non-sexual abuse is the most conspicuous type of abuse. Behaviors in this category include physical battering such as kicking, hitting, biting, choking, pushing, hair-pulling, bodily throwing, and assaulting with weapons. Frequently, the abuser targets specific areas of the body such as the abdomen of a pregnant woman, back of the head, breasts or genitals. Many abusers are careful to injure only parts of the body not easily seen by the casual observer.

Sexual Abuse and Violence

Sexual violence is the type of abuse most likely to occur and the least likely to be perceived, acknowledged, detected or reported. Because discussions of sexual practices are taboo in many groups and because females are generally socialized to provide sexual services for males, many victims do not know that they have been sexually abused. Unused to the idea that sex can be pleasurable for both participants and that desire can be mutual, many women believe they are obliged to participate in sex with their partners regardless of their wishes or the level of pain the sexual behavior may cause them. The shame many people feel when they perceive they have been assaulted also lessens the likelihood that victims will report.

Sexual abuse includes physical attacks on breasts or genitals, sexual sadism, forced sexual activity and the forced viewing of sexually explicit material or pornography. Sexual and non-sexual abuse escalate with time and can be accompanied by life-threatening acts or threats (Walker, 1979).

For elderly women, repeated vaginal rape is the most prevalent type of sexual assault (Ramsey-Klawsnik, 1991). Women who have communication disorders (including developmental disabilities) are the likeliest target of perpetrators of sexual assault (Protection and Advocacy, 1986; Abrams, 1992).

Psychological/Emotional Abuse

Psychological and emotional abuse do not occur in a vacuum. We are socialized to accept that males and those who "take care" of us have the power (and in some cases the right and duty) to define the reality of our lives, to require obedience to their demands and to use physical force if compliance is not forthcoming. We are also socialized to believe that females are . . . These beliefs may be either superficially positive/negative dependent on numerous factors and perspectives. Each person is a human being who has been socialized/indoctrinated with belief systems. The imposition of these beliefs are abusive in and of themselves; they can foster further psychological as well as physical violence.

While psychological abuse can occur without physical abuse, the victim always experiences psychological abuse when there is physical abuse. Although the effects of the physical and psychological mistreatment may not be observable, they are multiple, traumatic and long-lasting.

Psychological abuse can range from name-calling and verbal assaults to protracted and systematic efforts to dehumanize, sometimes with the goal of driving the victim to suicide or insanity (U.S. House Select Committee on Aging, 1990, p. 17). The most common form of psychological abuse cited by the U.S. House Select Committee on Aging (1990) and Hickman (1992) is the constant threat by care givers to throw the survivor into the street, or have them institutionalized. For some people with disabilities, threats also include withholding medication and access to the bathroom, as well as not getting the person out of bed or out of their wheelchair into bed.

The tactics abusers use to control their victims permeate the whole of the family's life and may also include:

abusing or threatening to abuse other family members and friends,
intimidation,
extreme controlling behavior, and
isolation.

Material (Financial) Abuse and Exploitation

For people with disabilities and a growing number of elderly, poverty is an overwhelming reality. Our society generally approves of the person who has the most social and personal resources making decisions about how those resources are allocated. This typically means that the male non-elderly, and able-bodied control family resources. Because both the abuser and survivor believe (or in many cases know) that the survivor is less able (or unable) to obtain resources that will meet their minimum needs, the impact of the financial abuse is significant. Common forms of financial abuse involve the theft or conversion of anything of value and is usually accomplished by physical mistreatment, psychological abuse or deception, fraud, deceit, and misrepresentation.

Violation of Rights

Perpetrators of family violence violate the rights of their victims. Perpetrators of adult and elder abuse may dictate living place, arrangements, safety and sanitary conditions; restrict physical mobility and medical treatment; remove personal property; violate privacy; and prohibit the survivor from complaining and seeking help.

Types of Neglect

Neglect may be characterized as *active neglect* (passive abuse), or *passive neglect.* Behaviors in this category include the withholding of medication, medical treatment, food and personal care necessary for the well-being of the survivor.

Active Neglect or Passive Abuse

Active neglect is most likely to exist in a family where there is ongoing violence and abuse. It is a direct attempt to manipulate, humiliate, control and punish the victim. perpetrators of active neglect intentionally fail to fulfill their caretaking obligations by consciously inflicting physical or emotional stress or injury on the victim. Examples include depriving the survivor of a wheelchair, eyeglasses, medication, food, dentures or life support services (i.e., clear breathing tube).

Passive Neglect

Passive neglect is the most understood category of mistreatment. It is the category in which there is the most sympathy for the perpetrator and that most social service programs were designed to ameliorate. In most cases passive neglect

> is the tragic result of well-meaning family members, friends, or other persons who assume the care of . . . a person but who are incapable of meeting that person's needs. They may not be up to the task for many reasons. The home care of a frail adult (and some people with disabilities) is more taxing than

most people think. The physical, emotional, and financial costs can be enormous, particularly when the dependent older person [or person with some types of disabilities] is bedfast, incontinent, or the victim of a long-term, behavior-changing illness (Douglass, 1987, p. 5).

Home care of some people with disabilities and frail elderly can involve performing procedures (i.e., assisting in bowel and bladder functions, cleaning wounds and tubes, etc.) that are demanding and unpleasant, providing financial assistance that may exceed the family's resources and expending emotional and physical energy beyond the care giver's capacity. Taken singularly, these issues seem trivial or manageable but increase in importance as family members give up education, retirement, vacation, home improvement and other plans to care for a family member.

Patterns of Abuse

The abusive practices perpetrators use are interrelated and are part of a culture that facilitates males, and younger, able bodied people gaining and maintaining power over family members.

I was physically, emotionally and verbally abused in my thirteen year marriage. I cannot say that it was totally because I am disabled. Certainly family of origin and upbringing had a direct effect. (I was not hearing impaired when growing up). I grew up in a troubled home and married into a troubled alcoholic marriage. I do believe, however, that the disability gave my husband reason to oppress me and feel better than me. It also kept me in an abusive marriage much longer because I could not see my way out. I was doubly isolated—hearing impaired and living in a lonely, abusive marriage (Doucette, 1986).

Intermittent reinforcement is a common pattern of mistreatment.

An 80-year-old woman (unable to walk because of a stroke) who lived with her 54-year-old son was found to be suffering from a staph infection from laying in her urine-soaked, feces-covered bed for three weeks. She also showed signs of bruises and lacerations around her face. She said that her son had to work so he could not help her to the bathroom and was too busy to change the bedding. Last week her son hit her because he did not like the smell of her room.

The woman also related that her son would fix her wonderful meals several times a month. Most mornings he would sing to her although, occasionally, he would fly into a rage and refuse to feed her breakfast. He gave her a bath and bought her a new mattress, nightgown and sheets last month on her birthday.

The woman feels frightened of her son, but also says that she tries to not eat or drink much so that she doesn't have to use the bathroom. She believes that she is a burden and that her son is good to let her stay with him. She says that she tries to say the right things to him but sometimes maybe she uses the wrong tone or asks for too much.

Her son admits that he "looses it" sometimes, but that his mother is better off with him than with strangers in a nursing home.

The mother and son have lived together for ten years. During that time the son has hit his mother 30 or 40 times and has sold much of her antique furniture to purchase a power boat for himself.

Intermittent Reinforcement is a social-learning theory asserting that behavior that has been reinforced on a random and variable basis (without prediction) is the most difficult behavior for a victim to adjust to psychologically and for perpetrators to extinguish. Typically, the abuser gains more and more power by acting in ways that appear to be random. Sometimes he acts positively while at other times he acts negatively (intermittent reinforcement) toward the same or similar situations (Walker, 1979). The survivor, therefore, loses her ability to predict the perpetrator's reaction to her or to anything else.

Similarly, the perpetrator intermittently reinforces his own behavior. Because he is out of touch with his feelings, he does not connect his beliefs and feelings with his actions and consequences of those actions. The abusive person is rarely in touch with any feeling other than anger (Ewing, et al., 1984, p. 3). Therefore, when he consciously or subconsciously experiences unacceptable feelings or thoughts he transforms them into feelings of anger and rage.

Thus, normal thoughts and feelings such as "I am using all of my retirement money to buy medication for mother." "I feel guilt and shame that I cannot deal with my wife's disability. A real man could." "I feel trapped by my obligations." "I feel frightened about what will happen to me when I get old." "I feel guilty that my son is 30 years old and still functions at the level of a six-year-old; I can't handle this anymore"—are translated into feelings of anger and rage.

Although people who are abusive may perceive that occasionally they "go too far," they believe that abuse is a legitimate and appropriate response to anger. Consequently, the abusive person's behavior is reinforced by his belief in the "rightness" of that behavior. The pain and chaos which results from mistreatment also diverts attention from what the perpetrator believes are his unacceptable emotions (i.e., fear, sadness, abandonment, shame, guilt, loneliness). His resulting experience of relief when he no longer experiences the precipitating thoughts and feelings also serve to reinforce the abuse.

Because the abusive family member is typically responding to feelings and thoughts that he does not know he has—and is therefore not discussing his distress with the survivor—his behavior appears random and unpredictable. The apparent "randomness" and "unpredictability" of his behavior serve as intermittent reinforcement for both the survivor and the batterer. Neither of them can accurately predict when the perpetrator will respond negatively or positively.

Add to this our culture's belief that a person can "cause" someone else to think or feel a particular way (i.e., jealously, cheerfully) or to behave in a particular way (violently, sexually), the survivor translates the abuser's negative or positive responses into: "I must have done something to cause him to behave the way he does." The perpetrator also points out what the victim has done to "set him off" or "push his buttons."

Compounding the effect these beliefs are beliefs of some people with disabilities and the elderly: "I should have died instead of burdening my family." "My condition would drive anyone to violence." "He feels so stressed in trying to take care of me; I don't blame him for losing control sometimes." "I feel ashamed that I cannot take care of myself." "I feel ashamed that I married (or raised) someone who treats me like this."

So when the perpetrator participates in loving, caring, behavior one time and mistreats the survivor the next, they both believe that it is the victim's behavior or "condition" causing his responses. She believes her happiness (and ultimately her life) depends on her ability to please and "fix" him. The "good" responses, mixed unpredictably with the abuse, serve as intermittent reinforcement for her to minimize and deny the mistreatment.

Adaptations to Mistreatment

Adaptations to mistreatment are varied and complex. To the untrained observer, many survival tactics and perceptions may seem to be "self-defeating personality disorder," "paranoia," "masochism" or similar behavior and character disorders. Adaptations in cases where mistreatment is occurring are attempts at adjusting to an environment of terrorism in which complete escape is seen as impossible. The following are some principal adaptations of most victims of prolonged trauma. These and other adaptations vary from person to person and change over time.

Learned helplessness is a psychological theory that describes what happens when a person loses the ability to predict that their actions will produce a particular outcome. Because the abused family member tries to protect herself and her family as best she can she will choose only those actions that have a high probability of being successful.

Learned helplessness, therefore, is a "survival-focused" (as opposed to an "escape-focused") adaptation to repeated, intermittent abuse such as family abuse or incarceration in a concentration camp during times of war.

As the mistreatment and isolation continue, and probably escalate, a shift in the survivor's comprehension of the situation occurs. She increasingly perceives escape as impossible. While she may continue to work at her paid job, eat, clean house, take care of children, laugh with co-workers and appear self-confident and independent, *surviving* the abusive relationship becomes the focus of her life at home.

In the survivor's eyes, the batterer becomes more and more powerful. The victim may see adult protective services and other agencies as less and less able to help (Walker, 1979; Quinn and Tomita, 1986). She may feel trapped and alone. She will likely develop a variety of coping mechanisms she believes will help her and her family stay alive. These mechanisms may include withdrawal, asking permission to do even trivial things, compulsiveness, manipulation, substance abuse, denying mistreatment and asking that charges be dropped if mistreatment is detected.

Post Traumatic Stress Disorder (PTSD) is a psychological condition that many abuse victims develop. PTSD is a collection of psychological systems. Battered Women's syndrome, Rape Trauma syndrome, Battered Child and Child Sexual Abuse Accommodation syndrome are all considered subcategories of PTSD. A single severe, traumatic event may bring on this disorder as can repeated trauma. PTSD may be mild or severe, transient or chronic. There are three major groups of psychological symptoms:

> Cognitive disturbances, such as recurrent intrusive memories of previous traumas, flashbacks, night terrors;

> High arousal or anxiety symptoms such as sleep pattern disruption, avoidance, numbing; and

> Depression responses including minimizing and denying the danger from violence.

The Stockholm syndrome is another common consequence of prolonged mistreatment and was originally coined to describe the reaction of hostages to their captors, and it can be applied to battered women and elder abuse victims.

The identifying reaction is characterized by a strong emotional bond between the two involved in a severe power imbalance: captor/hostage, batterer/survivor, abusive caretaker/elder or person with a disability. The two depend upon each other: the captor for his feelings of power and dominance, the victim for her life. *The survivor learns to accommodate to the abusers demands, often incorporating abusive belief systems as her own in extreme cases.*

The survivor develops feelings of fear and hopelessness about her situation. This is especially true for women who have the additional terror from threats that the batterer will harm people she loves, and for women who have sought help from the criminal justice system or adult protective services only to have them fail to respond to her pleas. The survivor attempts to emphasize that abuser's "kind" behavior and minimize his "aggressor" response. Since abusers/captors have the ability to seriously injure and kill, they are seen as gracious for providing essential services and sparing the survivor's life. Even though he is the one who initiated the mistreatment, the abuser is the only one there to console and provide services to the survivor after threatening or mistreating her.

Survivors grow to fear change and outside interference. Hostages fear situations like shootouts and abuse victims fear more beatings or the withholding of medication, or other life sustaining services. *The fear of what happens if they don't comply with the aggressor, as well as incorporation of the aggressor's values and behaviors as a coping strategy, keeps them from reaching out.*

Techniques (dependency, debility and dread) used by the captors during times of war to create "brainwashing" are in many ways the same techniques used by abusers on their victims. Not surprisingly, survivors display virtually the same survival adaptations to this "brainwashing" as do prisoners of war.

People who mistreat family members do not consciously lay out strategies for brainwashing the people they abuse. They simply interact with their victims the way they have been socialized to believe will work for them. Professionals have refined these abusive patterns and use them to brainwash prisoners of war.

Although it is true that the life experience of the survivor prior to contact with the abuser has a significant impact on her perception of the situation and her survival adaptations, most victims are exposed to at least some level of these three techniques.

Debilitation may result from deprivations occurring individually, serially or simultaneously. The most common deprivations are food, sleep, and human contact. When a victim experiences significant deprivation, she

> becomes paradoxically dependent on [her] torturer for these things. The only person who can provide these reliefs is the torturer, and in the induced abnormal environment where deprivation and stress are the norm and other social contacts are withdrawn, the victim becomes dependent on him as the sole source of support. Occasional unpredictable, brief respites, when among other things the torturer becomes a sympathetic listener, make the victim obligated toward him (Bettelheim, 1947, p. 46).

It is not uncommon for an abuser to physically lock up his victim or tie her up or deprive her of food, sleep and contact with other people. Many abuse victims report being prevented from going to sleep or awakened in the middle of the night by the abuser's long verbal haranguings. His physical ability to overpower her, his psychological abuse, deprivation and isolation, combined with societally perpetuated debilitating factors (economic, cultural and psychological) increase the dependency of the victim on him. These factors also increase the likelihood that the survivor will not report, will deny to police and adult protective services that anything is wrong, and stay with the perpetrator and comply with his demands.

Dependency is culturally driven. In much the same way that guards and prisoners of war experience a power differential when they are thrust into those positions, husbands in traditional patriarchal marriages and family caretakers have historically been given much power and authority by law and currently by custom. Therefore, caretakers need apply little or no manipulation or coercion for a considerable power and resource differential to exist between them and their victims. In such cases, dependency is a given.

Even today, with increasing egalitarian values, the elderly and disability rights movements, great power, resource and status differences exist between those who are identified as caretakers and those to be taken care of. These differences are continually reinforced through a variety of formal and informal sanctions, actions and inactions.

Dread is the feeling that requires constant attention and devours a tremendous amount of psychological and emotional energy. It is a feeling of constantly walking on eggshells. It is a product of the cycle of violence: never knowing when he will be loving and gentle or when he will be abusive. The feeling of dread is an all-consuming anticipation and terror of further violence. It becomes an involuntary response that strikes at the very core of the survivor. It is not just a fear of death. If it were only a fear of death, some victims would eagerly choose death and be done with it. Indeed, some survivors pray for death and some commit suicide.

The feeling of dread is a spontaneous reflex—a knee jerk reaction— that catapults the victim in survival behavior—trying to minimize the amount of pain she and other family members will experience. Therefore, noncompliance to the abuser's demands becomes more dangerous, and psychological "symptoms" become more pronounced as she anticipates and fears future mistreatment.

After one or more episodes of mistreatment, the survivor can be reminded of the past violence and the danger of further mistreatment by the abuser giving a particular look, word, nod of the head, facial movement or gesture. These signs may trigger the same psychological and physiological response in the survivor as if she were being abused again. Those who have developed PTSD actually re-experience parts of other incidents of mistreatment in their mind, adding to the psychological terror of the current incident.

Dependency, debilitation, dread, when executed in the proper measure over time, significantly alter a person's self-perception and lead to the psychological and behavioral adaptations described. When a survivor is no longer subjected to these factors, when she experiences safety, she often regains her previous self. Some victims more rapidly heal from the abuse when they attend a group with other victims; others may need the assistance of a therapist trained to work with survivors of violence. But, for the possibility of healing to occur, survivors need the violence and threat of violence to end permanently.

Other Adaptations developed by survivors include a wide range of behaviors that attempt to mask, mitigate or control the terrorism victims are experiencing. The most common adaptations include:

self medication through substance abuse
somatization of terror
withdrawal or isolation
stoic behavior

manipulative behavior

in some cases very passive, while in others, very provocative behavior

dependence on others to provide answers to questions or problems

THE SOCIAL CONSTRUCTION OF FAMILY ABUSE

Cultural Beliefs

Family violence is fundamentally a social phenomenon and is therefore not an issue so much of individual pathology as of societal pathology. Sexist social and cultural beliefs permit and encourage abuse toward females. Ageism and able bodyism, in the same way, encourage discrimination against and abuse of the elderly and people with disabilities (Marshall, 1986; Quinn and Tomita, 1986).

Additionally, our society assigns family roles and responsibilities on the basis of age, sex/gender as well as the nature and extent to which one is perceived to be able-bodied rather than on ability, competence and interest. Our cultural beliefs create roles in which the person identified as inferior becomes trapped and victimized. Some of those beliefs include:

males and male work are superior to females and female work;

boys are born and should be bred to be strong, aggressive, productive, able-bodied leaders until they are in their 60s, then they are to retire and let younger males take over;

girls are born and should be bred to be nurturing, loving, gentle caretakers who obey male family members and are responsible for maintaining a home in which to nurture men and children;

able-bodied people and their work are superior to people with disabilities and their work;

the elderly and people with disabilities don't contribute materially to society; they draw from social services money that could be used for other things;

real families are composed of able-bodied people: a father, mother and a small number of children—all other relational forms (including widowhood) are deficient, broken, perverse, invalid, or inadequate;

violence is a legitimate, appropriate and, in some cases, necessary means of obtaining and insuring the maintenance of power and control;

one person can *cause* another person to think or feel a particular way: "You make me happy." "You make me sad." "You make me hit you." "You turn me on." "You push my buttons." "You made me spend money on your medication that I could have spent on a new dress." "You are causing us to use Tom's college fund money to keep you alive."

love excuses or sanctions violent, abusive or neglectful behavior;

it is permissible to hit members of one's family, especially if it is to "teach them a good lesson";

winning is everything.

Perpetrators and Survivors

There is no "typical" abuser, victim or survivor. While some abusers love their family members and do not want to use violence, others do not love the family members, feel comfortable using violence and do not care whether the family member stays, leaves, lives or dies. Likewise, some victims love the family member who is mistreating them, do not want to see him hurt and just want him to stop the mistreatment; others hate their abuser and would like him to go away and leave them alone or to die.

Mistreatment may be the general, long-term and firmly embedded style of family interaction engaged in by all members of the family. It may be short-term and situational. Several members of the family may engage in mistreatment of one person, or one person may mistreat several others. There are countless variations of patterns of mistreatment.

Characteristics of people who are at risk of mistreating the elderly and people with disabilities include (Kosberg, 1988; Abrams, 1992; Hickman, 1992):

internalized cultural beliefs discussed above;
abuse subtances;
mental or emotional problems, including acting out negative feelings;
come from a family where violence was the norm;
feel stressed;
feel dependent on victim;
have unrealistic expectations;
socially isolated, alienated and has poor self-image
immature;
strong feelings of obligation rather than attachment;
poor self-control;
secretive;
blames victim.

Mistreatment is learned behavior that can be modified and changed. The key to changing behavior is found in identification and containment of the perpetrator's mistreatment, by giving him immediate, consistent no-violence messages and consequences.

> He would have stopped the violence long before if the police had arrested him in the beginning. In the beginning, he was afraid of the police. He was afraid of going to jail and losing his job. But when he saw that the police were not going to touch him, he came right back and the violence got worse, and he got bolder (U.S. Attorney General's Task Force on Family Violence, 1984, p. 4).

People are abusive toward their family members because, in the short term, it works and they can get away with it. Although the mistreatment masks his real feelings, the abuser believes that abuse "releases" or "fixes" them. Mistreatment also results in a change in behavior of the individual at whom it is directed. The result is a deeply embedded cycle of violence in which the whole family is trapped.

As pointed out by Ewing, et al. (1984),

> Violence is men's response to pain, via a circuitous, sometimes hidden, route. The man who batters is rarely in touch with any feelings other than anger. Anger is men's easy emotion. Anger is always there, ever present, as the emotion which veils hurt, fear, pain, loss and anxiety. Literally speaking there is no "reason" that men batter . . . there is only the violence at the moment, when unresolved feelings and cognition, covered with hurt-become-anger-become-rage, explode in an irrational act of "control." What [he perceives] is out of control, the batterer will beat into control. Violence controls; therefore in the short run, violence works (p. 3–4).

Perpetrators of family violence abuse and neglect come from every walk of life. They represent a wide range of mental health—from the "normal" person who underestimates the physical, emotional and financial commitment to in-home care of a family member—to the man who uses his male (or able-bodied or non-elderly) privilege and power to dominate his family—to the psychopathic person who stalks, tortures and kills his family and others. The "reasons" people abuse and neglect family members is a complex mix of psychological and cultural factors.

The "reasons" for perpetrator's actions are directly related to the perception and characteristics of the perpetrator and have virtually no relationship to the actual characteristics and needs of the survivor (Koopman-Boyden and Wells, 1979; O'Malley et al., 1980; Cicirelli, 1983; Wolf, 1989). Determinants of whether someone will mistreat a family member center around the family member's perception:

of the needs of the victim,
of circumstances where mistreatment is appropriate,

that he is dependent on the victim,
that his problems come from outside himself,
that others cause him to lose control,
that change is undesirable or frightening.

When a person holds the above beliefs, is highly impulsive, immature and easily excitable, the stage is set for mistreatment.

The relationships of perpetrators of abuse and neglect are filled with extremes of action and emotion that our everyday lives seldom match. The fulfilling relationships they crave are the opposite of the ones they create. Tormented by the inconsistency, they escalate their abuse in an attempt to coerce the family member into filling their emptiness. Identifying the cause of their distress as outside themselves, these perpetrators don't address their own needs and feelings, hence the love and security they crave become increasingly illusive.

Frequently perpetrators feel frightened, inadequate, isolated, victimized, empty, abandoned, and worthless. Because males are socialized to believe that they are invulnerable, unemotional, active in controlling the world and people around them, and abuse is a necessary and legitimate way to control their environment, they act out abusively. This abuse creates crises that remain more immediate, tangible, real and compelling than the surrounding "ordinary" stimulations that they perceive constantly threaten to disrupt their lives. It also keeps the focus on the victim's problems rather than the perpetrator's.

Depriving a person of medication, food, bathroom privileges, change of dressing, and the like, creates more crisis for all family members, (as does the infliction of physical and psychological injury). The focus shifts from the perpetrator to the victim, and what should be done to, with, for and about the victim.

People who resort to mistreatment use power to gain control over those whom they have assigned responsibility for their lives and feelings. They seek to establish control by violating basic human rights and by using physical, sexual and psychological violence coupled with economic deprivation while occasionally lavishing affection and gifts, isolating their victims from social supports; and creating crisis and chaos (Ewing, et al., 1984).

Abusers tend to rationalize their behavior through a belief system that maintains:

1. What I am doing is not wrong.
2. If it is wrong, I will not be caught.

3. If I do get caught, I can talk my way out.
4. If I cannot talk my way out, I can control the consequences and they will be light (Ewing, et al., 1984, p. 4).

A primary goal of perpetrators is to draw everyone (family members as well as "outsiders") into their belief system. They present a facade of innocence and ignorance and ignorance of the mistreatment to the outside world. If questioned, the perpetrator generally describes mistreatment was "self-inflicted" by the victim.

Providing services that address only the needs of the family member who is engaged in passive neglect, will fail to curb most mistreatment. Those services do not address the true nature of the mistreatment occurring in the majority of cases, and may serve to increase the lethality of the situation. Perpetrators of mistreatment of a family member require maximum intervention, containment, and treatment. When effective consequences are not forthcoming, perpetrators believe that they have drawn everyone into their belief system. They systematically get farther and farther into their abuse system and farther and farther from the true cause and effect of their beliefs and behavior. Without effective intervention, the perpetrator has no reality check that will insure that his behavior is appropriate.

Victims/Survivors are found in every segment of society. Characteristics of who will be mistreated vary widely, however, their adaptations to mistreatment tend to follow the patterns discussed previously.

Most able-bodied, non-elderly women who are battered leave violent relationships. Fewer and fewer stay. However, those who stay do so perhaps due to legitimate dependency. Typically, a battered woman will leave a violent relationship three to five times before she feels safe enough and has established enough resources to make the break permanent (Walker, 1979). Because a batterer is most violent when he perceives that his partner is leaving him (whatever that means to him), battered women must be very cautious in their preparations and in their leaving.

The more the victim needs the perpetrator, the less likely she will be able to physically and emotionally access help (Bolton and Bolton, 1987; Ramsey-Klawsnik, 1991). Many people with disabilities and elderly people have little access to or knowledge of help, and therefore are unable to take even the first steps toward leaving. Access means being accepted into a homeless or battered women's shelter, having literature that is consumable (e.g., braille, audio tapes, large type, etc.), appropriate communication systems (e.g., TTD, sign language interpreter) and barrier free environment (attitude as well as physical).

There are increasing numbers of women who are disabled as a result of domestic violence (Hickman, 1992). When people with disabilities who are mistreated make contact with agencies that provide them with appropriate services and safety, they leave the abusive situation with the same regularity as do non-disabled and non-elderly people (Abrams, 1992; Hickman, 1992). Many factors combine to keep a survivor in a battering relationship. Such factors include fear, lack of perceived alternatives, scarcity of social and personal resources, social expectations, and habituation to abuse. These factors make the cost of leaving an abusive relationship for most victims almost as high as staying. They are created by the victim's socialization and her experience. They are created by society's perpetuation of mistreatment, through excusing abusive behavior, blaming victims for being in the abusive situation and failing to detect abuse, and then failing to protect or support survivors even if the mistreatment is detected.

The Cycle of Violence

Battered women are not constantly being abused, nor is their abuse inflicted at totally random times. One of the most striking discoveries in the interviews was of a definite battering cycle that these women experience. Understanding this cycle is very important if we are to learn how to stop or prevent battering incidents. The cycle also helps explain how battered women become victimized, how they fall into learned helplessness behavior, and why they do not attempt to escape (Walker, 1979, p. 55).

The cycle of violence approach may be applied to spouse and elder abuse but special considerations must be made when applying this concept to the latter. That is, few documented cases of elder abuse involve violence between spouses. More often than not, abuse is perpetrated by a care giver or relative of a younger generation. In spite of this, and given that spouse abuse is so prevalent, it seems logical and practical to discuss this problem cross-generationally. Although it is not the same in all situations where abuse exists, Ewing, et al. (1984), describes the cycle of violence as consisting of four phases:

1. Tension Build-up
2. Explosion

3. Guilt and Remorse
4. Hearts and Flowers

An adaptation of that cycle is presented here to reflect mistreatment in family relationships that may or may not involve the marriage of the abuser to the victim.

The four phases of the cycle of violence are the loving, kind supportive phase; the tension or build up phase; and the explosion or serious mistreatment phase and the guilt and remorse phase.

While it is generally recognized that a perpetrator will typically increase the frequency and severity of abuse each time the cycle is repeated (Walker, 1979), the loving, kind supportive phase may not exist in all family situations and **THERE ARE NO GUARANTEES HE WILL NOT USE LETHAL FORCE (intentionally or accidentally) THE FIRST TIME HE MISTREATS THE FAMILY MEMBER.** The same is true of the second or the third incident, and so on. Therefore, **EVERY INCIDENT OF MISTREATMENT MUST BE CONSIDERED POTENTIALLY LETHAL.**

Phase One: Loving, Kind, Supportive Phase

The loving, kind, supportive phase is the first stage in the process and looks the same in a family in which there is mistreatment as in one where there is none, at least at first. In marital relationships, the elderly couple initially spend time together talking about themselves, laughing, having fun and buying each other presents. The perpetrator generally asks questions about the victim's life, hopes and dreams. He will later use this information against her. The perpetrator also expresses jealousy and wants all of her attention. Because of socialization, she typically interprets his behavior as "true love" and thinks this is great.

As time passes, and the cycle repeats, his "loving attention" becomes controlling and conditioned upon her compliance with his demands. He also feels guilt, shame and fear about his abusive behavior and tries to minimize the abuse by lavishing gifts and attention.

In other family relationships where mistreatment exists, there may be periods of loving and caring behavior. At first this behavior may be appropriate, and later, as in marital relationships, be conditioned upon compliance with the demands and mood of the perpetrator as well as the extent of guilt experienced by the perpetrator. This phase tends to be shorter than the tension phase and may disappear over time. The man is usually contrite, justifies his behavior by blaming the victim, offers excuses such as drinking and promises that it will never happen again. And he means it until the next time.

The survivor is least likely to be amenable to intervention at this time, particularly if the cycle has not had many repetitions (intermittent reinforcement) because it is the period when she receives the most rewards for the status quo. Often, in this phase the victim is reminded of an earlier time when the abuser behaved in a similar loving and nurturing manner with no observable mistreatment. In contrast, the abuser may be more amenable to intervention at this time because, although he is trying to divert attention from his abusive behavior, typically, he is remorseful and wishes to decrease his stress. Later in the phase, if he believes that he has again "won over" his victim (i.e., the victim will not cause further trouble) or that he has "gotten a hold of himself" and can handle his "burden," he is less and less amenable to intervention.

During the height of this phase, both parties minimize the violence and may actually forget and distort what happened. When that occurs, repetition of the cycle is surely inevitable. It is impossible for people to consciously change their behavior if they do not remember it; they cannot learn from past experience if they do not know what they did, thought or felt.

Phase Two: Tension or Build-Up

The second phase of tension-building may last a week, months or years. It will usually occur more frequently as the cycle is repeated. It is characterized by increasing verbal, minor physical abuse as well as active and passive neglect and a decrease in loving communication. Sometimes, only minimal levels of mistreatment are sufficient to frighten the victim into submission here; she knows what will happen if she does not comply with his demands. This is a time when the survivor may be amenable to resources in the community and may, if physically and mentally able, even seek out a member of the clergy, a physician or another authority figure she trusts. She tries to keep the perpetrator as calm as possible, fearing any escalation in tension will also increase his dangerousness.

Sometimes a victim who has been through the cycle before senses that an acute battering incident, Phase Three, is about to occur. She may do things she believes he will explode over. Sometimes she does this in front of other people. Her goal is to get the abuse over with while his abuse level is still relatively low. This may also be an attempt to alert others to the mistreatment she has been suffering. If others are around or she is able to name the time or place where he mistreats her, she believes that she is in a better place to defend herself and obtain help.

The abuser may also feel increased tension, but will deny this to himself and others. By such denial he is able to keep from admitting that "the problem" is within him. It is also the basis for his unwillingness to seek help; he thinks he can handle anything if he is "just man enough" to control himself and his environment.

Phase Three: Serious Mistreatment Phase

In the third phase, the tension has exceeded the perpetrator's ability or desire to control his angry feelings and abusive response. If he has mistreated a family member before, he knows that his "stress" seems to "vanish" when he is abusive. If he has not mistreated someone before, he will learn that abuse works to decrease his stress, and change the victim's behavior. Thus, the acute battering phase begins. If law enforcement intervenes, it is often at this time. If there are serious injuries requiring medical care, they usually occur during Phase Three.

It is important to note that any family member may "initiate" the acute battering phase. This is different from "asking for it" as the common myth suggests. Rather, if the survivor "initiates" the battering phase, she creates the illusion of controlling the place and time of the event. It does not make her an abuser, too. In this situation, she hopes that if he mistreats her now, the abuse will relieve his tension before it is so great that he becomes lethal.

Immediately following this phase the perpetrator and the survivor are more amenable to intervention. She is hurt and frightened and he often feels guilty, humiliated and ashamed. Both are highly motivated for the abuse to stop. An arrest at this time with immediate consequences would be the best intervention to stop the violence from recurring.

Phase Four: Guilt and Remorse

In the first several times the perpetrator engages the cycle, he typically feels guilty and remorseful. He then tries to lessen these feelings by telling the victim that he is sorry, that "it will never happen again," and lavishing gifts and attention on her. This then leads into the first phase of love and support. As time passes, he increases his justification for the abusive behavior and may decrease his feelings of guilt and remorse.

To summarize, in the first part of Phase One, the perpetrator and victim believe the relationship is good. As the cycle repeats, they believe that things are getting better each time they enter this phase; and do not want to talk about bad things when things are so "good." Later when this phase no longer exists, there may be hope that it will return at some future time.

In Phase Two, neither family member addresses the mistreatment because they hope that if both ignore the problem, things will get better. The survivor may feel that things are already too tense and if she just behaves "right," all will be well. They both think that if the victim would only be less demanding, more sensitive, giving and understanding and not "push his buttons," he would not "lose it" and mistreat her.

In Phase Three, neither one is in any condition to discuss issues logically and rationally. In Phase Four, both believe that conditions are getting better, so why rock the boat. According to learning theory, repetition of patterns of beliefs and behaviors recur for two basic reasons. First, the drop in tension is psychologically reinforcing; and second, the lack of perception of a cycle makes Phase Four perceived as intermittent or random and variable reinforcement.

CONCLUSION

The problem of elder abuse and neglect presents a formidable task for the adult protective services intervenor. This chapter addresses the problem of elder abuse and neglect by utilizing the established literature from the concomitant area of family violence: spouse abuse. There are many useful parallels between elder abuse and spouse when addressing the newly recognized area of domestic abuse of the elderly.

This chapter illustrates the application of spouse abuse to elder abuse by outlining the hidden phenomenon of elder abuse. Like spouse abuse, elder abuse in domestic settings occurs behind closed doors and may not be readily apparent to adult protective services investigators. The issue of detection will likely present important challenges to the investigator pertaining the possibility of intervention. Also like spouse abuse, the problem of elder abuse must include adequate operational definitions as applied to practice. When defining elder mistreatment, there are many parallels one can make while remaining cognizant that elder abuse victims and spouse abuse victims, while at times similar, do have different issues which each confronts.

Both domestic abuse of spouses and elders is socially constructed. That is, domestic abuse is defined by the cultural beliefs which are indicative of a particular society. American society possesses cultural belief patterns which reinforce abusive behavior as a satisfactory manner of resolving conflict. Within this cultural pattern one can find evidence of the cycle of violence. This position maintains that violence is learned through having experienced violence at an earlier period in life. Abuse is then perpetuated later in life based on this socio-cultural learning of domestic abuse. In domestic abuse, one can label the key players as perpetrators, victims, and survivors. More recognition must be made, however, to the reality that in the domestic abuse of the elderly this delineation is not as clear-cut. That is, the domestic violence perpetrator in elder abuse and neglect cases may also be a victim in need of services.

REFERENCES

Abrams, M. (1992). Elder Abuse Prevention Project, Denver, CO. Interview.

Aiello, D. & Capkin, L. (1984). Services for disabled victims: elements and standards. *Response to the Victimization of Women and Children, 7* (4), 14.

Anetzberger, G. (1989). Implications of research on elder abuse perpetrators: Rethinking current social policy and programming. In R. Filinson, and S. Ingman, (Eds.), *Elder abuse: Practice and policy.* New York: Human Sciences Press.

Bettelheim (1947). Individual and mass behavior in extreme situations. In T. M. Newcome and E. L. Hartley (Eds.), *Readings in Social Psychology.* New York: Holt, Rinehart and Winston.

Block, M. R. & Sinnott, J. D. (1979). *The Battered Elder syndrome: An Exploratory Study.* College Park: University of Maryland, Center on Aging.

Bolton, F., Bolton, S. (1987). *Working with violent families: A guide for clinical and legal practitioners.* Newbury Park, CA: Sage.

Cicirelli, V. (1983). Adult children and their elderly parents. In T. Brumaker (Ed.), *Family relations in later life.* Beverly Hills, CA: Sage.

Coalition of provincial organizations of the handicapped (1987). Proceedings from the workshop on disabled women's issues. Winnipeg, Canada.

Doucette, J. (1986). *Violent acts against disabled women.* Toronto, Ontario: The Disabled Women's Network Toronto.

Douglass, R. L. (1987). *Domestic mistreatment of the elderly.* Washington, DC: Criminal Justice Services, American Association of Retired Persons.

Ewing, W., Lindsay, M. and Pomeranz, J. (1984). *Battering. An amend manual for helpers.* Denver, CO: Abusive Men Exploring New Directions.

Federal Bureau of Investigation (1989). *Uniform crime reporting handbook.* Washington, DC: U.S. Government Printing Office.

Finkelhor, D., and Pillemer, K. (1989). Elder abuse: Its relationship to other forms of domestic violence. In G. Hotaling, D. Findelhor, J. Kirkpatrik, and K. Straus (Eds.), *Coping with family violence: Research on policy perspectives.* Beverly Hills, Sage.

Groce, N. (1988). Special groups at risk of abuse: The disabled. In M. Straus (Ed.), *Abuse and victimization across the life span.* Baltimore, MD: Johns Hopkins University Press.

Hickman, S. (1992). Executive Director, Domestic Violence Initiative for Women with Disabilities. Interview.

Hudson, M. F. (1986). Elder mistreatment: Current research. In K. A. Pillemer and R. S. Wolf (Eds.), *Elder abuse: Conflict in the family.* Dover, MA: Auburn House.

Island, D. and Letellier, P. (1991). *Men who beat the men who love them: Battered gay men and domestic violence.* Binghamton, NY: Haworth.

Kempe, H., Silverman, F. N., Steele, B. F., Droege-Mueller, W., and Silver, H. K. (1962). The battered child syndrome. *Journal of the American Medical Association, 181*(4), 327–346.

Koopman-Boyden, P. G. & Wells, F. (1979). The problems arising from supporting the elderly at home. *New Zealand Medical Journal, 89,* 265–272.

Kosberg, J. I. (1988). Preventing elder abuse: Identification of high risk factors prior to placement decisions. *The Gerontologist, 28*(1), 43–50.

Kutza, E. A. (1985). Benefits for the disabled: How beneficial for women? In M. J. Deegan and N. A. Brooks (Eds.), *Women and disability: The double handicap.* Oxford: Transaction Books.

Lau, E. & Kosberg, J. (1978). Abuse of the elderly by informal care providers: Practice and research issues. Paper presented at the 31st Annual Meeting of the Gerontological Society, Dallas, TX. 21 November.

Lobel, K. (Ed.) 1986. *Naming the violence: Speaking out about lesbian battering.* Seattle: Seal.

Marshall, A. (1986). Battering and ageism. *Minnesota Coalition of Battered Women News, 5* (5), 1.

O'Malley, H., Segars, H., Perez, R., Mitchell, V., and Kneupfel, G. (1980). *Elder abuse in Massachusetts: A survey of professionals and paraprofessionals.* Boston: Legal Research and Services for the Elderly.

Phillips, L. R. (1983). Abuse and neglect of the frail elderly at home: An exploration of theoretical relationships. *Journal of Advanced Nursing, 8*(379), 24–35.

Pillemer, K., and Finkelhor, D. (1986). *The prevalence of elder abuse: A random sample survey.* Durham, NJ: Family Violence Research Program, University of New Hampshire, Family Research Laboratory.

Protection and Advocacy, Inc. (1986). *Special advocacy report on domestic abuse and neglect of adults with disabilities.* Chicago, IL: Protection and Advocacy.

Quinn, M. J. & Tomita, S. K. (1986). *Elder abuse and neglect: Causes, diagnosis, and intervention strategies.* New York: Springer.

Ramsey-Klawsnik, H. (1991). Elder sexual abuse: Preliminary findings. *Journal of Elder Abuse and Neglect, 3*(3), 73–77.

Rathbone-McCuan, E. (1980). Intergenerational family violence and neglect: The aged as victims of reaction and reverse neglect. Paper presented at the International Congress of Gerontology, Tokyo, Japan.

Renzetti, C. (1988). Violence in lesbian relationships. *Journal of Interpersonal Violence, 3,* (4), 381–399.

Straus, M. A., Gelles, R. J. & Steinmetz, S. K. (1981). *Behind closed doors: Violence in the American family.* New York: Anchor.

U.S. Attorney General's Task Force (1984). *Report on family violence.* Washington, DC: U.S. Government Printing Office.

U.S. House Select Committee on Aging (1990). *Elder abuse: A decade of shame and inaction.* Washington, DC: U.S. Government Printing Office.

Walker, L. E. (1979). *The battered woman.* New York: Harper and Row.

Wolf, R. S. (1989). Perpetrators of Maltreatment. In R. T. Ammerman, and M. Hersen, (Eds.), *Treatment of family violence: A sourcebook.* New York: John Wiley.

Chapter Three

ADULT PROTECTIVE SERVICES AND ELDER SELF-ENDANGERING BEHAVIOR

BRYAN BYERS AND RICHARD A. LAMANNA

Much has been written on the problem of elder abuse and neglect (Davidson, Hennessey, and Sedge, 1979; Rounds, 1984; Johnson, O'Brien, and Hudson, 1985; Pillemer and Wolf, 1986; Quinn and Tomita, 1986; Breckman and Adelman, 1988). Prior research has focused on the identification of elder abuse and neglect (Dozier, 1984; McDowell, 1989; Sengstock, McFarland, and Hwalek, 1990), the measurement of this phenomenon (Brown, 1989; Dolon and Blakely, 1989; Pillemer and Moore, 1990), and issues which concern the professional gerontologist and adult protective services worker in addressing day-to-day victim needs (Ferguson, 1978; Bookin and Dunkle, 1985; Coleman and Karp, 1989; Kapp, 1990; Mixson, 1991).

Most prior research has dealt with abuse and neglect perpetrated by others. Although this topic is very important, little attention has been given to the social problem of self-endangering behavior. The limited amount of attention which has been given to self-endangering behavior has primarily focused on one particular variety; this would be "self-neglect" (McCuan and Fabian, 1992). While self-neglect is the dominant form of self-inflicted harm encountered by the adult protective services investigator, we use the term self-endangerment in referring to this and other types of self-inflicted harm discussed below.

Self-endangering behavior is very different in practice than abuse and neglect perpetrated by others. An important distinction here rests with the difference in the source of the harm. While battery, exploitation, and neglect perpetrated by others deals with an "offender" external to the victim, the focus of self-neglect shifts the perpetrator away from others and to the "self." However, and unlike the other forms of elder abuse and neglect, this does not suggest that the behavior is criminal. Self-neglect and self-abuse are the only behaviors, fitting within the elder abuse and neglect purview, which are not considered criminal. In spite of this, however, self-neglect and other forms of self-endangerment may still lead to adult protective services intervention which is also common to other forms of abuse and neglect.

Self-neglect, the most common term used to describe self-endangerment, occurs when the individual does not provide for the self as society might expect. While this pattern most often involves elderly individuals, it may also afflict disabled adults. Although we realize that the vast majority of elderly citizens are self-sufficient and do not demonstrate this pattern, the statistical pattern which seems to emerge among the elder abuse and neglect population reveals that lapses in self-care in the form of self-neglect occurs frequently.

Such lapses in self-care may involve inadequacy in such basic necessities as food, clothing, shelter, or medical care. Although a person of any age associated with responsibility for the self might be afflicted with this, the primary focus has been on the elderly. Since lapses in self-care among the elderly can involve many different types of situations as there are many gradations of this behavior. For instance, the behavior can be fatal. In other instances, it can seem quite benign and may be interpreted as a question of lifestyle. In any case, it seems to differ in both theoretical and practical ways from abuse or neglect inflicted by others.

We have three objectives which focus on the relevance to practitioners. First, we provide the reader with an understanding of the kind of behavior which might constitute self-endangering behavior by using self-neglect case illustrations. Second, we attempt to clarify the ways in which various types of self-endangering behaviors have been defined by researchers and lawmakers. Third, an attempt is made to move toward a conceptualization of self-endangerment. Fourth, prominent practice related issues involving cases of self-endangerment are briefly introduced and discussed.

ELDER SELF-NEGLECT LITERATURE

Most of the previous research on the topic of self-neglect is found within the medical, nursing, and psychiatric literature (Clark, Mankikar, and Gray, 1975; Clark, 1975, Cornwall, 1981; O'Rawe, 1982; Cybulska and Rucinski, 1986). This resulted in part because those coming into contract with the self-neglectful were often physicians and nurses within hospital settings. These were the individuals who were forced, often by default, to address the problem. Two early researchers in this area commented that at one time there was an absence of any organization to which cases of self-neglect could be reported and action obtained (Macmillan and Shaw, 1966), and this may have been a contributing factor in elder self-neglect being dealt by medical organizations. As a result, much of the early writing in this area focuses on "diagnosis" and "treatment" which is consistent with medical parlance.

However, with the growth of interest in geriatrics, social gerontology, and the advent of adult protective service programs specifically designed to address the problems of elder abuse and neglect, this topic is no longer exclusively in the medical domain and is now addressed within many communities (Quinn and Tomita, 1986). Current research is found primarily within the elder abuse and neglect literature. This shift in focus is due primarily to an increasing recognition that the topic of elder abuse and neglect is relevant not only to the medical field, but also to social services. Therefore, with a broadening research interest in social gerontology, and more attention given to elder abuse and neglect, the topic of elder self-neglect has been given additional attention (Administration of Aging, Dept. of HHS, 1980; Burr, AOA, 1982; Blanton, 1989; Coleman and Karp, 1989; Sengstock, Hwalek, and Petrone, 1989; Iris, 1990; Byers, 1991; Mixson, 1991; Keigher, 1991; McCuan and Fabian, 1992).

Given the nature of attention which has been given to self-endangering behavior, and self-neglect in particular, there has been little effort to define the type of behavior (Byers, 1991; McCuan and Fabian, 1992) which might constitute self-endangerment. Instead, previous efforts have largely been more applied in nature by focusing on appropriate and effective community level responses to such matters. Although it has been stated that defining abuse and neglect is a difficult task (Galbraith, 1989), much research has focused on such practical responses. While such research is important and vital to the practitioner, definitional research which relates to practice issues also has relevance. Without clear definitions of abuse and neglect, effective intervention is hampered.

In summary, the empirical examination of elder self-neglect has been limited and has come primarily from the medical field. The reason for this previous focus is due to the fact that medical personnel, by default, were the practitioners who addressed this problem. Since the 1960's, however, interest in social gerontology and adult protective services has grown. Due to this interest and growth, there is now a new dimension of scholarly and practitioner interest in the problem of elder self-neglect.

DEFINING ELDER SELF-ENDANGERING BEHAVIOR

Defining elder abuse and neglect is a formidable task and the literature devoted to this is scant (Cornell and Gelles, 1985; Pillemer and Wolf, 1986; Wolf and McCarthy, 1991; McCuan and Fabian, 1992). As a result, defining and conceptualizing self-endangerment also presents a challenge. To our knowledge, only one researcher (Hudson, 1989, 1991) attempts to provide clear empirical referents to elder neglect which could be extended to many cases of self-endangerment. A more recent treatment by McCuan and Fabian (1992) does attempt to offer definitions and their work takes a multidisciplinary approach to the problem by focusing on medical and social service dimensions. However, most published research in this area, while addressing important practitioner issues, fails to make the definition of such behavior explicit. Much of the time it seems the literature takes the definition of such behavior for granted.

Part of the problem of conceptualizing and defining self-endangerment may actually exist on a practical level. In an analysis of state reporting systems on elder abuse, it was noted that " . . . confusion centers around the issue of classifying and tabulating incidents of self-abuse/neglect . . . " (National Association of State Units on Aging and American Public Welfare Association, 1986, p. 2, executive summary). A definitional study conducted by Hudson (1991) revealed similar findings. An ensemble of "experts" in the field of elder abuse and neglect were convened to elicit their input on abuse and neglect definitions, and it was revealed that "self-neglect" was difficult to define. Further, in some instances the participants did not mention the "self" as much as other distinctions when discussing neglect (Hudson, 1991). These findings are not surprising in light of possible perceptual differences regarding self-neglect among social service, elder abuse, and protective service workers. Furthermore, definitions are most likely dependent on some interpretation of general legal descriptions. This leads to the possible assumption that there may be a wide array of interpretations found in practice. The consequence of this is a lack of standardization from state to state (Traxler, 1986).

Legal Definitions

Some of the problem surrounding the definitional and conceptual issues may center on jurisdictional differences in legal definitions of self-endangering behavior. Approximately 18 states have "Self-Neglect" included in their elder abuse laws according to a joint study by the National Association of State Units on Aging and the American Public Welfare Association (NASUA/APWA, 1986). The states include Alabama, Colorado, Connecticut, Florida, Iowa, Kentucky, Maryland, Mississippi, Nevada, New Mexico, North Carolina, Ohio, Oklahoma, Tennessee, Texas, Utah, Virginia, and Wisconsin.

Despite the fact that "self-neglect" is included within some state statutes, this does not mean that the concept is clearly defined or that the definition provided is useful in practice. Practitioners may actually dictate what may or may not constitute abuse and neglect through interpretation of state statute, field decision making, and discretion. Therefore, some states attempt to define the behavior, while others do not, and adult protective service investigators in all states may create working definitions which are subsequently used in practice.

A state survey of elder abuse laws by Traxler (1986) found that 41 states were found to have legislation to cover neglect, while only three covered "self-neglect" (Louisiana, Texas, and Wisconsin) and two included "self-abuse" (Missouri and Ohio). This may be contrasted with findings from the NASUA/APWA which maintain there are 18 states where self-neglect is outlined within protective services law (NASUA/APWA, 1986). Interestingly, Louisiana is included in the NASUA/APWA self-neglect list but not in the Traxler study, and Ohio is classified as having "self-neglect" legislation by the NASUA/APWA while Traxler claims Ohio covers "self-abuse." The reason for the discrepancy may rest in how the state statute covering neglect is defined. That is, if the statute includes provisions for the "self" within the neglect statute, it may have legitimately been overlooked. The criteria for defining self-endangerment may be found in state statute or practitioner interpretation. Most often, a combination of both may be the source of working definitions of self-endangerment.

In a more recent survey of state adult protective service laws, Thobaben (1989) identifies additional gaps in the detection of self-endangering behavior. In this study, several states outline provisions in the law for situations which do not constitute "abuse," "neglect," or "exploitation." For instance, six states list "abandonment" (California, Connecticut, Idaho, Rhode Island, Washington, Wyoming) which may or may not include self-endangerment. One state (Michigan) includes "endangerment," but this might depend on how the term is defined in practice. That is, endangerment could mean harm inflicted by the "self" or by "others." Probably the closest indication of self-endangerment in state law may be found in the Nevada statute with the use of the term "living in hazardous conditions" and "emergency situation" as used in West Virginia. Self-neglect, self-abuse, and self-endangerment are not used by Thobaben (1989) in illustrating state law. Provisions for self-endangerment can easily be overlooked in state adult protective services law, while it is clear that such cases are indeed dealt with in practice.

An example of how certain states might be overlooked with regard to self-neglect may be found in the Kentucky law. Kentucky, which participated in the Traxler survey of state statutes, is classified in his study as having no special provision for self-neglect. However, the Kentucky state adult protection law states something different. In addition to a statement of other-inflicted abuse or neglect, the Kentucky law does state that abuse or neglect may also involve "a situation in which an adult, living alone, is unable to provide or obtain for himself the services which are necessary to maintain his health or welfare . . . " (State of Kentucky, Protection of Adults, 1978, 1986; 209.020(7)). Therefore, a legal definition of self-neglect does exist in Kentucky. However, this definition leaves open the possibility that elders who exhibit self-neglectful behavior regardless of the source (the person chooses to live in squalor vs. an inability of the person to obtain adequate services) may be labeled identically in terms of attributions yet there are clearly different causes.

There are other examples of how this might occur. For example, the State of Indiana does not specifically offer a definition of self-neglect within its Adult Protective Services Law. However, a detailed definition for such behavior is outlined within the Indiana Administrative Code (I.A.C.) for "neglect," i.e.:

> Neglect means that the endangered adult (the term used in Indiana to define the abused adult, who possesses some mental or physical disability, and is in need of protective services) . . . is unable or fails to provide adequate food, clothing, shelter or medical care." (Indiana Administrative Code, 1987).

Although this definition is used within Indiana to define neglect and self-neglect, one can look further and find additional references to self-neglectful behavior. For example, if one looks at the Indiana Adult Protective Services legal definition of an "endangered adult," which encompasses "adult abuse," "elder abuse," abuse and neglect perpetrated by others, and self-neglect/abuse. On close examination, it is clear that self-neglect would be included even though the definition is provided elsewhere. To illustrate, the following classification is taken directly from the Adult Protective Services Law, Indiana Criminal Code (4-28-5-2, 1990). An "Endangered Adult" is "... an individual who is at least eighteen (18) years of age and who:

> (1) Is incapable by reason of insanity, mental illness, mental retardation, senility, habitual drunkenness, excessive use of drugs, old age, infirmity, or other incapacity, of either managing the individual's property or providing *self-care* or both; and
> (2) Is harmed or threatened with harm as a result of:
>
> > (A) *Neglect;*
> > (B) Battery; or
> > (C) Exploitation of the individual's personal services or property.

As one can readily see, the concept of self-neglect and self-endangerment are dealt within in the law. However, one must thoroughly review the law in order to detect the provisions and definitions for self-endangerment and definitions must be compared to field practices common to such cases (Byers, 1991).

Most state legal definitions of self-endangering behavior are quite broad and sometimes vague. Part of the reason for this may be the desire to allow as much field discretion as possible concerning case interpretation by protective service personnel. The available definitions do not vary much and most seem to address the absence of care within certain areas such as medical, nutritional, housing, and clothing needs. Usually, the absence of such self-care leads to some form of harm. To illustrate, Ohio defines self-neglect as:

> the failure of an adult to provide for himself the goods or services necessary to avoid physical harm, mental anguish, or mental illness.... (§5101.60 (K)).

As one can see, the State of Ohio not only includes some definition of what self-neglect may be (failure to provide basic goods and services), but it also includes the possible consequences.

Yet another example of legislatively defined self-neglect may be drawn from the Texas State Human Resources Department which is almost identical to the Ohio definition:

> "Neglect" means the failure to provide for one's self the goods or services which are necessary to avoid physical harm, mental anguish, or mental illness ... (§48.002 (4)).

The basic characteristics of neglect provided by the National Association of State Units on Aging/American Public Welfare Association remain intact for many state statutes given the above examples. Most state laws which include provisions for "neglect" largely focus on the " . . . deprivation of basic services . . . " and also " . . . the lack or absence of responsibility of care." (NASUA/APWA, 1986, p. xi). Extending this to self-neglect, this may be termed the failure to provide to the self basic necessities of life and survival. An example of this may be found in the 1990 U.S. Congressional Report, *Elder Abuse: A Decade of Shame and Inaction*. Within that report self-neglect is defined as " . . . the withholding of medication, medical treatment, food and personal care necessary for well-being from oneself" (p. 18). This is what is normally found within such definitions while sometimes mentioning possible consequences of the absence of such care.

Although those states and jurisdictions which do include self-neglect and other forms of self-endangerment within state law provide some definition for the behavior, these definitions can be vague and imprecise. Many legal definitions simply state that self-neglect constitutes a failure to provide the self with "services" but the specific nature of this condition is left to adult protective services investigator judgment. Other than a multidisciplinary approach taken by McCuan and Fabian (1992), an empirical factorial survey approach taken by Byers (1991) and a case study approach by Byers and Hendricks (1990), we are not aware of any other research which examines self-neglect case characteristics empirically. In order to further address this issue, we now turn to the various non legal definitions found within the literature.

Non-Legal Definitions

The following discussion centers on non-legal definitions of self-neglect, and other forms of self-endangerment found in the literature. Included are a discussion of self-neglect, the senile recluse, and self-injurious/self-destructive behavior. These definitions provide much more detail than those found in state statutes and may better illustrate the nature of this social problem.

Self-Neglect. Perhaps the earliest treatment of this topic was by R.S. Stevens in the 1963 medical article, "Self-Neglect in the Elderly." Stevens (1963, p. 88) describes the self-neglectful person in the patient population as follows:

Fundamental to the conception of the Welfare State is the proposition that there is a certain level of subsistence, below which no citizen should be allowed to sink, and it may be supposed that this implies a reasonable standard of personal and domestic cleanliness and care.... Because there are grades of squalor of lesser importance it is necessary to define the term "extreme squalor." This cannot be done in one word, but involves a complex of various combinations of characteristic features. The extreme squalid dwelling is always utterly filthy. Thick layers of dust coat every object that can be dimly discerned in the darkened rooms (the light of a candle or torch may be necessary), tattered remnants of curtains droop at the windows, which are dark with accumulated grime, soot and grease. One's foot falls softly in the deep pile of dirt on the floor.... Faded wallpaper hangs in dreary strips that brush the face, plaster crumbles at a touch.... Molding food, half-emptied tins, and used crockery are seen in odd corners. Always, inevitably, there are stacks of old newspapers which may be scattered about... Heaps of empty jam-jars.... may grace a corner of the room. Somewhere, on a bed, or in a broken chair ... one finds the patient. Pale skin with dirt deep-grained, the palms of the hands black, the clothes, unchanged these many months, adherent to the body. Beside or around there may lurk one or several cats and perhaps an infinity of lesser living creatures.

Here the author maintains that the self-neglect case involves a person living in "extreme squalor." Much of what Stevens says pertains to a deterioration of living conditions which fall far below community standards, or the degree to which one may live free from harm.

Duncan Macmillan and Patricia Shaw (1966) defined what appears to be self-neglect as "senile breakdown" and linked this to deterioration of living conditions. They refer to "senile breakdown" in this way because " ... with the exception of one psychiatric patient [they] found it only in the senile epoch." (Macmillan and Shaw, 1966, p. 1032). They describe the typical case as follows:

The usual picture is that of an old woman living alone, though men and married couples suffering from the condition are also found. She, her garments, her possessions, and her house are filthy. She may be verminous and there may be feces and pools of urine on the floor. These people are often tolerated for years by the neighbours, who may suddenly decide that they cannot stand this state of affairs any longer and report the case to various organizations, such as the police or the health department. By this time conditions are usually so bad that many organizations have to spend disproportionate amounts of time and energy in trying to put them right, often with little result. ·

These authors conclude that social isolation, a certain type of personality, bereavement, and alcoholism were important causal variables in their 35 elder self-neglect patients (Macmillian and Shaw, 1963, p. 1037). Further, the elder self-neglect victim seems to resent the community, all it stands for, and longs for isolation and self-sufficiency (Macmillian and Shaw, 1963).

Clark, Mankikar, and Gray (1975) also examined medical patients in England suffering from what appeared to be "Diogenes syndrome" or self-neglect. They define self-neglect as follows (p. 366):

> All had dirty, untidy homes and a filthy personal appearance about which they showed no shame. Hoarding of rubbish (called "syllogomania") was sometimes seen. . . . All were known to the social services departments and a third had persistently refused offers of help. An acute presentation with falls or collapse was common, and severe physical diagnoses could be made. . . . The mortality, especially for women, was high (46%; most of the survivors responded well [to hospital and medical treatment] and were discharged. Half showed no evidence of psychiatric disorder and possessed higher than average intelligence. Many had led successful professional and business lives, with good family backgrounds and upbringing. Personality characteristics showed them to tend to be aloof, suspicious, emotionally labile, aggressive, group-dependent, and reality disorienting individuals . . . Twenty-eight [of 30] lived alone. . . .

Typically, according to these authors, the self-neglect victims in their sample lived in deplorable conditions, had medical conditions, and previously lived "normal" lives.

The following more recent definition provides yet more detail than the state statutes provided earlier and includes a broader range of behaviors which are believed to constitute self-neglect (Quinn and Tomita, 1986, p. 52–53):

> Self-abuse and -neglect mean that an individual is failing to provide the necessities of life for himself such as food, clothing, shelter or adequate medical care, and reasonable management of financial resources. It ranges from poor grooming and eating habits to disintegration of the body through ignored medical care. The financial assets of the individual may be wasted. With the elderly, it is usually associated with the increasing severity of mental and/or physical impairments, but it can also be part of a life style such as is frequently seen with alcoholism or drug abuse. It can include filthy and unhealthy living environment with animal droppings in the house or dissipation of bank accounts or other assets. Some elders in this category isolate themselves from those who would care for them. They show physical signs of self-neglect such as dirty matted hair, layers of clothing inappropriately arranged, clothing inappropriate to weather conditions, lack of food in the refrigerator, or food that is decayed and moldy.

Such a definition may include many types of behavior which practitioners in this area may not consider self-neglect. For instance, the terms "appropriate" and "reasonable" impute value judgments. One particular addition made by Quinn and Tomita, not mentioned in other descriptions, is that of " . . . reasonable management of financial resources" (1986, p. 52). This concept is defined by Byers and Hendricks (1990) as it pertains to the self-neglect case. They refer to financially-based issues of self-neglect as "financial self-neglect" (p. 205). Such self-neglect may include not paying utility bills and other necessary debts to assure one's personal safety, independence, and self-sufficiency. An interesting contrast found between Clark et al. (1975) and Quinn and Tomita's (1986) description is the disagreement of the victim's mental health status. While Clark, et al. (1975) maintain that their contact with self-neglect victims indicates they generally do not suffer from mental illness, Quinn and Tomita (1986) seem to disagree.

Like Traxler (1986), Quinn and Tomita (1986) do not seem to make a distinction between "self-neglect" and "self-abuse," while Macmillian and Shaw (1963) and Clark, et al. (1975) do not mention "abuse." At times the terms "neglect" and "abuse" are used synonymously which may elicit additional confusion. However, one should recognize that "abuse" may imply more intentionality than "neglect" when applied to the self. This does not mean, however, that self-neglect is always "passive." It might also be quite "active" as is sometimes the case when a person may willfully choose to live a life of isolation and squalor shunning dependence and embracing independence and self-sufficiency (Quinn and Tomita, 1986; Coleman and Karp, 1989).

Senile Recluse. Not everyone addressing this topic uses the term "self-neglect" or "self-abuse." For instance, Post (1982, p. 180–181), in an attempt to shed light on elder self-endangerment, defines these individuals as "senile recluses" and describes them as follows:

> They come to notice because neighbours become concerned with the nuisance caused or because a final illness is suspected. In fact, nearly half of them die soon after admission, usually to a geriatric facility. Where psychiatric or psychological assessment has been possible, a characteristic picture tended to emerge. Men and women have been found to be equally affected. Most lived alone, but a few shared their seclusion with a sibling, more rarely a spouse. Senile recluses as a group are of average or above average intelligence, and possibly persons belonging to the middle and upper classes predominate. Poverty is conspicuous by its absence: considerable sums of money are often found hidden among the filth and shambles of the home. Recluses have always been independent, quarrelsome, and secretive people, who come increasingly to reject contact with others except perhaps an occasionally visiting relative:

they may literally barricade themselves in their homes and only venture out occasionally.

This description of the senile recluse characterizes the self-neglectful elder in a similar manner as the previous descriptions, but Post avoids calling the above characteristics a "syndrome" or "Diogenes" as do others (Cybulska and Rucinski, 1986).

The term "Diogenes syndrome" has been used by several authors (Clark, et al., 1975; Clark, 1975; Cornwall, 1981) to describe the self-neglect condition. The originates from the Greek Philosopher Diogenes of Sinope, because he was allegedly self-sufficient, begged, and sought out the company of others. Few, if any, self-neglect cases involve these latter traits. Further, Post (1982) maintains that the senile recluse's behavior " . . . marks the end stage of a personality disorder." (p. 181). This statement contradicts other medical researchers in this area who maintain that the self-neglectful do not, as a group, possess any discernable psychiatric or psychological abnormalities (Macmillan and Shaw, 1963; Clark, et al., 1975; Clark, 1975; Roe, 1977).

As for the issue of the "Diogenes syndrome" being used as the term to describe self-neglect, we also find it to be inaccurate for the same reasons as Post (1982) and Cybulska & Rucinski (1986). Although self-neglect does seem to have a few characteristic features (Macmillian and Shaw, 1966), the term "diogenes" should be replaced with self-neglect when describing this form of self-endangerment.

Self-Injurious/Indirect Self-Destructive Behavior. Another branch of research in the area of self-endangerment addresses a phenomenon known as "Self-Injurious Behavior" (S–IB) (Kastenbaum and Mishara, 1971) or "Indirect Self-Destructive Behavior" (ISDB) (Farberow, 1980; McIntosh and Hubbard, 1988). Both of these depict the individual as a person who may not engage in any overt self-destructive behavior. The potential exists to do the self harm which is manifested in "subintentional and other indirect methods" (Kastenbaum and Mishara, 1971, p. 79), depicting the person as "unconscious" and unaware that the behavior is intended to harm the self, and the effect of the behavior is considered long term (Farberow, 1980, p. 16). In other words, the behavior may be "covert," "less obvious," or a "slow," self-destructive method (McIntosh and Hubbard, 1988, p. 37). Farberow, summing up this type of behavior states that:

... self-destructive behavior takes many forms. In its most familiar form, we see the overt behavioral manifestations which result in death, injury, or pain consciously inflicted upon the self, or we hear the verbal warning that self-harm is intended or death is planned. The behavior is visible, and the effect is immediate. Indirect self-destructive behavior is distinguishable from direct self-destruction by at least two criteria, time and awareness. The effect is long-range and the behavior may span years; the person is usually unaware of or doesn't care about the effects of his behavior, nor does he consider himself a suicide.

ISDB may involve such life-threatening behaviors as refusing medication, not following physician orders, smoking or drinking against medical advice, refusing to eat, or placing oneself in a "hazardous environment" (Kastenbaum and Mishara, 1971, p. 78). The ISDB person also tends to be a "loner" with "few sources of external support" (Farberow, 1980, p. 25).

These characteristics may be found in self-neglect and "senile recluse" cases as well. McIntosh and Hubbard's (1988) case study of ISDB appeared very much like self-neglect or the senile recluse. It seems plausible that the only difference may be in the label one might attach to the behavior. Therefore, what distinguishes the two? Perhaps the answer to this question rests with the "intent" of each individual. That is, two individuals may engage in identical behavior which may seem "self-endangering," yet, one might be considered ISDB because the person wishes to commit suicide, or to do the self harm, and the other does not. To label all instances of self-destructive behavior as self-neglect, ISDB, or anything else would seem shortsighted given the important differences in the intention that may exist.

ELDER SELF-ENDANGERMENT CASE ILLUSTRATIONS

In order to enhance an understanding of the phenomenon under study here, we provide below actual cases of self-endangering behavior which have been labeled as "elder self-neglect." All of the cases share the common characteristic features of self-neglect. That is, each case includes some discussion of how the victim resides in isolation from the community and amongst squalor.

The Select Committee on Aging, House of Representatives, 101st Congress released the report, *Elder Abuse: A Decade of Shame and Inaction* in 1990. Within that report are accounts of various types of elder abuse and neglect, and an entire section is devoted to cases of "self-neglect."

The following brief vignettes deal with self-neglect and are taken directly from that report (pp. 18–23).

- In Mississippi, a 64-year-old woman whose husband lived in a nursing home tried to live at home alone with 48 dogs. Social workers who came to investigate reported that her home was filthy and that the woman, Mrs. K., had not had a bath in years. In addition, four dead dogs were removed from the home.
- In Texas, a social service volunteer was shocked to find an impoverished elderly Hispanic couple lying in a room amidst swarms of cockroaches in conditions she likened to a horror movie.
- An 84-year-old North Dakota woman lived on a rural farm with 20–40 cats in her home. The woman told a visiting nurse that she sometimes ate the cat food and she told how she prepared it. Further investigation showed that there were dried cat feces and newspapers encrusted with cat feces all over the floors. The living room had garbage piled high in one corner. The woman's clothing was filthy and she was disoriented to time and place.
- An 80-year-old Idaho woman lived by herself, although totally deaf and almost blind and suffering from bouts of confusion. She could not manage her financial affairs and, as a result of not paying bills, her light and heat had been turned off. She also was unable to cook for herself and subsisted mostly on junk food snacks.
- An elderly Massachusetts man in his mid-sixties had become disabled and increasingly dysfunctional due to a stroke, which in turn led to his becoming emaciated and isolated. A home visit revealed that he had no food, had never received services after his stroke and had no money. The bathroom was encrusted with feces and the home had no refrigerator. The housing project had shut off his stove because he had left the gas on several times.
- An elderly gentleman from North Dakota was found on the floor of his bedroom, unable to move. Police officers had to kick the door open in order to enter the home. He was taken to the hospital by a relative and was described as being in very poor condition. The house was in a state of disarray—the man said all he had eaten was a piece of ham on a bun the day before. The whole house was unsanitary, garbage lying all over. The man was very dirty and had urinated on himself.

From the very same report, an account of an Indiana case is given. The case vignette is included under the heading "Physical Abuse and Neglect" but also involves self-neglect. The case, as it appears in the congressional report, is as follows:

- A 75-year-old Indiana woman was beaten by her 52-year-old son, who lived with her. She suffered bruises and contusions. The son was a victim of self-neglect, who drank heavily and had psychotic tendencies but refused to go to the Veterans Administration Hospital for tests.

More detail illustrates this case's complexity. The elderly woman in the case will be referred to as Mrs. A, the self-neglectful son is Mr. B, and Mr. B's half-brother is Mr. C.

• The Adult Protective Services Unit in the area where Mrs. A lived received a call from older adult case management that there was an elderly woman in very poor physical health living with her son. The son was reported to be an alcoholic and was given primary responsibility for her care. A joint home visit was made in order to assess the situation from an adult protective services perspective. The investigation found the home in complete disarray, dirty dishes all over the house, unsanitary cooking conditions in the kitchen and roaches in the home. The son, Mr. B, had a demeanor in which his emotions would fluctuate often. He maintained that he "did what he could for his mother" in terms of care. Mr. B was an Air Force veteran who was a jet mechanic and often commented on how his knowledge was "ancient history" which seemed indicative of his low self-esteem.

Mrs. A was a widow of a prominent attorney. She was rather well known also. She had her own radio talk show at a time when it was very uncommon for a female to hold such a high status in broadcasting. Upon entering the home, she was found in a back bedroom. Mrs. A was almost completely bedridden and relied on her son to help her with many activities around the house. Dried feces were evident on her housecoat and she often wore sunglasses inside the home in order to hide her black eyes. The investigation supported the allegations of abuse toward the mother from the son and the son's own self-neglect due to his severe drinking. When questioned about physical abuse, neither the son nor the mother would admit that any abuse was occurring. Contact was then made with the only other local relative, a step-brother to Mr. B, Mr. C. He was very concerned over the treatment of Mrs. A but felt powerless to do anything.

The local Adult Protective Services Unit maintained very close contact with Mrs. A, Mr. B, and Mr. C. Often, the unit would do unannounced visits in order to detect possible, continuing abuse. For the most part, each subsequent visit yielded the same result: evidence of abuse and a denial that it was occurring. As the case became more advanced, the unit discussed the possibility of a court order to remove Mrs. A from the home for her own protection or even criminal charges of battery against her son. These options were not easily used since neither party would admit the abuse was occurring and Mrs. A was mentally competent and appeared to be protecting her son (a protective order cannot be used if the victim is competent and criminal charges cannot realistically be authorized unless the victim or offender admit that the act has occurred).

One day, the case seemed to reach a crisis point in terms of the son's self-neglect and the abuse. He had been on a long drinking binge and had

reportedly (from neighbors) been beating his mother at night. A home visit
was made by the unit and the step-brother. During the visit, emotions ran
high. Mr. B threatened to attack the investigators, so the police were called.
Several police units converged on the scene and Mr. B was arrested for public
intoxication and subsequently charged with battery. The charging process was
made possible because Mrs. A stated during that final visit, "I'm sick and tired
of you pulling me out of bed, throwing cold water on me and beating me in the
middle of the night."

This case dealt with both self-neglect and battery in which the self-
neglectful person became abusive, at least in part, due to self-endangerment
in the form of excessive alcoholism. Wolf and McCarthy (1991) maintain
that such cases may be characteristic of elder abuse situations because
they involve " . . . multiple types of mistreatment over extended periods
of time." (p. 498). That is, it is not uncommon to find a situation which
involves combinations of battery, exploitation, and neglect.

In contrast, the following case deals only with self-neglect. This article
is from the same jurisdiction as the previous case as documented in a
regional newspaper (*South Bend Tribune,* August 7, 1988, p. B-1).

• During a very hot summer, the Adult Protective Services Unit received a
report of adult endangerment from a local public library branch. The library
employee reported that for several months an elderly couple, Mr. and Mrs. D,
would come to the library branch and spend the entire day. This did not alarm
the library employee, but the couple's strong odor, the fact that they cut all the
coupons out of the newspapers, and that they would take gallons and gallons of
water out of the public restroom in plastic milk jugs did concern her. An
attempt was made by the local County Health Department and Adult Protective Services to visit the couple at home. No one was found there, but an
external examination of the home indicated that the couple may be living in
squalor.

An attempt was then made by Adult Protective Services to visit the couple at
the library they reportedly visited often. They were found at the library and
were approached for an assessment. They adamantly refused any assistance or
intervention and were quite angry with the offer. They were very suspicious
and agitated over the thought of any type of "interference" in their lives.

A few days later, the unit received a call from City Code Enforcement
indicating a crisis at the couple's home. Adult Protective Services went immediately to the home. Upon arrival, various emergency medical, fire, police, Code
Enforcement, and the local media were present.

A neighbor had called the police and emergency medical personnel because
Mrs. D was observed knocking on a window from inside the home and crying
for help. Emergency personnel arrived and forced their way into the home.
Inside they found the couple severely dehydrated. They were taken to the

hospital emergency room. Adult Protective Services, and other municipal personnel, went into the home after the couple had been removed. The couple had been using one corner of the living room as a bathroom and feces and urine were found there. The couple never threw anything away. They had garbage and trash piled in all areas of the home from the floor to the ceiling. They had devised a series of "paths" to navigate around the trash. In addition, there was at least eighteen inches of compressed trash on the floor.

They had not had utility service to the home in several years and heated the home in the winter by burning trash in the gas furnace. Although they lived as though they had no money at all, a financial investigation revealed that the couple had over $300,000.00 in 32 separate accounts, with a local bank. The couple's health was so poor, and the dehydration so severe, that they were placed in a local nursing home directly from the hospital for further convalescence.

This case is consistent with most of the descriptive elements of self-neglect. The physical conditions of the home typify extreme squalor. Their physical appearance indicated that no personal hygiene had taken place for quite some time. They were able to exist in this condition until external factors (in this case, the weather) interacted with other, more chronic, characteristics of the situation thus creating the crisis.

Many of these cases either go unnoticed by the community or neighbors do not wish to become involved until a crisis situation necessitates action. This was the case for the following gentleman. This case comes from Byers and Hendricks (1990, pp. 209–210).

• Mr. F, a white male approximately 79 years of age, was reported to the local Adult Protective Services Unit. The caller alleged that the man, who lived alone, was a danger to himself and others. The basis of the allegation was that the alleged victim was breaking the windows out of his own home from within the house and was threatening to those who came near. The investigating adult protective services worker, accompanied by two police officers, visited the home immediately. Upon entering the dwelling, strong odors were noticed. An inspection of the dwelling revealed Mr. F sitting on a bed in the front room of the house. He was able to walk but seemed somewhat confused. The general living conditions in the home were poor with little sanitation. Further, little food was present. Soon thereafter, another elderly man appeared at the door claiming to be Mr. F's caretaker. Upon questioning this person, it was revealed that he did little more than pay Mr. F's essential utility bills (while not paying taxes and other debts) and to buy him fast-food which he delivered to the home. . . .

For Mr. F., it was not so much an instance of shunning outside assistance as it was a matter of losing, or perhaps never having, the necessary level of social support. Other than this, the case resembles the previous descriptions offered.

Each of these cases have elements in common. First, there is a lack of self-care. Self-neglect is frequent, serious and dangerous within the elder abuse and neglect victim population. The above cases offer the reader some working knowledge of the nature of self-neglect as it pertains to adult protective services practice and the domain of self-endangering behavior. Second, social and physical deterioration is not uncommon. Socially, the nature and extent of social support may erode or deteriorate. Physically, the person may experience very serious health problems which are often the reason s/he comes to the attention of the community. Third, at times the self-endangerment case victim is disoriented as to time and place. One should not assume, however, that their living conditions are always indicative of mental confusion since the two may or may not be associated. The self-endangerment case will ultimately be known to the community. Usually knowledge of these cases is the result of chronic squalid living conditions which become known to the community through some crisis. This may often be a health condition. These seem to be some of the more common descriptive elements of self-endangerment cases.

It is our hope that the reader has a working understanding of the conceptual and definitional problems associated with these types of cases and a better understanding of what type of behavior might constitute self-endangerment in practice. However, what is lacking in these illustrations is a clear definitional understanding of what might constitute self-endangerment.

TOWARD A CONCEPTUALIZATION OF SELF-ENDANGERING BEHAVIOR

All of the behaviors discussed thus far (self-neglect/abuse, senile recluse, and S–IB/ISDB) fit within the purview of self-endangering behavior. This leaves us with a collection of legal and non legal descriptions of self-endangerment, and some effort to conceptualize and define these with the use of non legal approaches. However, in an effort to go beyond this, and to gain better understanding of self-endangerment, one must strive for additional clarity.

We advocate going beyond the notion of "knowing it when you see it" which is prevalent in practice and is reinforced by vaguely stated legislative and non legal descriptions. Definitions of this form of behavior are not self-evident. While we can appreciate the probable reality that the "...practitioner's concern in cases of self-neglect is not with definitions..." but with the cultural value conflict between autonomy and protection (Mixson, 1991, p. 35), we believe definitions to be essential to this latter concern and to the continued viability and ethical practice of adult protective services.

In spite of what appears to be a scant treatment of self-endangering behavior in the literature given its significance for practice, there does seem to be some common ground which connects the various patterns described. That is, they all involve some type of destructive behavior to the self. For simplicity, we may refer to all four of these patterns as constituting "Self-Endangering Behavior" (S–EB) since they all may pose some psychological or physical risk to the individual. S–EB may be defined, then, as any behavior which poses some physical or psychological risk to the individual which is done intentionally, or unintentionally, to the self which may or may not be linked to functional dependence. The "functionally dependent" are those "individuals whose illnesses, disabilities, or social problems have reduced their ability to perform self-care and household tasks in an independent manner" (*Age Words*, 1986). One might also extend this reasoning to suggest a dichotomy between "direct" forms of self-endangering behavior, or DSEB, and "indirect" (ISEB).

Second, each of these behaviors seems to suggest that the person is isolated from society or the community and may lack adequate social support. This is clearly the case for instances of self-neglect and the senile recluse, but less clear for the self-destructive behavior typology. A third area of commonality rests in the notion that each of these types of behavior involve a violation of some community standard of crisis proportions concerning how to live. Typically, some standard is violated; some group finds the behavior inappropriate; action may eventually be taken against the person in order to correct these lifestyle infractions.

To summarize, then, the previous discussion centers on defining self-endangering behavior through a presentation of legal and non legal definitions of self-neglect, self-abuse, senile reclusive behavior, and self-injurious/indirect self-destructive behavior. One may refer to these three behaviors as forms of "Self-Endangering Behavior" (S–EB) while the "senile recluse" is a type of person who may engage in S–EB. S–EB may include any intentional or unintentional behavior which places life or health in jeopardy.

More specifically, self-neglect refers to the failure of the individual to provide for one's self what society expects in the area of self-care, nutrition, medical care, clothing, and/or shelter. Such matters, depending on their severity, could involve value conflicts in lifestyle preferences between the elder and the person charged with the responsibility of investigation of providing "protective services." Self-abuse is the intentional infliction of harm upon the physical or psychological self which does not necessarily result in death (suicide would be the most extreme form of self-abuse but would constitute another, much broader, category not considered here). Indirect self-destructive behavior is any self-endangering behavior which is intended to cause "premature death" (a term used by Kastenbaum and Mishara, 1971) but is not overt or direct in appearance. Therefore, this type of self-endangerment may be considered a form of suicide (McIntosh and Hubbard, 1988). The senile recluse (Post, 1982) is not a type of behavior but a type of person likely to engage in self-endangering behavior.

ADULT PROTECTIVE SERVICES AND SELF-NEGLECT

Definitions of self-endangerment seem to come from different orientations. That is, their source may be legal or non-legal. The designation of "self-neglect" as a category of self-endangerment seems most relevant to the adult protective services practitioner. This designation may or may not call for some "corrective" action in the form of paternalistic intervention. Such steps largely depend on the severity of the case and the philosophical orientation of the individual adult protective services worker. Therefore, the self-neglect label may not necessitate paternalistic intervention since some professional case interpretation may conclude that it would not be prudent or least restrictive.

The important distinction, then, appears to rest on whether the person is perceived to be in need of assistance based on an inability to provide for the self versus whether the person should be allowed to live as he/she may have chosen. As a result, it appears that there may be very real consequences for the client or victim depending on how self-endangerment is defined since such definitions will undoubtedly guide adult protective service intervention.

The elder self-neglect case is likely to be the most challenging and frustrating an adult protective services worker will address as there are many issues which confront the worker. Often, the elder self-neglect victim coming to the attention of adult protective services is not willing to accept offers of assistance. In other words, many are "involuntary" clients who shun the thought of anyone "interfering" in their lives. This is a frustrating reality in practice which can contribute to worker burnout. Due to the reality that many of these victims can and do refuse assistance, the elder self-neglect case is usually one of the more challenging forms of neglect the worker will encounter.

An important aspect of adult protective services practice is arranging what are referred to as "protective services" for the endangered adult. These "services" are intended to do two things. First, the services are meant to address the problem and alleviate, or reduce, the threat to the elder. Second, the services are intended to allow the alleged victim the most personal freedom and choice or be "least restrictive." Many of the services arranged through APS may be considered "social services" such as case management, counseling, meals-on-wheels, or some type of financial management assistance. Some of the more restrictive types of intervention, or how "services" might be implemented, include a petition for a Protective Order where an endangered adult is required to be in "receipt" of protective services, submit to guardianship, or be civilly committed to a mental health facility. These latter more restrictive options are used sparingly.

The worker must not only navigate within the social service and organizational framework of adult protective services, but s/he must also remain cognizant of societal values and preferences. Although the investigator is influenced by the needs of the client and the evidence in the case, the value structure undoubtedly has an impact. In addition, the worker is required to examine the adult protective services case through investigation, reach a conclusion or finding, and recommend a solution if the case is substantiated. The investigator must do all of this while following the principle of least restrictiveness. The individual's ability to make choices and have personal freedom runs deep within our cultural ethos and in adult protective services practice.

SUMMARY AND CONCLUSION

Within this chapter we present case illustrations of self-endangering behavior of one variety (self-neglect), examine legal and non legal definitions of self-endangering behavior, and attempt to move toward conceptualizing self-endangerment. Self-neglect, the most dominant form of self-endangering behavior found in the practice literature, is not always defined in state adult protective services law, but it will almost always be dealt with in practice. Most state law defines the behavior as an inability, or a lack of desire on the part of the individual to engage in adequate levels of self-care. In some instances, perhaps, self-neglect may be confused with life-style and personal choice and this can create a dilemma for the practitioner.

However, self-neglect (although dominant in adult protective services practice) is just one form of behavior found in the literature which depicts a person not engaging in self-preservation. The others include self-abuse, senile recluse, and Indirect Self-Destructive Behavior. Each of these behaviors fit under the purview of Self-Endangering Behavior (SE–B) used here to describe any behavior which is a threat to health or life. However, the presence of SE–B as a concept does not detract from the need to use the other definitions (e.g., self-neglect, self-abuse, senile recluse, and ISDB) in empirical research. What is needed is more precision in defining the category of self-endangering behaviors.

Our intent here is to introduce the topic of self-neglect and other forms of self-endangering behavior while emphasizing the empirical research and practitioner issues. While not detracting from the obvious importance this research has had, we contend that additional efforts need to be focused on definitional and conceptual studies which may aid the practitioner.

REFERENCES

Administration of Aging. (1980). *Elder abuse.* Washington DC: U.S. Dept. of Health and Human Services, Office of Human Development Services.

Blanton, P.G. (1989). Zen and the art of adult protective services: In search of a unified view of elder abuse. *Journal of Elder Abuse & Neglect, 1,* 27–34.

Bookin, D. & Dunkle, R.E. (1985). Elder abuse: Issues for the practitioner. *Social Casework, 1,* 3–12.

Breckman, R.S. & Adelman, R.D. (1988). *Strategies for helping victims of elder mistreatment.* Newbury Park, CA: Sage.

Brown, A.S. (1989). A survey on elder abuse at one native American tribe. *Journal of Elder Abuse & Neglect, 1,* 17–38.

Burr, J.J. (1982). *Protective services for adults: A guide to exemplary practice in states providing protective services to adults in OHDS programs.* Washington DC: Administration on Aging, Office of Human Development Services, U.S. Dept. of Health and Human Services.

Byers, B. (1991). *Measuring judgments of responsibility attribution and the self-neglectful elder: The case of adult protective services investigators in the criminal justice system.* Unpublished doctoral dissertation. University of Notre Dame.

Byers, B. & Hendricks, J.E. (1990). Elder financial self-neglect and exploitation: An adult protective services response. *Journal of Free Inquiry and Creative Sociology, 18,* 205–211.

Clark, A.N.G. (1975). The diogenes syndrome. *Nursing Times, 71,* 800–802.

Clark, A.N.G., Mankikar, G.D., & Gray, I. (1975). Diogenes syndrome: A clinical study of gross neglect in old age. *Lancet, 1,* 366–368.

Coleman, N. & Karp, N. (1989). Recent state and federal developments in protective services and elder abuse. *Journal of Elder Abuse & Neglect, 1,* 51–63.

Congress of the United States of America (101st, Second Session). (1990). *Elder abuse: A decade of shame and inaction.* Select Committee on Aging, U.S. House of Representatives. Washington, D.C.: U.S. Government Printing Office.

Cornell, C.P. & Gelles, R.J. (1985). Elder abuse: The status of current knowledge. In B. B. Hess & E. W. Markson (Eds.), *Growing old in America* (3rd ed.). New Brunswick: Transaction Books.

Cornwall, J.V. (1981). Filth, squalour and lice. *Nursing Mirror, 153,* 48–49.

Cybulska, E. & Rucinski, J. (1986). Gross self-neglect in old age. *British Journal of Hospital Medicine* (July).

Davidson, J.L., Hennessey, S. & Sedge, S. (1979). Additional factors related to elder abuse. In M.R. Block & J.D. Sinnott (Eds.), *The battered elder syndrome: An exploratory study.* College Park, Maryland: Center For Aging, University of Maryland.

Dolon, R. & Blakely, B. (1989). Elder abuse and neglect: A study of adult protective services workers in the United States. *Journal of Elder Abuse & Neglect, 1,* 31–49.

Dozier, C. (1984). *Report of the elder abuse and neglect assessment field instrument.* Atlanta, GA: Atlanta Regional Commission.

Farberow, N.L. (Ed.). (1980). *The many faces of suicide: Indirect self-destructive behavior.* New York: McGraw-Hill.

Ferguson, E.J. (1978). *Protecting the vulnerable adult.* Ann Arbor: Institute of Gerontology.

Galbraith, M.W. (1989). A critical examination of the definitional, methodological, and theoretical problems of elder abuse. In R. Filinson & S.R. Ingman (Eds.) *Elder abuse: Practice and policy.* New York: Human Sciences Press.

Hudson, M.F. (1989). Analyses of the concepts of elder mistreatment: Abuse and neglect. *Journal of Elder Abuse & Neglect, 1,* 5–26.

Hudson, M.F. (1991). Elder mistreatment: A taxonomy with definitions by delphi. *Journal of Elder Abuse & Neglect, 3,* 1–20.

Indiana Administrative Code. (1987). *Volume 3: Titles 410 to 470.* Indiana Legislative Council.

Indiana Criminal Code. (1990). *State of Indiana.* Adult Protective Services. Burns, 4-28-5.

Iris, M.A. (1990). Uses of guardianship as a protective intervention for frail, older adults. *Journal of Elder Abuse & Neglect, 2,* 57–72.

Johnson, T.F., O'Brien, J.G. & Hudson, M.F. (Eds.). (1985). *Elder neglect and abuse: An annotated bibliography.* Westport, CT: Greenwood.

Kastenbaum, R. & Mishara, B.L. (1971). Premature death and self-injurious behavior in old age. *Geriatrics,* July, 71–81.

Kapp, M.B. (1990). Evaluating decisional capacity in the elderly: A review of recent literature. *Journal of Elder Abuse & Neglect, 2,* 15–30.

Keigher, S.M. (1991). Informal supportive housing for elders: A key resource for preventing self-neglect. *Journal of Elder Abuse & Neglect, 3,* 41–60.

Macmillian, D., & Shaw, P. (1966). Senile breakdown in standards of personal and environmental cleanliness. *British Medical Journal, 2,* 1032–1037.

McDowell, D. (1989). Aging America: Images of abuse. *Journal of Elder Abuse & Neglect, 1,* 1–8.

McIntosh, J.L. & Hubbard, R.W. (1988). Indirect self-destructive behavior and the elderly: A review with case examples. *Journal of Gerontological Social Work, 13,* 37–48.

Mixson, P.M. (1991). Self-neglect: A practitioner's perspective. *Journal of Elder Abuse & Neglect, 3,* 35–42.

National Association of State Units on Aging/American Public Welfare Association. (1986). *A comprehensive analysis of state policies and practices related to elder abuse.* Washington, D.C.: NASUA/APWA.

O'Rawe, A.M. (1982). Self-neglect: A challenge for nursing. *Nursing Times, 78,* 1932–1936.

Pillemer, K.A. & Moore, D.W. (1990). Highlights from a study of abuse of patients in nursing homes. *Journal of Elder Abuse & Neglect, 2,* 5–30.

Pillemer, K.A. & Wolf, R.S. (Eds.). (1986). *Elder abuse: Conflict in the family.* Dover, MA: Auborn House.

Post, F. (1982). Functional disorders: Description, incidence, and recognition. In R. Levy & F. Post (Eds.), *The psychiatry of late life.* Oxford: Blackwell.

Quinn, M.J. & Tomita, S.K. (1986). *Elder abuse and neglect: Causes, diagnosis, and intervention strategies.* New York: Springer.

McCuan, L.R. & Fabian, D.R. (1992). *Self-neglecting elders: A clinical dilemma.* Westport, CT: Auburn House/Greenwood.

Roe, P.F. (1977). Self-neglect. *Age and Ageing, 6,* 192–194.

Rounds, L.R. (1984). *A study of selected environmental variables associated with non-institutional settings where there is abuse or neglect of the elderly.* Ph.D. Dissertation, University of Texas at Austin.

Sengstock, M.C., Hwalek, M. & Petrone, S. (1989). Services for aged abuse victims: Service types and related factors. *Journal of Elder Abuse & Neglect, 1,* 37–56.

Sengstock, M.C., McFarland, M.R. & Hwalek, M. (1990). Identification of elder abuse in institutional settings: Required changes in existing protocols. *Journal of Elder Abuse & Neglect, 2,* 31–50.

South Bend Tribune. (August 7, 1988). Dilemma arises when elderly unable to live independently. Page B-1.

State of Ohio. *Ohio State Code.* Section § 5101.60. Definitions.

State of Kentucky. 1978, 1986. *Protection of Adults.* 209.020(7).

State of Texas. *Texas State Code.* Section § 48.002. Definitions.

Stevens, R.S. (1963). Self-neglect in the elderly. *British Journal of Geriatric Practice, 2,* 88–91.

Thobaben, M. (1989). State elder/adult abuse and protection laws. In R. Filinson & S.R. Ingman (Eds.), *Elder Abuse: Practice and Policy.* New York: Human Sciences Press.

Traxler, A.J. (1986). Elder abuse laws: A survey of state statutes. In M.W. Galbraith (Ed.), *Elder abuse: Perspectives on an emerging crisis.* Kansas City, KS: Mid-American Congress on Aging.

U.S. Dept. of Health and Human Services. (1986). *Age words: A glossary on health and aging.* Washington, D.C.: DHHS.

Wolf, R.S. & McCarthy, R.S. (1991). Elder abuse. In B.B. Hess & E.W. Markson (Eds.), *Growing old in America (Fourth Edition).* New Brunswick: Transaction Books.

Chapter Four

LEGAL AND LEGISLATIVE DIMENSIONS

M. Steven Meagher

INTRODUCTION

Recent decades have witnessed keen interest in meeting the needs of particular classes of victims. Abuse of the elderly is one of the latest forms of family-related violence to be discovered, following spouse abuse and child abuse (Karmen, 1990). Abuse of the elderly is not a twentieth century development and historical accounts abound prior to the current interest (Stearns, 1986).

The extent of the problem of the abuse of the elderly is difficult to accurately assess, similar to the situation with spouse and child abuse. Nonetheless, the National Aging Resource Center on Elder Abuse estimated there were two million instances of physical, emotional and financial abuse of the elderly in 1988 (McGovern, 1991). Abuse of the elderly may be on the upswing or reported incidents of abuse may have increased. For example, it is estimated that the incidence of elder abuse in Massachusetts increased one hundred percent in the period 1984 to 1990 (Graham, 1990). Obviously, it is difficult to determine if the increase represents a true increase in the occurrence of elder abuse or more of a willingness of victims to report or an increased capability of service providers to detect the abuse, neglect and exploitation of the aged and to provide intervention.

The mistreatment of the elderly and the attention received by the legal system in the 1970's closely parallels the focus on the abuse and neglect of children in the 1960's. The discovery of both of these classes of victims created stereotypes characterizing these victims as helpless and defenseless against what were typically described as young, middle-class perpetrators (Utech and Garrett, 1992). These generalizations, later proven to be somewhat mistaken, dominated both the public and legislative mind-set and were influential in the development of the statutory response to the social problems associated with both elder and child abuse.

Past research has revealed that the public generally views the elderly in a negative sense, depicting them as weak, dependent, in poor health, isolated and unintelligent (Secombe and Ishii-Kuntz, 1991). With this perception, the interest in protecting this growing segment of the American public took on many of the same faces as the efforts to protect victims of spouse and child abuse. Similar to the instances of other special needs victims, the emerging concern with the protection of aging citizens resulted in the enactment of victim-specific legislation at the federal and state level. In the late 1970's, the specter of abuse and neglect of the elderly gained the eye of the American public and resulted in discussion in hearings before various United States Congressional committees, publications in scholarly and scientific journals, and media attention (Steinmetz, 1978; Block and Sinnott, 1979; Douglass et al., 1980).

As is the case with any new legislative effort, the passage of laws designed to safeguard the elderly necessitated the development of enforcement mechanisms to make legislative intent a reality and generated legal and public debate as to the extent of the abuse of the elderly and the appropriateness of expanded social intervention. The intent and goal of protection of the aged has been generally well received, but the means of implementation and effectiveness have experienced the same obstacles and shortcomings as other endeavors dealing with special classes of victims.

This chapter will center upon the legislative and legal issues in the realm of adult protective service law at the state and federal levels. After historically reviewing the evolution of these laws, focus will shift to the present status of federal legislation and the fashion in which the various states have confronted the protection of elderly citizens. An overview of legal issues will follow, focusing on matters that confront caregivers to the elderly and the social and criminal justice agencies that typically encounter both the victims and offenders of elder abuse.

LEGISLATIVE DEVELOPMENT OF
ADULT PROTECTIVE SERVICES

When abuse of the elderly is mentioned, the common conception is that of the older American who is physically abused by a relative or other caregiver or who is swindled out of a life's savings by an unscrupulous relative or business person. If society perceived only a need to investigate these matters, the existing criminal laws of our states and the federal government would be sufficient. However, the elderly, very similar to abused children, were viewed as being in need of special forms of protection—protection that would demand that caregivers and professionals who became cognizant of instances of abuse, neglect and exploitation would report these matters in the event the elder victim was unwilling or unable to do so. Additionally, it has been viewed that in many instances there is need to guarantee that the welfare of the abused senior be monitored and possibly the duty to make life critical decisions be vested in someone other than the victimized elder. The result has been the creation of a system of adult protective service.

Defining abuse, neglect and exploitation of the elderly has not been a simple task and this difficulty is reflected in the myriad of statutes enacted at both the state and federal levels. Poertner (1986) noted that legal definitions of abuse of the aged are varied, ranging from passive neglect to severe physical abuse, including death. The wide-ranging legal delineation of abuse of the elderly subsequently resulted in variable protective service programs, modes of service delivery and legal application of statutory provisions and sanctions.

The legal focus on the needs of the elderly has centered not only on legal mandates that allow prosecution of abusers but also on the provision of services that will assist the elderly victim in coping with the victimization. Sengstock and Barrett (1986) maintain that adequate care of the elderly victim of abuse, neglect or exploitation necessitates services such as court advocates, legal assistance to the elderly in processing both civil and criminal actions against abusers, and the provision of legal counsel in formal court actions and in out-of-court actions involving the victim and the offender.

The appearance of laws and statutes designed to protect the elderly reflects neither the discovery of a new category of crime nor a new category of victim. Rather, the emergence of legislation is indicative of efforts to bring to society's attention the special needs of this particular class of victims. The legislative efforts in this area have served not only to legally protect the aged but have further served the social purpose of similar movements in raising the public consciousness regarding abuse of the elderly. The enactment of laws in the area of adult protective services communicates the message that abusive behaviors are unlawful while at the same time reflect the moral message that these same behaviors constitute socially reprehensible conduct (Heisler, 1989).

While the recent history of legal intervention in this area is relatively short, dating to the 1960's, the pattern of recognition follows the track of other similar efforts, most notably spouse abuse and child abuse. This pattern is generally a four stage process involving, first, a class of individuals experiencing injury or harm; second, the individual's perceiving the harm as undeserved, unfair or unjust and thus perceiving themselves as victims; third, the perceived victims seeking social or official recognition of the victimization; and finally, the official declaration of victimization and the creation of forms of support or protection (Viano, 1989).

Initially, attention to the elder citizen as a victim dealt with the misperception that the elderly were more likely to be the victims of violent crime. Experience and perception did not meld, yet the movement to focus on the aged victim intensified as not the probability but the possibility of victimization propelled this emerging class of victim to the forefront (Reid, 1987). Once subject to inspection, the victimization of the elderly took on a different angle—the abuse of the elderly by caregivers, family members, and acquaintances. In noting that abuse of the elderly involves not only violent crime but withholding care, theft of savings and earnings, and verbal abuse, the nation was chastised by the chairman of a subcommittee of the United States House of Representatives Select Committee on Aging "domestic violence against the elderly is a burgeoning national scandal" (New York Times, 1980).

Creation of adult protective services legislation caught on quickly. The initial legislative attention to elder abuse culminated in the majority of state laws being enacted in the early 1980's (Thobaben, 1989). Presently, all fifty states have enacted legislation to protect the elderly from domestic abuse and neglect and forty-two states provide certain types of caregivers and professionals must mandatorily report instances of suspected abuse or neglect (Ehrlich and Anetzberger, 1991).

Yet, there is considerable deviation in the state laws. For example, among states mandatory reporting of suspected violations range from anyone with such knowledge to specifically designated professions such as medical personnel and social caseworkers. The variability in the scope and nature of the state statutes generates wide fluctuations in the definition of adult protective service laws and mandatory reporting requirements (Quinn, 1985). From this flows public and professional confusion and misperception of the true nature of the problem and means by which it is to be addressed. The common thread in the legislative efforts of the various states is evident in that the various adult protective services laws all address the prevention, detection, reporting and treatment of elder abuse, neglect and exploitation.

These fifty statutory endeavors tend to define abuse as any intentional or willful infliction of physical injury, confinement of an unreasonable nature, mental or physical intimidation, or punishment of a nature that causes physical or mental harm. Statutorily, neglect generally refers to the failure of the caregiver or the aged person to provide services or goods that are deemed necessary to prevent physical or mental anguish or physical harm. Exploitation is most usually defined as the improper or illegal use of an elderly or disabled person's resources for the fiscal or personal gain of a caregiver (Foelker, et al., 1991).

State efforts to statutorily address the issue of elder abuse were the products of two forces. As with any social problem that eventually receives public attention, the normal forces generating political action were at work. The decades of the 1970's and 1980's saw the "awakening" of the political influence of social movements and following the trail of those evoking legislation in the areas of spouse abuse and child abuse, the interest groups championing the protection of the elderly were able to garner the attention of politicians.

The second impetus for action by the states was the federal government. In 1987, the United States Congress amended the Older Americans Act of 1965. The amended act represented the federal government's mandate that the states provide services to prevent abuse of aged citizens. The legislation required state Offices on Aging to ascertain those agencies within each respective state involved in the prevention, identification and treatment of abuse, neglect and exploitation of the elderly. Further, the states were directed to determine the extent to which the service needs of the elderly were not being fulfilled (Foelker et al., 1991). While direct service provision is handled through state and local agencies, the federal government exercised its capacity to influence and attempt to standardize the manner in which states make available services to the elderly through the provision of fiscal assistance.

Given that the legal intervention into the area of elder abuse is of relative newness, it is not surprising that the fine tuning of adult protective service statutes continues. At present, the majority of states are actively engaged in the revision of previously enacted protective statutes. In most instances, there is no initiative to create new adult protective services legislation but rather to amend existing legislation. Reflecting the public concern and support of intervention efforts for the protection of the elderly, the governors and legislators of the majority of states actively support the strengthening of adult protective service statutes (American Association of Retired Persons, 1989).

STATE ADULT PROTECTIVE SERVICES LEGISLATION

The interest in the protection of elderly persons from abuse, neglect and exploitation has resulted in a proliferation of state laws, all similar in intent but different in approach. Several aspects of the variability of these statutory initiatives is of focal concern due to the manner in the various states approach the protection of adults deemed incapable of protecting their own interests.

The pattern in which these state enactments emerged demonstrates the slow or cautious approach to the passage of adult protective services laws. As revealed in Table 1, Nebraska and North Carolina pioneered the way with the remainder of the states and the District of Columbia following suit. It was not until after the passage of the 1987 amendment to the Older Americans Act of 1965 that all states provided specific legislation for the protection of the aged.

Despite the variability in state adult protective services statutes, there are common themes that pervade and these become evident when each of the fifty enactments are examined. The foremost noticeable characteristic is the *parens patriae* approach of overseeing the affairs of elders in much the same fashion as parents protect the interests of children. This approach is formulated upon the premise that government has an obligation and a right to take care of minors and others who cannot legally take care of themselves (Oran, 1985). The states, then, have adopted legislatively a stance that elders who are subject to abuse, neglect or exploitation may be in circumstances that dictate that government assume full or partial control of their affairs in order to shield them.

The mechanism by which the various laws allow the state to protect the elderly rest on the intervention of governmental agencies and their employees. All of the statutes mandate intervention be of the least restrictive nature possible so that the privacy and self-determination rights of the victim be recognized. This strives to respect the constitutional rights of the elderly, in the legal vein, and to respect the issues of human dignity in a moral vein.

Intervention techniques available through the enactments of the states

Table 1
Year of Initial Enactment of Adult Protective Services Law

1973	*1974*	*1976*
Nebraska	South Carolina	Alabama
North Carolina	Tennessee	Kentucky

1977	*1978*	*1979*
Arkansas	Florida	New York
Connecticut	New Mexico	
New Hampshire		
New Jersey		
Utah		

1980	*1981*	*1982*
Kansas	Georgia	Delaware
Minnesota	Hawaii	Idaho
Missouri	Maine	Louisiana
Oklahoma	Nevada	Massachusetts
Vermont	Ohio	Michigan
	Rhode Island	Montana
	Texas	
	West Virginia	
	Wyoming	

1983	*1984*	*1985*
Alaska	Arizona	Indiana
California	Illinois	
Colorado	Iowa	
Oregon	Maryland	
	Washington	
	Wisconsin	
	District of Columbia	

1986	*1988*
Mississippi	North Dakota
South Dakota	Pennsylvania

are varied. In particular situations, the laws allow for the appointment of a conservator or guardian for the elderly victim. This represents a situation in which a judicial decision warrants to a third party the legal right and duty to take care of the elderly person or the elderly person's property due to the legal inability or unwillingness of the elderly victim to take care of his or her own affairs (Oran, 1985). Such decisions are generally rendered when it is determined that the elderly victim is not competent to make sound determinations with respect to matters dealing with personal care and finances. Closely associated with this concept is the ability to appoint a guardian ad litum for the aged person, in which case the guardian ad litum represents the interests of the elderly victim in the court or administrative hearing setting when the victim is not in a physical or mental condition to do so personally. This action is of particular importance in instances in which the elder victim is confronted with an involuntary placement hearing. In circumstances in which a guardian or conservator has been appointed, some state laws provide for annual reporting on the part of the guardian or conservator with reports being filed with the state agency or department responsible for implementing adult protective services. Unfortunately, some state laws do not mandate such reporting and the possibility of further exploitation of the elderly is possible based on prior actions to protect these victims. Similarly, the court may give to a third party power of attorney for the abused aged in which case there is not a determination of incompetence on the part of the elder but rather a recognition that the elder may need assistance in carrying out future decision-making.

One of the main strengths of any adult protective service legislation is the requirement that known instances of abuse be reported to authorities. At present, forty-three of the fifty-one legal jurisdictions mandate reporting of known instances of the abuse, neglect or exploitation of the elderly. Generally, the laws mandate that professionals (i.e., medical personnel, law enforcement personnel, social caseworkers, and the like) report incidents. However, a few states mandate that anyone who possesses such knowledge report the incident. The remaining eight jurisdictions rely on voluntary reporting of incidents and several of the jurisdictions providing for mandatory reporting allow voluntary reporting by persons not specifically covered by the mandatory reporting requirement.

Of the states mandating reporting of instances of suspected abuse, neglect or exploitation, thirty make the failure to report a misdemeanor criminal offense and two make the failure to report a civil infraction. Two states, Arkansas and Minnesota, provide for a combination of civil and misdemeanor penalties for failure to report and one state provides that in addition to possible misdemeanor criminal penalties, offenders will be reported to professional licensing organizations for possible sanctions. Of the states making the failure to report a misdemeanor, six (Alabama, California, Louisiana, South Carolina, Tennessee and West Virginia) provide for jail confinement as a possible sanction. The remainder of the states providing for mandatory reporting of suspected cases, and those states relying on voluntary reporting of suspected cases, provide no penalty for the failure to report.

The omission of mandatory reporting requirements or the provision of no penalty for failure to notify authorities of instances of suspected abuse are often criticized. Given the basis for adult protection as an inability of certain aged to protect their own interests, the failure to mandate reporting of such incidents does not assure the possibly abused, neglected or exploited will come to the attention of those agencies who are legislatively required to provide services and protection.

The time frame for reporting suspected cases is also of key concern. The vast majority of statutes require an immediate verbal report to the agency responsible for carrying out the investigation with a written report to be filed within a specified time frame, usually twenty-four to seventy-two hours. However, some states allow up to five days for the filing of any type of report and a few allow an unspecified time frame. Obviously, if the elderly citizen is in fact in danger of physical harm or exploitation, any unnecessary delay in initiating the investigatory process places the victim at further risk.

With respect to the time frame within which the investigation must begin, many of the state laws simply mandate that the investigation begin "immediately" or "promptly" upon the receipt of the complaint. A few states specify a time frame, with the range being from one to ten days. States providing for longer or unspecified time frames for reporting, generally mandate that the investigation must begin immediately if there is reason to believe the elderly victim is in a life threatening situation or if physical harm may occur if immediate intervention is not undertaken.

The agency receiving the report and holding responsibility for investigating the alleged abuse, neglect or exploitation is most usually a state department of human services or a similar agency. A few of the states provide that law enforcement agencies be notified and some states require that reports be filed with an office for the aged. It is of further interest to note that almost sixty percent of the jurisdictions do not maintain a central registry of complaints to assist investigating agencies in resolving complaints or assist caregivers in seeking information regarding possible victims.

In an effort to provide some consistency in the protection of abused adults, Thobaben (1989) proposed guidelines for state legislation. These guidelines provide:

1. Persons covered by the law should be anyone eighteen years of age or older who lacks the functional ability to care for and protect themselves.
2. Clear definitions of abuse, neglect and exploitation should be used.
3. Reporting should be mandatory for all health and social services personnel who have reason to believe an incapacitated person is a victim of abuse, neglect or exploitation. Voluntary reporting should be available to any other individual.
4. Failure to report should be a misdemeanor crime and the professional should be reported to the appropriate professional licensing agency.
5. Any person reporting a suspected incident should enjoy both civil and criminal immunity if the report is made in good faith and without malice.
6. All reports should be treated as confidential unless disclosed with the consent of the reporting party or due to judicial action.
7. Verbal reports should be required on an immediate basis with written reports required within a specified time period.
8. A single state agency should be mandated to accept reports and maintain a central register of complaints.
9. There should be a specified time period for the initiation of the investigation to verify and assess the complaint.
10. The minimum content of a statewide service plan should be specified.
11. Services should minimally include emergency response, placement services, guardianship services, and a community services inventory.
12. The legislation should mandate that necessary funding be provided.
13. To protect the due process rights of the victim, the law should provide for the refusal of services by competent adults and incompetence must be proven through the judicial process.
14. Penalties for violation of the law by caregivers should be specified.
15. Public education and training for service providers should be mandated.

Thobaben (1989) notes that none of the existing state legislative efforts in this area approach the proposed model law yet maintains that unless comprehensive state laws that provide both the legal foundations and the requisite funding are created, the ability to adequately protect adults incapable of protecting themselves will be difficult to achieve. Additional support for the adoption of these model guidelines can be found in earlier studies that revealed state adult protection laws failed to live up to expectations due to a lack of clear definitions of elder abuse and specifically identifying target victims (Satz et al., 1984) and most cases came to the attention of caregivers who fell outside the narrowly described professionals covered by the mandatory reporting provisions (Faulkner, 1982).

FEDERAL ADULT PROTECTIVE SERVICES LEGISLATION

While the federal government first demonstrated interest in the plight of senior citizens with the enactment of the Older Americans Act in 1965, it was not until the late 1970's that specific interest in abused elderly became evident. In 1981, the Select Committee on Aging of the United States House of Representatives issued its report, *Elder Abuse: An Examination of a Hidden Problem,* and for the first time an attempt to define the nature of elder abuse and determine its scope and extent was undertaken by the federal government.

At this time, federal legislators likened the problem of elder abuse to other forms of domestic violence—spouse and child abuse—and began to tailor the federal response to the problem like the previous efforts in these other fields. Rinkle (1989) observes that federal efforts favored the mandatory reporting requirements inherent in child abuse legislation over the general domestic violence standards that believed that problems flowed from the existence of a dysfunctional family, with the prevention, treatment and investigation provisions accompanying such measures.

There were a series of proposed federal legislative initiatives to address the issue of elder abuse in the early 1980's yet none were successful until 1984. In that year the Family Violence Prevention and Treatment Act was approved by both the House of Representatives and the Senate. The act, in addition to providing grant monies to the states, mandated research on the occurrence of elder abuse. It was also in 1984 that the reauthorization of the Older Americans Act required that additional attention be given to the problem of elder abuse. As a result of these legislative measures, the federal government adopted the stance that abuse of the elderly should be approached in the same fashion as the federal efforts to address child abuse.

The efforts at the federal level were largely the product of Representative Claude Pepper. It was through the committees chaired by Representative Pepper that the two above mentioned acts emerged (Rinkle, 1989). After 1984, the bent of federal activities in the area of elder abuse shifted slightly. There was a marked shift from focusing on elder abuse that occurs within the confines of the family setting to one that focuses on the institutional abuse of the elderly. There developed a keen interest in the impact of inflationary medical costs and health insurance issues that frequently placed the elderly in situations that could lead to abuse, neglect and exploitation at the hands of family members and other caregivers. As pointed out by Rinkle (1989), many federal legislators feel many of the problems of elder abuse can be prevented or handled if the associated problems of institutionalized care and catastrophic health care are adequately addressed.

Such sentiment resulted in the enactment in 1990 of the Nursing Home Reform Amendment. This federal action addressed the problem of abuse of the elderly in the institutional setting by providing civil and criminal relief.

LEGAL CONCERNS AND ISSUES

The enactment of legislation at both the state and federal level has resulted in nationwide provision of adult protective services. Yet, there is concern that the creation of a specific class of victims of abuse, neglect and exploitation may not be the most appropriate vehicle for dealing with the problems encountered by the elderly. Fattah (1989) observes that abuse of the elderly is related to and symptomatic of other problems, notably poverty, exclusion from existing social networks, a sense of powerlessness, residential segregation and perceptions of vulnerability and further posits that undue emphasis on criminal victimization will possibly ignore or create an aura of mystification concerning these pressing social issues. Kosberg (1988) adds lack of community resources, continuing intrafamilial cycles of abuse, and personal hedonism on the part of caregivers as societal contributors to the mistreatment of the elderly.

When the social conditions facing the elderly are combined with the problems inherent with those individuals who tend to subject the aged to victimization, the ability of the legal system to address the issue is strained at best. Kosberg (1988) described the high risk caregiver as exhibiting one or more social problems, including substance abuse, suffering dementia, confusion or mental illness, inexperienced in providing care to persons in physical or mental need of assistance, and living in family environments that are overcrowded, isolated and lack support. Giordano and associates (1992) found that in instances of financial exploitation of the elderly, the typical offender was a son, daughter or friend who demonstrated problems with steady employment, a physical or mental impairment and difficulty establishing and maintaining relationships.

The amalgamation of the social factors surrounding the elderly victim and victimizer are ones that are largely out of the realm of control of those providing adult protective services. These factors are representative of the social milieu in the nation and have been relegated to the legal dominion due to any other reasonable alternative. Popular media accounts and scholarly literature discuss the breakdown of the extended family in American society and the issues of the care of the elderly take on added significance. Advances in health care and changes in lifestyles have resulted in ever-increasing life expectancies with senior citizens becoming the fastest growing segment of the population. As life expectancy has increased, so have the responsibilities of those who must care for the aged and the ailing (Graham, 1990). Whereas in the past, the elderly and the ill were cared for by the extended family, today there is reliance on government agencies and private institutions to provide this care. Failure to adequately address the special issues surrounding the ability of the elderly to function meaningfully and safely in society have culminated in the need to provide for legal avenues to assure some modicum of a quality life for the aged.

As is the case with legislation focusing on other special classes of victims, adult protective services legislation may very well be the signal that our society is unable to effectively deal with complex social issues and, as a last resort, has relegated the matter to the realm of the legal and criminal justice systems (Fattah, 1989).

Along the same track, Matthews (1988) asserts that adult protective service legislation is well intentioned but may actually be counterproductive to its averred goals. He contends that these laws may imply that merely by age a person is incompetent or infantile in nature and this in

turn encourages ageism and contributes to the existing biases and preju-
dices that may generate abuse, neglect and exploitation of the elderly.
Matthews (1988) also states that the administration of adult protective
services must not abridge the constitutional rights of victims and states
must comply with due process requirements and seek the least restrictive
alternatives in extending protection to adults.

Concern with the legal rights of elderly victims is of importance.
Thobaben (1989) sees the issues of the legal rights of victims falling in
two areas. First, there is a conflict between the state's obligation to protect
vulnerable adults and respecting the privacy and self-determination
rights of dependent adults. Many abused elderly report a desire to
remain in the abusive circumstances rather than surrender their personal freedoms as frequently perceived in the instance of institutionalization (Yurkow, 1991).

Second, mandatory reporting laws may transgress the confidential
relationship existing between the elderly client and the professional
rendering services. Such concerns create the likelihood that professionals may fail to report suspected incidents of abuse, neglect and
exploitation if there is any perception that the adult protective services
are less than adequate and beneficial. A survey of physicians concerning
compliance with mandatory reporting laws revealed medical doctors
were not confident in their ability to accurately recognize elder abuse,
neglect and exploitation. The physicians also reported a lack of confi-
dence in the ability of the state to effectively investigate alleged offenses
in a timely fashion and to deliver subsequent services (Daniels et al.,
1989). The same research discovered that physicians felt that if the
detection and treatment of elder abuse were to be effective, increased
funding is essential.

To heighten the recognition of the seriousness of the abuse, neglect
and exploitation of the elderly and the importance of reporting its
incidence, the American Medical Association in 1992 issued its first ever
written guidelines on the issue. These regulations urge physicians and
other health care providers to be more alert to the signs of mistreatment
or neglect of older patients by their families or other caregivers (Russell,
1992).

In an interesting attempt to make not only professionals but others
aware of the necessity of reporting aged abuse to proper authorities, the
More-Jones Advertising Company sponsored at its own cost a television

and newspaper based public relations campaign in the Denver metropolitan area to increase awareness of elder abuse (Mahoney, 1992).

Efforts to protect the abused aged generate two major concerns when considering the constitutional rights of the elderly. There is the need to protect the victim from those individuals or institutions that place him or her at jeopardy, physically, emotionally or financially, and a need to protect the elder from unwarranted intrusion on the part of adult protective services agencies. As discussed earlier, there are legal procedures for the assignment of guardians or conservators but in many instances the adult victim is in need of assistance prior to this occurrence. As a result, advocacy groups for elders are taking on importance. For example, the National Academy of Elder Law Attorneys has been formed to safeguard the rights of elders who are allegedly the victims of physical and financial abuse and are brought into the process of adult protective services (Denver Post, 1989).

The enactment of laws designed to protect adult citizens from abuse, neglect and exploitation are effective only if the laws are effectively and adequately enforced. In many circumstances, the attempt to legislate solutions to social problems has unfortunately rendered less than desirable results. In assessing the procedures attendant to the mistreatment of the elderly, Ehrlich and Anetzberger (1991) discovered that all fifty state departments of health were aware of elder abuse reporting laws but there appears to have been little progress in implementation. The researchers found that none of the state departments of health had in fact developed protocols for identification of abuse and referral of victims and saw the largest contributing factor as the diffusion of authority among agencies for human services, offices of the aging and law enforcement. The United States House of Representatives Select Committee on Aging (1990) reported that 86 percent of states delegated investigative responsibility to departments of social service, 8 percent to departments of elder services and 2 percent to an ombudsman office. The Committee also found that thirty percent of states placed secondary responsibility on law enforcement agencies.

As previously discussed, there is considerable variability in the provisions of the various state statutes. Consequently, it is not possible to develop standardized response formats in each of the states. In each of the states, there is need for one agency to assert control over the coordination of the contributions of agencies holding some share of the responsibility for the enforcement of adult protective statutes yet this is generally not the case. Ehrlich and Anetzberger (1991) contend that the state agency in the most appropriate position to oversee this coordination is the state department of health due to its interest in elder abuse as a public health issue and its position as a neutral party in the process of investigating complaints and providing services to elderly victims.

The passage of legislation at the state and federal levels is significant in that it has created a system, albeit a somewhat inconsistent and diverse one, for protecting the interests and well-being of aged who are not able to do so. Yet, even if the various adult protective services were written in the most ideal frame and rendered maximum protection while recognizing the legal rights of the elderly, there is a major governmental factor that must be added to the picture to make the process viable. This key variable is funding.

This problem takes on critical proportions, particularly in light of government fiscal issues. For example, in a 1990 congressional hearing conducted by Representative Joseph Kennedy of Massachusetts, it was reported that abuse of older persons by younger family members is rising dramatically while at the same time the level of government funding for adult protective service programs and enforcement is decreasing (Foster, 1990). Hagedorn (1990) echoed this finding by revealing that many states lack the funds to enforce laws requiring reports in the instance of abuse, neglect or exploitation of the elderly and further lack the fiscal resources to provide protective and rehabilitative programs for both the victims and the offenders.

Perhaps one of the most dramatic examples of the fiscal crunch being felt in the provision of adult protective services is in Wisconsin. Despite a doubling of reported cases of elder abuse in a three year period, the Wisconsin Department of Health and Social Services failed to include any funding to address the problem in its 1990/91 fiscal year budget (Drake, 1989).

In the administration of adult protective services, a review of the legal dimensions dictates scrutiny of the role of those government actors that may be called upon to assist the elderly. Similarly, there are legal implications for service delivery on the part of non-government caregivers who function as caregivers to the elderly.

At the level of government actors, whenever a particular behavior is criminalized the first thoughts swing to the police and the prosecutor and the application of the strictures that are statutorily and constitutionally imposed on these individuals in the job setting. From this perspective, the investigation of alleged abuse, neglect or exploitation of the elderly must follow the same guidelines as the processing of any criminal matter. Yet, adult protective statutes create the real possibility that government actors outside law enforcement will most likely come into the picture in the processing of elder abuse cases. The applicability of constitutional and statutory mandates to non-law enforcement personnel will become critical to successful case processing if matters reach the stage of criminal prosecution. While different standards are applied to the police and prosecutors due to their powers of arrest and charging, non-law enforcement government actors will possibly find handling elder abuse cases will propel them into the workings of the legal and criminal justice systems.

Case workers in departments of social welfare or similar agencies will be forced to take note of their activities, keeping in mind that cases involving the elderly may eventually move from the realm of casework to the realm of case prosecution. Much in the same vein that social caseworkers dealing with children's issues in the 1970's, caseworkers assigned to the elderly will require specific training so that proper and well intentioned actions one day do not jeopardize the instance in which the client is no longer simply a person in need of services but in fact a person who has been subject to abuse, neglect or exploitation. These workers will need to be cognizant of factors such as watching for and preserving physical evidence of abuse, the need for and methods of taking proper statements from both victims and alleged offenders, and the necessity of referring cases at the earliest recognizable moment to the appropriate authority for investigation.

Non-government personnel serving the elderly as caregivers and as professionals acting in the legitimate capacity, will confront a variety of issues. The first and foremost issue will be the need to provide legal, ethical and appropriate care for the aged in their trust without contravening the laws designed to protect the elderly. In short, caregivers and professionals may not behave in any manner in which the elder client is placed in jeopardy of being abused, neglected or exploited.

A second area of concern for private sector persons serving the elderly is the requirement to report suspected cases of abuse to appropriate authorities. This presents both a legal requirement for the service provider and recognizes the moral and ethical demand that the welfare of the elderly be monitored by those in a position to do so. Failure to report may, in and of itself, result in the criminal prosecution of the negligent caregiver.

Both of the above scenarios present the distinct possibility of civil prosecution for the caregiver or professional who intentionally abuses and elder, conducts business so that others within the agency are able to abuse the elderly, or fail to report the abuse and further subject the aged person to continued abuse, neglect or exploitation. In all likelihood, it is the potential threat of civil action that will prompt the private sector to more diligent attention to the plight of the elderly. Not only does the care provider or the employer face the risk of civil prosecution and the loss of revenues and capital resources as the result of a successful suit, but the liability and malpractice insurers of these individuals and businesses have demanded stricter compliance with statutory provisions so as to minimize risk exposure, costly litigation and potential losses.

CONCLUSION

The issue of abuse of the elderly has entered the social consciousness in the same manner as the concern with abused children. In many respects, the two groups are viewed in the same light—helpless and powerless. As a result of the public's growing awareness of the problem and the growing political savvy and power of proponents of protection of the elderly, the issue has moved from the social arena to the legislative and legal bailiwick.

Efforts to guarantee that the elderly are not subjected to abuse, neglect and exploitation due to their potential inability to protect their own interests have resulted in the enactment of specific laws for this new category of victim. The existing criminal laws of this country, and its component states, already provided the basis for the investigation of physical abuse and neglect of the aged and for instances of financial exploitation. Yet, there was a recognized need to provide a mechanism by which elderly persons, who either could not or would not report instances of abuse, could be brought to the attention of governmental agencies that would act to protect the elderly.

As a result of intense pressure upon legislative bodies, each of the fifty states and the federal government have enacted various legislative initiatives designed to protect the elderly citizenry. While there is considerable variation in the nature and scope of these laws, the intent is two-fold. First, they guarantee that possible instances of abuse, neglect and exploitation are reported to authorities. Second, where appropriate, they place some agency or person in the position of being responsible for the welfare of the elder victim.

Adult protective service laws raise concerns regarding the respect of the privacy and self-determination rights of the elderly and the confidentiality rights of the elder client of professionals (e.g., physicians, caseworkers, etc.) who may be directed to report suspect cases. Such concerns cannot be taken lightly since the intent of adult protective service law is to protect the elderly and insure the ability to lead as normal and dignified life as possible. The intent is not to subject every elderly person to treatment as an irresponsible child.

The actions of state and federal legislators generate social policy concerns far beyond the intent to offer protective services to the elderly. New programs necessitate the expansion of existing services and agencies or the creation of new agencies altogether. Funding for programs, also the responsibility of legislative bodies, must be provided. Yet, most legislative bodies appropriate funds in measures that are separate and distinct from enabling legislation. Legislative endorsement of a particular program, in this instance the protection of elderly adults, does not insure adequate financial resources will be available for program implementation. There is always that the well-intentioned fervor that leads to the passage of substantive laws in the area of adult protective services will be lost or misdirected in the budgeting process. With the present status of state and federal government budgets, provision of services for the elderly is in competition with every other governmentally funded operation. At present, the evolution of law to protect the elderly has moved from infancy to the stage of full development. The test, in the next several years, will be whether the implementation of these laws does in fact result in protection of the elderly from those who would abuse, neglect and exploit.

REFERENCES

American Association of Retired Persons. (1989). *Summary of State Legislative Action Concerning Treatment and Services for Victims of Crime with Emphasis on Older Victims. Washington.*

Block, M.R. & Sinnot, J.D. (1979). *The Battered Elder Syndrome: An Exploratory Study. College Park: Maryland Center on Aging.*

Congress panel hears of physical abuse of the elderly. (1980, April 22). *New York Times,* B, 1:1.

Cordes, R. (1992). Nursing homes held accountable for abuse, neglect. *Trial, 28*(8): 11–14.

Daniels, R.S., Baumhover, Lorin A. & Clark-Daniels, C.L. (1989). Physicians' mandatory reporting of elder abuse. *The Gerontologist, 29*(3): 321–327.

Douglass, R.L., Hickey, T. & Noel, C. (1980). *A Study of Maltreatment of the Elderly and Other Vulnerable Adults.* Ann Arbor: University of Michigan Institute of Gerontology.

Drake, T.S. (1989, January 26). Elder abuse plan proposed. *Chicago Defender,* 6:3.

Ehrlich, P. & Anetzberger, G. (1991). Survey of state public health departments on procedures for reporting elder abuse. *Public Health Reports, 106*(2): 151–154.

Fattah, E.A. & Sacco, V.F. (1989). *Crime and Victimization of the Elderly.* New York: Springer.

Faulkner, L.R. (1982). Mandating the reporting of suspect cases of elder abuse—an inappropriate, ineffective and ageist response to the abuse of older adults. *Family Law Quarterly, 16*(1): 69–75.

Foelker, G.A., Jr., Holland, J., Marsh, M., & Simmons, B.A. (1990) A community response to elder abuse. *The Gerontologist, 30*(4): 560–562.

Foster, C. (1990, September 27). Elder abuse on the rise. *Christian Science Monitor,* 6:4.

Giordano, J.L., Yegidis, B.L., & Giordano, N. (1992). Victimization of the elderly: individual and family characteristics of financial abuse. *Arete, 17*(1): 26–37.

Graham, R. (1990, October 19). Secret suffering. *Boston Globe,* 1:1.

Hagedorn, A. (1990, June 25). States lack funds to deal with rising elder abuse. *Wall Street Journal,* B, 1:1.

Heisler, C.J. (1991) The role of the criminal justice system in elder abuse cases. *Journal of Elder Abuse, 3*(1): 5–33.

Karmen, A. (1990). *Crime Victims,* 2nd ed. Pacific Grove: Brooks/Cole.

Kosberg, J.I. (1988). Preventing elder abuse: identification of high risk factors prior to placement decisions. *The Gerontologist, 28*(1): 43–50.

Mahoney, M. (1992, October 19). Riveting pro bono campaign spotlights elder abuse. *Denver Post,* C, 2:1.

Matthews, D.P. (1988) The not so golden years: the legal response to elder abuse. *Pepperdine Law Review, 15*(4): 653–676.

McGovern, K. (1991, November 5) Elderly often easy victims for merciless scam artists. *Denver Post,* E, 1:5.

Oran, D. (1985). *Law dictionary,* 2nd ed. St. Paul: West.

Over 65 group's mounting concerns receive assistance through elder law. (1989, April 10). *Denver Post,* D, 3:1.

Poertner, J. (1986). Estimating the incidence of abused older persons. *Journal of Gerontological Social Work, 9*(3): 3–16.

Quinn, M.J. (1985). Elder abuse and neglect raise new dilemmas. *Generations,* Winter: 22–25.

Reid, S.T. (1987). *Criminal justice: Procedures and issues.* St. Paul: West.

Rinkle, V. (1989). Federal initiatives. In R. Filinson & S.R. Ingram (Eds.) *Elder abuse: Practice and policy.* New York: Human Sciences, 1989.

Russell, C. (1992, November 24). Abuse of the elderly alarms doctors. *Washington Post,* WH, 7:1.

Satz, M., Salends, E., Kane, R.A., & Pynos, J. (1981) *Elder Abuse Reporting: Limitations of Statutes.* Los Angeles: UCLA/USC Long Term Gerontology Center.

Secombe, K. & Ishii-Kuntz, M. (1991). Perceptions of problems associated with aging: Comparisons among four older age groups. *The Gerontologist, 31*(4): 527–533.

Sengstock, M. and Barrett, S. (1986). Elderly victims of family abuse, neglect and maltreatment. *Journal of Gerontological Social Work, 9*(3): 43–62.

Stearns, P.J. (1986) Old age family conflict: the perspectives of the past. In K.A. Pillemer & R.S. Wolf (Eds.) *Elder abuse: Conflict in the family,* Dover: Auburn House.

Steinmetz, S.K. (1978). *Overlooked Aspects of Family Violence: Battered Husbands, Battered Siblings and Battered Elderly.* Testimony presented to the United States House of Representatives Committee on Science and Technology. Washington.

Thobaben, M. (1989). State elder/adult abuse and protective laws. In R. Filinson & S.R. Ingram (Eds.) *Elder abuse: Practice and policy,* edited by Rachel Filinson and Stanley R. Ingram. New York: Human Sciences.

United States House of Representatives. (1979). *Elder abuse: An examination of a hidden problem.* Washington: Government Printing Office.

United States House of Representatives Select Committee on Aging. (1990). *Elder abuse: A decade of shame and inaction.* Washington: Government Printing Office.

Utech, M.R. & Garrett, R.B. (1992) Elder and child abuse: conceptual and perceptual parallels. *Journal of Interpersonal Violence, 7*(3): 418–428.

Viano, Emilio C. (1989). Victimology today: Major issues in research and public policy. In E.C. Viano (Ed.) *Crime and its victims,* New York: Hemisphere.

Yurkow, J. (1991). Abuse and neglect of the frail elderly. *Pride Institute Journal of Long Term Home Care, 10*(1): 36–39.

Chapter Five

ADULT PROTECTIVE SERVICES AND THE CRIMINAL JUSTICE SYSTEM

STEVEN CHERMAK

INTRODUCTION

Crime ranks among America's most significant domestic problems. Victimization occurs at alarming rates. Over 34 million people became victims of crime in 1990 (U.S. Department of Justice Statistics, 1990a), and close to 6 million violent crimes occur annually (U.S. Department of Justice Statistics, 1991). One in three violent crime victims suffer physical injury, and as a result one in ten spend at least one night in the hospital (National Organization for Victim Assistance, 1983). Criminal activity results in over 16 billion dollars in direct, personal, and financial losses (U.S. Department of Justice Statistics, 1990b). These figures exclude other secondary expenses such as lost time from work, medical costs and adding security to one's home.

One of the mechanisms used to address the crime problem is the criminal justice system, consisting of a police, court, and correctional component. Unfortunately, the majority of crimes that occur are never fully processed and are filtered out of the criminal justice system. Few suspects are caught, arrested, charged, tried, and convicted. For example, the difference between the total number of crimes that occur and those reported to the police is known as the "dark figure of crime." Citizens would rather not report their victimization then get the police involved. Of those crimes that are reported to the police, an additional amount are filtered out because police typically are unable to make an arrest. Moreover, even if the police can establish probable cause and arrest a suspect, prosecutors might refuse to charge because of skepticism regarding their ability to prove guilt beyond a reasonable doubt. Judges might dismiss charges, a suspect might be found innocent at trial, or a case may be filtered out of the system via a plea bargained agreement.

Historically, crimes that occur between family members have been automatically filtered out of this process. Family crimes were thought to be beyond the purview of the criminal justice system, and only of concern to social service agencies. Academics, advocacy groups, and the news media have all played instrumental roles shattering the myth that family violence is a private matter, altering the typical response to these crimes. For example, in the 1960s the victimization of children by their parents became an issue of national concern. Changes have occurred which reduce the number of child abuse cases filtered out of the process including mandatory reporting by medical and social service workers, training of police to recognize abuse cases, and allowing videotaped testimony. In the 1970s, stimulated in part by the women's movement, various responses to spousal assault were implemented to decrease the filtering out of domestic violence cases. These responses included: the growth of shelters for women; mandatory arrest policies; and the acknowledgement by the courts of the "battered spouse syndrome" (Ohlin and Tonry, 1989). These responses have helped to limit the number of family crimes filtered out of the criminal justice process which, in turn, has diminished the "second victimization" that can be caused from a victim's participation in the system.

Concern regarding the victimization of the elderly began to gain momentum in the 1980s lagging behind the interest in child and spouse abuse. Although the research literature examining these latter two areas has increased dramatically, understanding domestic abuse of the elderly is in its infancy. What responses have been attempted to limit the filtering out of elder abuse cases from the system? The balance of this chapter examines the response by the criminal justice system and adult protective services (APS) to elder abuse. Coordinated efforts between these two types of agency can be an effective response because it ensures that the problem is addressed while satisfying the needs of elderly victims. First, the extent of elder abuse and limitations in what is known are discussed. The second part of this chapter discusses the police and elder abuse by examining the police response, the links between police and APS, and how limitations can be addressed. The court response to elder abuse cases is considered in the third section. It examines prosecutorial awareness, the role of APS in court, and the sentencing of abusers.

VICTIMIZATION OF THE ELDERLY

The elderly are portrayed in the news as victims of conventional crimes such as murder, robbery, and rape. The robbery of an old, frail woman is an important news story (Lotz, 1991). These images contribute to the public's belief that the elderly are among the groups most frequently victimized (Finley, 1983; Fattah and Sacco, 1989). However, available victimization data indicates that the elderly are the least likely of all age groups to be victims of index crimes, although they are more likely to sustain an injury requiring medical care (United States Department of Justice, 1992a). Even minor injuries can cause serious and permanent damage because of the physical vulnerability of the aged (Liang and Sengstock, 1983). What these data do not reveal is the significant "dark figure" associated with elder crime. In particular, such standard data sources do not necessarily count the frequency of "elder abuse and neglect" cases which, when they occur, are often perpetrated by family members. Therefore, victimization of the elderly is allusive.

Even though elderly victims are less likely to be directly victimized than other age groups by index crimes, the threat of crime has a significant psychological and behavioral impact. For example, research does indicate that the elderly are more likely to be fearful of crime compared to other age groups (Yin, 1985). In terms of the problems that are most salient to the elderly, fear of crime is second only to their concerns about having food and shelter (Ashton, 1981). The elderly may accommodate these fears by adapting their behavior and lifestyle. Some are afraid to go outside alone, reduce interaction with other community members, and barricade themselves in their home: a type of self-imposed "house arrest" (Greenstein, 1977).

The elderly believe that the home is a place where they are protected from victimization. The reward for a lifetime of productivity. Is isolating themselves in their home a guaranteed safe haven? Data are becoming increasingly available which indicate that the home can be a dangerous, violent place. Gordon (1987) states, "The image of the elderly as victims of conventional "street" crime is being replaced by a view in which the family and private nursing home settings appears as more hazardous environments" (p. 126).

Extent of the Problem

In order to understand how the criminal justice system and APS responds to elder abuse, the nature and scope of the problem must be determined. Should criminal justice professionals be concerned? Is elder abuse significant enough that scarce criminal justice resources should be expended to address the problem? Would the money and resources be better spent addressing other types of problems? The following section discusses the available data on the prevalence of elder abuse, some of the limitations of what is known, and why so many elder abuse incidents are filtered out of the criminal justice process before ever coming to the attention of any service agency.

Recognition of elder abuse is just beginning because of the invisible nature of these crimes. Researchers started to examine the extent of the problem in the late 1970s (Quinn and Tomita, 1986; Fattah and Sacco, 1989), even though historical evidence indicates it has been a problem for centuries (Steinmetz, 1987). The interest that emerged in the 1970s was sparked, in part, by testimony at a congressional inquiry that concluded that elder abuse[1] was a "hidden problem" (United States House of Representatives, 1981). The following is one of the most frequently quoted conclusions based on the testimony provided:

> Elder abuse is far from an isolated and localized problem involving a few frail elderly and their pathological offspring. The problem is a full-scale national problem which exists with a frequency that few have dared to imagine. In fact, abuse of the elderly by their loved ones and caretakers exists with a frequency and rate only slightly less than child abuse (p. xiv).

These congressional hearings highlighted the need for information. The extent of the problem, whether states were addressing the problem, and how they were responding to it was generally unknown. A number of studies have attempted to document more precisely the prevalence of elder abuse since these early congressional concerns. The resulting estimates of abuse vary considerably ranging between 1 and 10 percent of elders sampled (Hudson, 1986; Tatara, 1990). For example, Gioglio and

---

[1]The focus of this discussion will be on elder abuse that occurs by the family. Institutional elder abuse, although closely linked to the problems with abuse that occurs in the home, will not be discussed in detail. There is not as much data available directly addressing some of the problems with institutional elder abuse (Tatara, 1990). This is, of course, an oversight that needs to be considered in future research. In addition, there is a broad range of crimes that are indicative of abuse. For example, physical abuse (battery), financial exploitation, psychological mistreatment, neglect, denial of basic rights, are all considered types of elder abuse. This chapter uses the term "elder abuse" in a very generic sense, including the different types of behavior.

Blakemore (1983) reported that approximately 1 percent of a random survey of elderly had experienced some form of abuse. Block and Sinnott (1979) found that 4 percent of 73 elders studied were victims of elder abuse. They then extrapolated from these figures to suggest that a million elders were victimized annually, and concluded that elder abuse was as common as child abuse. Other researchers have reported figures much higher. For example, Lau and Kosberg (1979) and Steinmetz (1981) reported that 10 percent of the elderly in their respective samples were victims of elder abuse.

The findings presented were tentative because these studies employed various methodologies, were of diverse quality, and defined elder abuse in a number of different ways (Tatara, 1990). Responding to these limitations, Pillemer and Finkelhor (1988) conducted the most comprehensive study to date on the prevalence of elder abuse. This study was "the first large scale random sample survey of the problem," surveying 2,000 elderly in Boston. These researchers concluded that physical abuse, neglect, or chronic verbal aggression occurred at a rate of 3.2 percent. They argued that if similar abuse rates were found across the country as in Boston, between 701,000 and 1,093,560 elders are abused annually (p. 54).

Finally, a more recent survey conducted by the Subcommittee on Health and Long-Term Care of the House Select Committee on Aging provide data of national significance (Tatara, 1990). The results from this survey of the states indicated:

> Abuse of the elderly is increasing nationally. About 5 percent of the Nation's elderly may be victims of abuse from moderate to severe . . . about 1 out of every 20 older Americans, or more than 1.5 million persons, may be victims of such abuse each year. This represents an increase of 1 percent of the elderly population, or 500,000 abuse cases annually since 1980 (p. XI).

These studies indicate the high prevalence of elder abuse. The existing data provides some indication that elder abuse is worthy of criminal justice attention. These numbers, however, are even more significant when coupled to the facts that the elderly population continues to grow, as well as the elderly's apprehension to report their abuse to the police.

America is getting older. The average life expectancy has increased significantly during the past century. For example, someone born in the early 1900s was expected to live, on average, about 50 years. Today, the average American is remaining active and healthy into their mid-70s. Quinn and Tomita state: "The fastest growing segment of the population is the group 75 and older, which means that more and more middle-aged adult children will have old-old parents, and four-generational families will become commonplace" (p. 15). By the year 2000, 1 in 5 citizens will be 65 or older, and the greatest increase (53 percent) will be among those 75 and older (Steinmitz, 1987). Concomitantly, it can be expected that elder abuse will continue to increase as more and more children have to care for older and older parents.

Crime victims are generally considered the principal gatekeepers of the criminal justice system (Gottfredson and Gottfredson, 1988; Gottfredson, 1989). Victims play a significant role deciding which crimes get filtered out of the process because of their unwillingness to report crimes to the police. Research has shown that most victims refuse to report for various reasons, such as fear of retaliation, embarrassment, and victims do not think that the police can do anything about it (United States Department of Justice, 1992b).

The problems inherent in reporting all types of victimization are exacerbated with cases of elder abuse because of the invisibility of these crimes and the oft found heavy reliance of the abused elder on the abuser. It is safe to assume that the available figures on elder abuse underestimate the problem, because the elderly often refuse to report domestic victimization. Researchers have acknowledged that a significant number of elder abuse cases are not reported to the police, resulting in limited understanding of the scope of the problem (Plotkin, 1988; Dolon and Blakely, 1989). Some of the available estimates indicate that only 1 out of 8 elder abuse cases is reported (United States House of Representatives, 1990).

The reasons why elderly victims refuse to report abuse to the police are similar to why all types of crime victims refuse to cooperate. Developing an understanding of these reasons will highlight some of the obstacles APS and police departments must overcome to develop an effective response to elder abuse. These reasons can be grouped under three categories: individual; family; and criminal justice.

One of the most salient individual factors is the abused parent's economic and emotional dependence on the family. For many abused elders, staying in the abusive situation and enduring the victimization is preferred over long-term institutional care in a nursing home (Albanese and Pursely, 1993). Elderly fear that they will be separated from the family if they report the abusive situation or fear that the abuser will retaliate. Moreover, some elderly victims are unable to recognize being abused or cannot report it because of physical and/or mental limitations. A victim's denial of abuse poses particular difficulties because of the elderly person's right to privacy. Individuals are unable to help the elderly victim because they lack the legal authority to intervene if the victim does not want to cooperate (Pagelow, 1989).

Family privacy also limits the number of abuse cases that come to the attention of authorities (Attorney General's Family Violence Task Force, 1988). The elderly sometimes refuse to report their victimization because of embarrassment and shame: How could they have raised a child to be so cruel? Abusers will constantly degrade the elderly victim to a point where the victim starts to believe that they are a burden to the family and deserved the abuse. Some elderly are reluctant to report the abuser because they fear that their child will be incarcerated in prison, alienating whatever family they have.

Finally, the elderly may refuse to report abuse because of limitations in the criminal justice system. Arcuri (1981) reported that the elderly lack knowledge about the operation of the system and generally think that the police are ineffective (p. 110). Some elderly victims assume that police reporting procedures are too complex and not worth the effort (Plotkin, 1988). Moreover, elderly are afraid that the police will question their credibility. Other researchers have documented the same sort of apprehensions among the elderly regarding the court system. Heisler (1991), for example, reports that the elderly lack a general understanding about the court process, that most fear facing their assailant in the courtroom, and think they will be put on trial when asked to testify (p. 6). According to Plotkin (1988), "Victims may also be wary of the legal process in general, may perceive it as impotent in solving domestic violence problems, or may simply not understand it" (p. 18).

The extent that elder abuse is a problem is yet to be precisely determined because of reporting problems. Available data underestimate the extent of the problem. In addition, the size of the problem will continue to increase because the elderly population continues to get larger due to medical advancements and population growth. The remainder of this chapter will examine how the various components of the criminal justice system have combined with APS to respond to this problem. Heisler (1991) reports "it is evident that all branches of the criminal justice system-law enforcement, prosecution, and courts-and community professionals have critical roles to play" (p. 8). What is to follow, then, is an examination of the responsibilities of APS, police, prosecutors, and judges in addressing elder abuse. The police and court sections both begin by discussing how each of these criminal justice components have responded to elder abuse. The extent that each is coordinated with APS is then discussed. Finally, each section concludes by discussing how limitations in the criminal justice response to elder abuse can be overcome.

ELDER ABUSE AND POLICE

The criminal justice response to elder abuse presents unique challenges in comparison to other forms of family abuse because of the limited contact the elderly generally may have with other members of the public. The elderly are generally less active, more dependent, and more isolated than other abused family members because of health limitations and their fear of crime. For example, children have regular contact with teachers, doctors, and neighbors while an elder who is less ambulatory may not see a concerned other for days on end.

The role of the police is particularly important in cases of elder abuse because they are one of the few service providers that may have direct contact with them. The police are in an unique position to assist this segment of the population (Yin, 1985). Police officers are relied upon by the public to address a wide variety of problems because they are well-known, constantly available, and easily accessible by telephone. The police are a constant presence in the community because of their visibility, increasing the likelihood that an isolated elder might come into contact with the police. Police need to be aware of the intricacies of elder abuse in order to effectively respond to the problem.

The initial interactions that the elderly have with the most visible member of the criminal justice system can significantly shape how the elderly reacts to the trauma caused by abuse. A positive experience at the initial stages of the process might diminish their apprehensions about getting involved. This will increase the likelihood that they will continue to cooperate if their case moves to other stages of the process.

This section examines the police response to elder abuse. Many of the elder abuse cases that come to the attention of the police are filtered out even if the elderly person reports their victimization because of limitations in the police response. The two major limitations in the police response is their level of awareness of abuse, as well as the extent that they are coordinated with APS in the delivery of services. These limitations and how they can be addressed are discussed.

Police Awareness of Elder Abuse

One of the more important legislative responses to elder abuse has been the implementation of mandatory reporting laws. A majority of states have enacted these laws, requiring specific professionals to report actual and suspected cases of elder abuse to protective services (Tatara and Rittman, 1992). These laws were enacted to encourage reporting among specific groups of professionals that have contact with the elderly. Typically, employees of law enforcement departments are among the mandated groups required to report suspected cases of abuse. Mandatory reporting laws, however, can only be of significance if these professionals are able to recognize cases of elder abuse when coming in contact with them. Existing research indicates there are a number of gaps in the mandatory reporting process, including police ability to detect abuse.

The seminal study examining the police response to elder abuse was conducted for the Police Executive Research Forum (PERF) by Martha Plotkin (1988). Nearly half of the 200 police departments surveyed reported that elder abuse was not a problem in their community (p. 17). This finding is inconsistent with existing research that has documented the prevalence of elder abuse. In part, police underestimation of the problem can be explained by the failure of departments to collect separate data on elder abuse. Elderly cases are typically classified within a generic family violence category, so many departments may be aware of the extent of the problem. Approximately 80 percent of the responding departments in Plotkin's study were unable to identify the number of elder abuse cases that came to their attention in the previous year (p. 20). Albanese and Pursely (1993) state that "police departments don't routinely classify offenses accordingly and since states don't routinely classify offenses accordingly and since states don't routinely keep records of elderly abuse cases, problems abound in trying to get a handle on what's going on" (p. 254).

Legal Awareness

A problem which compounds the limitations of failing to record these crimes as separate offenses relates to police awareness of their legal mandate. Responses to Plotkin's (1988) survey indicated that about one-third of the departments were unaware of existing state statutes related to elder abuse and neglect who actually had these types of law (p. 28). This oversight is significant because she also discovered that those departments that were aware of elder abuse and neglect laws were over twice as likely to have special programs to meet the needs of the elderly compared to departments that did not know about these laws. In sum, it appears that a number of departments are unaware of the extent of the problem because of classification problems and knowledge of existing legal mandates. However, when the police are informed about the problem, departments do tend to take specific measures to address elder abuse.

Characteristics of Elder Abuse

Another shortcoming of police awareness is their ability to detect the unique characteristics of abuse when exposed to these cases. Plotkin's (1988) research indicates that the most common concern across departments is to improve officer ability to detect evidence of abuse. These cases are filtered out because police officers are unable to recognize domestic abuse, and define it as such, even if the elderly reports their victimization. Officers may dismiss physical indicators of abuse, attributing injuries to being old, fragile, and accident prone. For example, bruises, burns, cuts, or welts might be thought to be injuries sustained in a fall. Furthermore, police may stereotypically question the credibility of the elderly victim, dismissing the complaint as paranoia or senility (King, 1984). Even when officers think that the elderly victim's complaint is legitimate, police may investigate it like they would any general crime of assault or fraud, and ignore the possibility that the perpetrator might be someone in the home (Plotkin, 1988).

Community Resource Awareness

Many instances of abuse could be prevented if the elderly were informed about services available in the community (Pagelow, 1989). There are a vast array of community services that exist, such as homehealth care, that can ease the burden of caring for elderly persons. However, police officer's ability to refer elderly victims to sources of help is limited because they may be unaware of these services. For example, a study conducted by Schack and Frank (1978) found that only 9.2 percent of 257 elderly who called the police for assistance actually reported that the department referred them to an alternative resource for help. This finding is supported by other research that indicates that police referrals to non-police social service agencies are rare (Loving, 1980; Dutton, 1984; Dolon, Hendricks, and Meagher, 1986).

A lack of police awareness of available resources is linked to a low regard for performing services for the community. Some police may think that the more important aspects of law enforcement are preventing crime, conducting investigations, and making arrests. These officers envision their primary role to be that of a "crime fighter" (Walker, 1989). However, the majority of calls received by police departments are for order maintenance and service behaviors, such as providing transportation to a hospital, helping someone locked out of their home, or providing assistance to someone whose car is stranded on the side of the road. The police evaluate the complaints and requests for assistance initiated by older persons less seriously because of their dislike for the service aspects of their job (Arcuri, 1981).

Level of Coordination Between Police and APS

Most state statutes require APS to work closely with police to handle elder abuse cases (Tatara, 1990). The degree that this coordination takes place is another important aspect of the current response to elder abuse. Strong, coordinated efforts can overcome the limitations of police officer awareness and decrease the number of elder abuse cases excluded from criminal justice processing. A report prepared by Tatara and Rittman (1992) for the National Aging Resource Center on Elder Abuse stated:

> Only when each state takes advantage of the immense number of possibilities for interagency action open to them in combating elder abuse, will we begin to make major improvements in alerting and educating the public about elder abuse and in changing the lives of our elderly citizens for the better (p. 11).

Police departments need to work closely with APS professionals in order to take advantage of each of their respective strengths. Both police and APS have strengths and limitations in how they respond to elder abuse. The strengths of each individual agency can be used to overcome the limitations of the other agency if closely coordinated and cooperative. For example, both APS and police have particular expertise in detecting certain types of abuse that they can use to educate each other. APS professionals have more expertise in detecting specific types of abuse such as neglect and psychological abuse, whereas police are more effective at proving physical abuse cases and establishing the paper trail necessary to successfully prosecute a financial exploitation case (Quinn and Tomita, 1986). Closely coordinated efforts between these two agencies will prevent duplication of effort, and make reporting less laborious for the elderly victim.

APS is responsible for coordinating the activities of the variety of agencies involved, and is often the lead agency in determining what services should be provided. Thus, APS professionals are the primary advocates that represent the special needs of elderly victims. For example, they serve as a liaison between the victim and police, and raise the consciousness of the police regarding the seriousness of these crimes (Eisenberg, 1991). They can encourage the victim to cooperate with the police overcoming some of the difficulties in getting elderly to report their victimization. These APS professionals are in a unique position to encourage this cooperation, because they may have already established a trusting relationship with an abused victim.

It is important that APS professionals understand the procedures and legal requirements of the criminal justice system so that they can collect the type of information needed to bring a case to the attention of the police. In addition, they can inform the police of other potential remedies and less drastic alternatives if arrest is inappropriate. APS will have a considerable amount of information about a particular elder's case because of their close working relationship with them, and can meet with the police early so that they can provide officers with useful information to assist them with their investigation. For example, they can provide names and phone numbers of witnesses, historical information regarding the relationship between the victim and the suspect, as well as medical concerns of the victim. If different incidents of abuse are reported to the police by the same victim, the APS professional can make sure that each responding officer has been briefed about existing reports. This information can be used to substantiate the existence of abuse increasing officer awareness, giving credibility to the victim's account, and convincing police that the victim's injuries were not the result of a fall or self-neglect.

On the other hand, the police can also play a pivotal role in effectively disposing of elder abuse cases. The 24 hour accessibility of the police increases the likelihood that the police might be the first person that responds to elderly victims in need. If police are well trained in recognizing the unique characteristics of these cases and can detect abuse when provided the opportunity, the police can provide an early warning to social service agencies, serving as a voice for an isolated elder.

The police are better prepared to deal with the abuser. This is territory more familiar to a responding police officer. Thus, when an APS professional expects danger, is threatened, or is having difficulties getting access to the victim, then the police can be used to check on the safety of the client. An abuser is more likely to allow APS into the home when accompanied by uniformed police officers because of the public's unconditional acceptance of their authority. In addition, when a case progresses to a point where an arrest is necessary and the abuser is removed from the home, the close coordination of APS and police improves the likelihood that it will be effectively disposed of when processed into the court system.

Problems with Coordination

If APS and police are well coordinated, investigations can be conducted concurrently avoiding duplication of effort. Investigations of elder abuse will be more thorough because each agency can concentrate on their respective strengths (Pagelow, 1989). However, the links between police and APS do not appear to be firmly established, resulting in the provision of inadequate services to the elderly. Research indicates that the degree of coordination between them varies widely across different states (Tatara, 1990). These coordination problems result from a number of factors including the "lack of familiarity about each other's role," the "lack of staff time to initiate efforts to develop formal relationships," the "differences in the professional cultures between the two types of agencies," and the "overall bureaucratic complexities in both types of agencies" (Tatar, 1990, p. 99).

Historically, a general mistrust has existed between law enforcement and social service agencies. Some social workers may believe that police officers are generally insensitive to the needs of crime victims. Conversely, some police may believe social workers are ignorant of the law and are a detriment to their ability to solve crimes. A study by Sengstock and Hwalek (1987) highlighted police lack of awareness of the type of cases handled by APS. These researchers found that even when departments made an effort to exchange information with APS, they would refer the wrong type of cases, such as landlord-tenant cases, persons with mental problems, and general domestic violence. Understanding the services provided by APS is an additional barrier that must be overcome in order to achieve the effective coordination of activities between these two agencies.

Improving the Police Response

Developing effective training programs is the single most effective strategy to address the limitations in police awareness of elder abuse. Dolon and Blakely (1989) state that there is "widespread belief that additional training is needed to improve the quality of services which are provided to victims of elder abuse and neglect" (p. 47). Numerous other researchers agree that officer training needs to be improved in order to be able to better address the problem (Goldstein and Wolf, 1979; Arcuri, 1981; Plotkin, 1988; Pagelow 1989; Karmen, 1990). Although there is a general consensus that modifying police training is a crucial factor, research indicates that most departments have yet to fill this void. For example, Plotkin (1988) found that only 20 percent of the police departments surveyed had a training program specifically geared towards explaining the unique characteristics of domestic elder abuse and neglect. Currently, police departments give cursory attention to elder abuse as part of general domestic violence issues during academy training. According to Heisler (1991), the police are unfamiliar with "the type of information needed to prove an elder abuse case and will not know the critical questions that must be asked. Many are untrained in the special methods required to investigate these cases" (p. 14). This results in additional traumatization for the victim and perhaps causes these cases to be excluded from further processing by the criminal justice system.

Training can be improved by sensitizing officers to the special needs of the elderly, discussing reasons for refusing to report their crimes, and documenting the indicators of abuse. Officers have to understand the aging process so that they do not overlook cases of abuse by attributing injuries to physical ailments. Improving police training to increase awareness expands the likelihood that an abuser will be charged because officers will conduct more thorough investigations. Police officers need to learn how to communicate with the elderly by asking the right questions to substantiate the elder's accusation.

Another limitation of the current police response is their knowledge of available community resources. There is some research that indicates that effective training programs increase the willingness of police officers to refer victims to social service agencies (Pearce and Snortum, 1983; Dutton, 1984). For example, the study by Dutton (1984) indicated that officers trained in crisis intervention were over *twice* as likely to make victim referrals compared to a group of officers that were not trained.

Effective training programs would increase officer willingness to use existing community resources because they would be more aware of the resources available, and could be provided with lists of available service agencies as part of basic or in-service training programs.

One encouraging aspect of the limited coordination between APS and law enforcement is the fact that both are willing to work with each other. Tatara and Rittmann (1992) report that the lack of coordination "does not necessarily stem from the lack of willingness by either party to work closely with the other" (p. 100). Part of officer training needs to be structured to develop an understanding of the roles and responsibilities of APS. Integrating this topic into training will improve the level of coordination between these two agencies. APS and police administrators need to work closely together so a consensus response to elder abuse is developed. This will allow both agencies to take advantage of their individual expertise: conducting joint investigations; sharing information between agencies; and supplementing each other's training needs. Strong coordination will also ensure the effective disposal of difficult cases.

In addition, there are other ways to strengthen the ties between police departments and APS. First, they can conduct joint training programs. At present, existing training is typically completed by officers at "in-house" training sessions (Plotkin, 1988). Using police and APS professionals to train officers will promote coordination between the two agencies and stimulate information sharing. This could be done during police academy training or on an in-service basis. APS professionals are aware of a multitude of existing community organizations that can fill the void in the services that need to be provided, so that the limited resources of each organization does not have to be expended.

Second, the ties between these two agencies can be strengthened through the use of inter-agency protocols. Protocols "insure an active, joint partnership in fighting elder abuse" (Tatara and Rittman, 1992, p. 10). Police departments can use these protocols to effectively detect elder abuse and neglect, and make early referrals to APS. Pagelow (1989) states, for example, that "intervention should be guided by standardized, preplanned protocols developed by interdisciplinary health care teams, much like those recommended for suspected child abuse" (p. 276). In order to further promote the possible joint coordination of investigation and service provision, jurisdictions may wish to consider creating a police-APS liaison who may be a police officer or a prosecutor's investigator.

Unfortunately, police and APS are not currently linked by these protocols. Tatara and Rittman's (1992) survey of the states indicated that the vast majority of states responding indicated that no formal protocols existed between APS agencies and state law enforcement agencies, although informal relationships between agencies exist.

ELDER ABUSE AND THE COURTS

It is the responsibility of the police to attempt to substantiate crimes reported by citizens. Police officers accomplish this by interviewing victims and witnesses, gathering evidence, and questioning suspects. If an officer gathers enough information to establish probable cause, the suspect will be arrested and booked. Police then present whatever information they have to a prosecutor. This initiates the court process. Prosecutors have a tremendous amount of discretion at each phase of this process. For example, prosecutors decide whether to charge and what charges should be brought against a suspect, whether a case should be tried, and what type of plea offers are extended in exchange for admitting guilt. Prosecutors are the principle court actors determining if elder abuse cases are filtered out of the criminal justice process.

Generally, prosecutors have been reluctant to pursue crimes that are committed by family members because of the perplexity of these cases. Research indicates that the prosecution of all types of family violence has been rare (Lerman, 1986; Pleck, 1989; Harshbarger, 1989; Elliot, 1989). Numerous reasons exist for the infrequent prosecution of family violence cases, including the limited availability of court resources, abusers not being thought of as a threat to society, and because prosecutorial perceptions that these crimes are not serious (Friedman and Shulman, 1990). In addition, prosecutors hesitate to pursue these cases because of concern about the victim. Prosecutors are afraid that family violence victims will refuse to cooperate as the case progresses, requesting that charges be dropped (Forst and Hernon, 1985).

Similarly, research indicates that criminal prosecution of elder abusers has been extremely rare (Crystal, 1987; Korbin, Anetzberger, Thomasson, & Austin, 1991). Legal interventions are considered to be a secondary solution to the problem (Dolon and Blakely, 1989). The typical response to elder abuse has been to focus on community based services and institutional placements rather than criminal prosecution because of the difficulties in gathering enough evidence to establish guilt beyond a reasonable doubt (Astrein, Steinberger, & Duhl, 1984). Thus, legal inter-ventions to elder abuse need to be closely linked with other types of services to improve the court response.

A number of reasons exist for the limited number of elder abuse prosecutions that mirror why all types of family violence cases get weeded out of the system. First, prosecutorial awareness of the necessary elements to establish abuse is limited. Since elder abuse is the most recently acknowledged type of family violence, prosecutors have rarely had to work on these types of cases, and have "virtually no experience in prosecuting domestic elder abuse" (Attorney General's Family Violence Task, 1988, p. 63). A recent study by Kromsky and Cutler (1991) found that attorneys had a limited understanding and awareness of technical aspects of all family violence cases, such as the cycle of violence and reasons why domestic violence victims stay in the abusive relationship, even though responses to child and spousal assaults have been in place over twenty years.

A second factor limiting the prosecution's ability to pursue elder abuse cases relates to courthouse limitations. Getting involved in the arduous court process may simply overwhelm elderly victims. Certain aspects of participating in the court system, such as long delays and numerous continuances, places particular hardships upon the elderly. The physical and financial limitations of the elderly are often not consid-ered by prosecutors. Elderly victims may not be able to afford the costs of court involvement, or are unaware of services available that could limit some of the costs. For example, arranging transportation to the court-house is difficult for the elderly because of their limited mobility. Moreover, when they do manage to arrange transportation, they often discover that the trial has been rescheduled wasting the energy and effort to arrive. The emotional wear-and-tear that results from these difficulties may frustrate the elderly victim, discouraging their contin-ued involvement.

Third, effective disposition of these cases is limited by the elder victims willingness to cooperate with the prosecution. Quinn and Tomita (1986) state that "very few cases of elder abuse and neglect reach the criminal justice court system, partly because of the elderly victim's reluctance or inability to ask that charges be pressed, especially if the charges are against a relative or someone she has known for a long period of time (p. 220). Elderly victims may be willing to pursue a case initially and testify in support of an emergency or protective order, but are not as likely to pursue the case to completion (Eisenberg, 1991, p. 80). Elderly victims may feel guilty about testifying against a family member, fear confronting the abuser in court, or may be pressured by the abuser to drop charges. Pagelow (1989) discusses that the only way that prosecutors can pursue these cases without the cooperation of the victim is "if there is strong evidence that a crime or crimes occurred, there is a corroborating witness, and it can be shown why the victim refuses to testify (e.g., fear of retaliation)" (p. 274).

Finally, prosecutors are reluctant to put elderly victims on the stand because they are not considered to be good witnesses. They suffer credibility problems because members of the public have a difficult time believing that the physical injuries incurred by the elderly resulted from abuse and not from an accident or fall. This reality, which is promoted through social stereotypes, may seriously hinder further case processing. In addition, elderly victims may have limited ability to recall some of the details of a crime because of partial memory loss (Quinn and Tomita, 1986), or are easily confused when cross-examined by a defense attorney (Albanese and Pursely, 1993). Prosecutors also fear that the elderly victim may not live long enough to be able to testify at trial. The reluctance of prosecutors to use elderly victims as witnesses severely limits their ability to prosecute abuse cases because they are typically the only witness that can provide direct testimony.

Improving the Court Response to Elder Abuse

Korbin et al. (1991) state that the cooperation between APS and court professionals is an important part of improving the court response to elder abuse:

> The criminal justice system should be seen as part of the community service system in providing necessary services for specific family problems affecting the elderly. This would mean both that the social service community would include legal intervention as an option and that the justice system would be sensitive to the needs and vulnerabilities of elders. Practitioners in aging, health, and social services should be encouraged to help abused elders seek legal solution for maltreatment when this strategy is appropriate (p. 14–15).

Currently, the links between these two agencies are not firmly established. The reasons for this lack of coordination parallel the limitations described with APS and police links. Prosecutors may mistrust APS professionals because they are unfamiliar with their role and the services they can provide to both the elderly and the court. Also, given the limited prosecution of elder abuse cases there has been little contact between APS and prosecutors.[2] Prosecutor's fear that court involvement by any individual outside of the direct courtroom workgroup (i.e., prosecutors, defense attorneys, judges) will upset the "going disposal rates" of cases. Finally, prosecutors may think that consulting APS on a case will disrupt the speedy disposition of cases. Prosecutors need to have more information regarding what APS can do in order to foster cooperation between these two types of agencies.

APS professionals can play a critical role acting as a liaison between prosecutors and elder abuse victims. According to Eisenberg (1991), "A high percentage of elder abuse cases require the involvement of social service providers to ensure that the client receives the support necessary during the stressful period of making major and permanent changes in the elder's life" (p. 78). An APS professional can accompany the elderly victim when interviewed by the prosecutor, demonstrating moral support and encouragement. They can be responsible for explaining the process before it begins so that they are prepared and not surprised by the length of time and delays that are part of the process. Moreover, the APS professional can help the elderly victim to understand the need for charges to be filed by the prosecution. These are matters that a prosecutor briefly alludes too and the elderly victim may be overwhelmed by the variety of tasks.

The professional can also help insure that the victim's participation needs are met by serving in the capacity of a "victim advocate." For example, they can remind the victim of upcoming court dates. They can help the elderly victim arrange transportation to court, so that the victim can arrive safely. The quality of support that the elderly victim receives throughout the court process will influence whether they will continue to seek help in the future, regardless of the final disposition of the case.

APS can also be of direct assistance to prosecutors. First, prosecutors need to rely on the expertise of APS, because it will improve their ability to establish guilt. APS professionals can provide written statements about recurring abuse, help locate a victim who might be in hiding, and can locate other potential witnesses, such as neighbors or friends that could corroborate the victim's testimony (Heisler, 1991). Albanese and Pursely

---

[2]The exception to this may be found in the state of Indiana where almost all of the thirty sum APS investigators work directly for a district attorney or prosecutor. Moreover, they are also sworn prosecutor's investigators.

(1993) state that "without independent and strong corroborative evidence it is very difficult to convict a family member of abusive acts toward an elderly member of the family" (p. 255). APS can make this easier for the prosecutor by providing a list of names and addresses.

The APS professional can also serve as a source of information, instructing the prosecutor about the victim's ability to withstand the court process. They will be familiar with the medical condition of the victim, and can discuss their specific concerns. They can instruct the prosecutor about the abused victim's competence as a witness, going over their testimony so it is more resistant to cross-examination. Finally, the professional can reaffirm the resolve of the victim to pursue a case to completion (Heisler and Tewksbury, 1991).

APS can also help establish guilt when the victim decides to no longer or are unable to cooperate with the investigation. According to Heisler (1991), "While in most elder abuse cases the victim will be called as a witness, there are some cases that may be proved even if the victim later becomes forgetful or is reluctant to testify" (p. 16). Charges may not be automatically dropped if problems arise. It is important that the APS professional carefully records and documents each incident of abuse increasing the options that are available to prosecutors regardless of the status of the victim. In addition, statements that are made to APS professionals by suspects are admissible at a criminal trial, as long as the professional was not working directly for the police when asking questions (Quinn and Tomita, 1986).

Second, the APS professional can be an important link between the prosecutor's office and the variety of other agencies that are involved in each elder's case. Plotkin (1988) found that other agencies, such as hospital workers, victim service workers, mental health workers, transportation services, and shelters, respond to the different needs of the elderly. If APS is linked closely with the prosecutor's office, the caseworker could serve as the central hub of information for each of the various agencies involved. For example, the use of medical evidence is an important factor in proving that the elderly person's injuries were not sustained in a fall or some other household accident. APS can provide the prosecutor's office with a list of medical experts who have expertise in discussing the unique physical and psychological limitations of elder abuse.

Third, prosecutors can make a number of internal changes that would increase their level of coordination with APS. For example, large offices could have one prosecutor handle family abuse cases so that they can establish a direct link to the different APS caseworkers. Moreover, offices can vertically prosecute these cases where the same attorney handles the case from the beginning of the court process through the end. This will allow the prosecutor handling the case to understand the unique difficulties of a particular case, as well as develop a trusting relationship with the victim.

Finally, prosecutors need to be more adequately trained in handling these cases (Harshbarger, 1989). A number of the training topics discussed within the police section apply to prosecutorial training. For example, prosecutors need to be trained to understand the aging process and understand the limitations of abused elderly. This would encourage prosecutors to make an effort to reduce the number of continuances, dismissals, and unnecessary court appearances keeping in mind the possible frailty of the elderly. Training would also help prosecutors realize the seriousness of the problem. Furthermore, prosecutors need to be trained in the role and responsibilities of APS, and how they can effectively use the APS professional to assist them with a case.

SENTENCING

The effective disposition of elder abuse cases involves various aspects of both social service and law enforcement agencies. APS needs to advocate for the services necessary to insure that the victim's needs are protected, and each component of the criminal justice system must validate the victim's experience. Eisenberg (1991) states:

> Legal advocates for victims of abuse must be prepared to pursue cases aggressively and seek non-traditional remedies or remedies borrowed from other areas of the law. Attorneys must be advocates for the creation and expansion of legal remedies that will expedite the identification and eradication of elder abuse, while, at the same time, protect the rights of older people and their families. . . . with the interaction of legal and social forces, substantial steps can be taken to reduce elder abuse and remedy such conditions when they do exist (p. 92).

One of the final steps of the court process is to decide what should be done with defendants when found guilty of committing a crime. Judges have a variety of sentencing options available and wide discretion to decide the disposition of a case. The different options available and the judicial discretion to use them is an important aspect of improving the response to elder abuse because of the unique characteristics of these cases. A number of variables could be considered by the sentencing judge, such as who would care for the elder, how the elder could be reimbursed for losses, and the risk of the abuser recidivating in the future. The current response to elder abuse often does not remedy the situation even though a defendant might be found guilty because the special needs of the victim are not considered at sentencing by judges.

According to Heisler (1991), the "traditional methods and approaches for dealing with elder abuse may have discouraged victims and service providers from turning to the criminal justice system for help" (p. 25). Sometimes the elderly person may be at risk, but there may not be enough evidence for the prosecutor to charge a suspect and obtain a conviction. Moreover, the criminal justice system remains geared towards punishment, which may not necessarily be the best method for remedying elder abuse problems. Indeed, some criminal justice and social service officials encourage less legal intervention to maintain privacy and avoid exacerbating the stressful situation (Zimring, 1989; Pagelow, 1989). These situations highlight the need to consider alternatives to prosecution and incarceration. Courts have broad abilities to create laws to meet the unique needs of these cases because of judicial discretion. Pagelow (1989) states:

> Responses by the criminal justice system to victimization of the elderly must be designed on a case-by-case basis, carefully considering many factors, including the victims' ages, their physical and mental health, and their attitudes, as well as the characteristics of suspects, intentionality, and environmental and interpersonal dynamics of the relationship (p. 275).

Judges need to consider the sentencing preference of the victim. Some elderly victims may want the abuser to be punished severely. Consistent with this line of reasoning, the courts could benefit at sentencing by allowing either a verbal or written victim impact statement. Judges can make defendants realize the seriousness of their conduct, making it clear to society that elder abuse is a public concern, not a private matter (Heisler, 1991). The importance of the crime to the victim is minimized if judges do not react properly in resolving the unique problems of elder abuse cases.

Other victims might prefer a sentence that is less drastic. One remedy that has a considerable amount of promise because of the unique difficulties of elder abuse cases is Alternative Dispute Resolution (ADR). The use of ADR has been fueled by the rediscovery "that many disputes that are conceptualized and treated as collisions of rights or win-lose adversarial contests, are indeed negotiable" (Adler, 1987, p. 61). A number of features of elder abuse discussed throughout this chapter make these cases prime candidates for ADR (Goldberg, Green, & Sangley, 1985). Elderly victims may be apprehensive about reporting and cooperating with the criminal justice system because of their fear of institutionalization. Instead of severing the ties between the elderly victim and the abuser, ADR attempts to resolve the family conflict. Both parties provide input as to the reasons for the difficulties in the relationship and these reasons are openly discussed. The flexibility of ADR can insure that the needs of both parties are considered. For example, the preference of the elderly to remain in the home could be considered. The abuser could be ordered to get treatment that is needed, such as drug or alcohol counseling, allowing them to stay out of prison and continue to provide some care for the elderly. Moreover, an abuser may be sentenced to any of a number of community-based correctional programs.

It is important that APS stays involved through the sentencing of a defendant and beyond to continually monitor the safety of the elderly victim. For instance, APS can inform a judge about the need of a protection order if the abuser again starts to threaten the victim. APS can advise the elder on when to initiate such a step, and tell them to not invite the abuser back into the home (Quinn and Tomita, 1986). They can also inform the judge regarding the preferred sentence of the victim. For example, APS can inform a judge about the victim's financial situation and suggest that the offender pay restitution to the victim. In addition, the professional knows the suspect as well as the victim, and can make recommendations at sentencing regarding the suspect's needs given that it has long been accepted in the area of elder abuse and neglect that the perpetrator is also often a victim.

CONCLUSION

Domestic abuse of the elderly has increasingly become a topic of concern subsequent to interest in other forms of family abuse. A number of studies have documented the prevalence of elder abuse, illustrating its significance. The initial response has been the creation of social service agencies such as APS whose purpose has been to advocate for the rights and needs of elder abuse victims. Limitations in the ability to respond to all types of cases have highlighted the need for these agencies to obtain additional help from other organizations, specifically the different components of the criminal justice system.

Criminal justice professionals have made some changes to help respond to the elder abuse problem because of political and public pressure. However, there are a number of limitations to their response. First, both police and prosecutors are unaware of the seriousness of the problem, are unable to recognize the unique characteristics of these cases, and fail to respond in a way that takes into account the special needs of these victims. Second, it appears that each component of the criminal justice system does not rely on existing community resources, such as APS agencies, for assistance in their response. Both types of agencies have individual strengths that can overcome the existing limitations in each. This limited awareness and lack of coordination results in a number of elder abuse cases being filtered out of *both* systems, resulting in unnecessary harm to the elderly.

A number of solutions can be implemented to prevent additional harm. For example, training of criminal justice professionals is one of the most important solutions because of limitations of the current response relates to understanding the problem, developing appropriate responses, and knowing existing community resources. Overcoming these limitations as part of basic, in-service, and special training sessions is an important starting point for improving the response. In addition, these organizations need to be more closely coordinated with APS agencies. The implementation of formal inter-agency protocols will stimulate coordination, and APS professionals can be used to fill police and court training needs to promote these links. Development of a coordinated response through increased training and forced interactions will improve the current response to elder abuse, ultimately making the elderly's home the safe haven that they hoped it to be.

REFERENCES

Adler, P. (1987). Is ADR a social movement? *Negotiation Journal,* 3 (1), 59–71.

Albanese, J.S., & Pursley, R.B. (1993). *Crime in America: Some existing and emerging issues.* Englewood Cliffs, New Jersey: Regents/Prentice Hall.

Arcuri, A.F. (1981). The police and the elderly. In D. Lester (Ed). *The elderly victim of crime.* (pp. 106–28). Springfield, Illinois: Charles C Thomas, Publisher.

Ashton, N. (1981). Senior citizens' views of crime and the criminal justice system. In D. Lester (Ed). *The elderly victim of crime.* (pp. 14–26). Springfield, Illinois: Charles C Thomas, Publisher.

Astrein, B., Steinberger, A., & Duhl, J. (1984). *Working with abused elders: Assessment, advocacy, and intervention.* Worchester, MA: University Center on Aging, University of Massachusetts Medical Center.

Attorney General's Family Violence Task Force. (1988). *Violence against elders.* Pennsylvania: Office of the Attorney General.

Block, M.R., & Sinnott, J.D. (1979). *The battered elder syndrome: An exploratory study.* College Park, Maryland: University of Maryland, Center for Aging.

Campbell, J.C. (1991). Public-health conceptions of family abuse. In D.D. Knudsen, & J.L. Miller (Eds). *Abused and battered: Social and legal responses to family violence.* (pp. 35–47). New York: Aldine De Gruyter.

Crystal, S. (1987). Elder abuse: The latest "crisis." *The Public Interest.* 88, 56–66.

Dolon, R., & Blakely, B. (1989). Elder abuse and neglect: A study of adult protective service workers in the United States. *Journal of Elder Abuse & Neglect,* 1 (3), 31–49.

Dolon, R., Hendricks, H. & Meagher, M.S. (1986). Police practices and attitudes toward domestic violence. *Journal of Police Science and Administration.* 14, 187–192.

Dutton, D.G. (1984). Interventions into the problem of wife assault: Therapeutic, policy and research implications. *Canadian Journal of Behavioral Science.* 16, pg. 281–297.

Eisenberg, H.B. (1991). Combatting elder abuse through the legal process. *Journal of Elder Abuse & Neglect,* 3 (1), 65–96.

Elliott, D.S. (1989). Criminal justice procedures in family violence cases. In L. Ohlin, & M. Tonry (Eds). *Family violence.* (pp. 427–480). Chicago: University of Chicago Press.

Fattah, E.A., & Sacco, V.F. (1989). *Crime and victimization of the elderly.* New York: Springer.

Finley, G.E. (1983). Fear of crime in the elderly. In J.I. Kosberg (Ed). *Abuse and maltreatment of the elderly: Causes and interventions.* (pp. 21–39). Boston: John Wright.

Forst, B. E., & Hernon, J.C. (1985). *The criminal justice response to victim harm.* Washington, DC: U.S. Department of Justice.

Friedman, L.N. & Shulman, M. (1990). Domestic violence: The criminal justice response. In A.J. Lurigio, W.G. Skogan, & R.C. Davis (Eds). *Victims of crime: Problems, policies, and programs.* (pp. 87–103). Newbury Park, California: Sage.

Galbraith, M.W. & Zdorkowski, R.T. (1984). Teaching the investigation of elder abuse. *Journal of Gerontological Nursing,* 10 (12): 21–25.

Gioglio, G.R., & Blakemore, P. (1983). *Elder abuse in New Jersey: The knowledge and experience of abuse among older New Jerseyans.* Trenton, New Jersey: New Jersey Department of Human Services.

Goldberg, S.B., Green, E.D., & Sander, F.E.A. (1985). *Dispute resolution.* Boston, Massachusetts: Little, Brown.

Goldstein, A.P. & Wolf, E.L. (1979). Police investigation with elderly citizens. In A.P. Goldstein, W.J. Hoyer, & P.J. Monti (Eds). *Police and the elderly.* New York: Pergamon.

Gordon, R.M. (1987). Financial abuse of the elderly and state "protective services":

Changing strategies in the penal-welfare complex in the United States and Canada. *Crime and Social Justice,* 26, 116–134.

Gottfredson, G.D. (1989). The experiences of violent and serious victimization. In N.A. Weiner and M.E. Wolfgang (Eds). *Pathways to criminal violence.* (pp. 202–234). Newbury Park, California: Sage.

Gottfredson, M.R. and Gottfredson, D.M. (1988). *Decision making in criminal justice.* Cambridge, Massachusetts: Ballinger.

Greenstein, M. (1977). An invitation to law enforcement. *Police Chief.* 44, 46–47.

Harshbarger, S. (1989). A prosecutor's perspective on protecting older Americans: Keynote address. *Journal of Elder Abuse & Neglect,* 1 (3), 5–15.

Heisler, C.J. (1991). The role of the criminal justice system in elder abuse cases. *Journal of Elder Abuse & Neglect,* 5 (2), 5–33.

Heisler, C.J., & Tewksbury, J.E. (1991). Fiduciary abuse of the elderly: A prosecutor's perspective. *Journal of Elder Abuse & Neglect,* 3 (4), 23–40.

Herzberger, S.D., & Channels, N.L. (1991). Criminal-justice processing of violent and nonviolent offenders: The effects of familial relationship to the victim. In D.D. Knudsen, & J.L. Miller (Eds). *Abused and battered: Social and legal responses to family violence.* (pp. 63–75). New York: Aldine De Gruyter.

Hudson, M.F. (1986). Elder mistreatment: Current research. In K.A. Pillemer & R.S. Wolf (Eds). *Elder abuse: Conflict in the family.* (pp. 125–166). Dover, Massachusetts: Auburn House.

Karmen, A. (1990). *Crime victims: An introduction to victimology (2ed).* California: Brooks/Cole.

King, N.R. (1984). Exploitation and abuse of older family members: An overview of the problem. In J.J. Costa (Ed). *Abuse of the elderly: A guide to resources and services.* (pp. 3–12). Lexington, Massachusetts: Lexington Books.

Korbin, J.E., Anetzberger, G.J., Thomasson, R., & Austin, C. (1991). Abused elders who seek legal recourse against their adult offspring: Findings from an exploratory study. *Journal of Elder Abuse & Neglect,* 3 (3), 1–18.

Kromsky, D.F., & Cutler, B.L. (1991). The admissibility of expert testimony on the battered-women syndrome. In D.D. Knudsen & J.L. Miller (Eds). *Abused and battered: Social and legal responses to family violence.* (pp. 101–109). New York: Aldine De Gruyter.

Lau, E., & Kosberg, J.I. (1979). Abuse of the elderly by informal care providers. *Aging.* September–October, 11–15.

Lerman, L.G. (1986). Prosecution of wife beater: Institutional obstacles and innovations. In M. Lystad (Ed). *Violence in the home: Interdisciplinary perspectives.* (pp. 250–295). New York: Brunner/Mazel.

Liang, J., & Sengstock, M.C. (1983). Personal crimes against the elderly. In J.I. Kosberg (Ed). *Abuse and maltreatment of the elderly: Causes and Interventions.* (pp. 40–67). Boston: John Wright.

Lotz, R.E. (1991). *Crime and the American Press.* New York: Praeger.

Loving, N. (1980). *Responding to spouse abuse and wife beating: A guide for police.* Washington, D.C.: Police Executive Research Forum.

Nathanson, P. (1983). An overview of legal issues, services, and resources. In J.I.

Kosberg (Ed). *Abuse and maltreatment of the elderly: Causes and Interventions.* (pp. 303–315). Boston: John Wright.

National Aging Resource Center On Elder Abuse. (1990). *Highlights of a national teleconference series: Law enforcement and elder abuse.* Washington, D.C.: National Aging Resource Center On Elder Abuse.

National Organization For Victim Assistance. (1983). *Campaign for victim rights/1983: A practical guide.* Washington, D.C.: National Organization For Victim Assistance.

Ohlin, L., & Tonry, M. (1989). *Family violence.* Chicago: University of Chicago Press.

Pagelow, M.D. (1989). The incidence and prevalence of criminal abuse of other family members. In L. Ohlin & M. Tonry (Eds). *Family violence.* (pp. 263–313). Chicago: University of Chicago Press.

Pearce, J.B., & Snortum, J.R. (1983). Police effectiveness in handling disturbance calls: An evaluation of crisis intervention training. *Criminal Justice and Behavior.* 10, 71–92.

Pillemer, K., & Finkelhor, D. (1988). The prevalence of elder abuse: A random sample survey. *Gerontologist.* 28 (1), 51–57.

Pleck, E. (1989). Criminal approaches to family violence, 1640–1980. In L. Ohlin., & M. Tonry (Eds). *Family violence.* (pp. 19–57). Chicago: University of Chicago Press.

Plotkin, M. (1988). *A time for dignity: Police and domestic abuse of the elderly.* Washington, DC: Police Executive Research Forum.

Quinn, M.J., & Tomita, S.K. (1986). *Elder abuse and neglect: Causes, diagnosis, and intervention strategies.* New York: Springer.

Regan, J.J. (1983). Protective services for the elderly: Benefit or threat. In J.I. Kosberg (Ed). *Abuse and maltreatment of the elderly: Causes and interventions.* (pp. 279–291). Boston: John Wright.

Schack, S., & Frank, R.S. (1978). Police service delivery to the elderly. *The Annals of the American Academy of Political and Social Science,* 438, 84–92.

Sengstock, H.C. & Hwalek, M. (1987). A review and analysis of measures for the identification of elder abuse. *Journal of Gerontological Social Work.* 10, 21–36.

Sharpe, G. (1988). The protection of elderly mentally incompetent individuals who are victims of abuse. In B. Schlesinger & R. Schlesinger (Eds). *Abuse of the elderly: Issues and annotated bibliography.* (pp. 64–74). Toronto: University of Toronto Press.

Steinmetz, S.K. (1981). Elder abuse. *Aging.* January–February, 6–10.

Steinmetz, S.K. (1987). Elderly victims of domestic violence. In C.D. Chambers, J.H. Lindquist, O.Z. White, & M.T. Harter (Eds). *The elderly: Victims and deviants.* (pp. 126–141). Athens, Ohio: Athens University Press.

Tatara, T. (1990). *Elder abuse in the United States: An issue paper.* Washington, DC: National Aging Resource Center on Elder Abuse.

Tatara, T., & Rittman, M. (1992). *Working relationships between APS/Aging agencies and law enforcement agencies: A short-term project.* Washington, D.C.: National Aging Resource Center On Elder Abuse.

U.S. Department of Justice, Bureau of Justice Statistics. (1992a). *Elderly victims.* Washington, D.C.: U.S. Department of Justice.

U.S. Department of Justice, Bureau of Justice Statistics. (1992b). *Criminal victimization in the United States, 1990.* Washington, DC: U.S. Department of Justice.

U.S. Department of Justice, Bureau of Justice Statistics. (1991a). *Violent crime in the United States.* Washington, DC: U.S. Department of Justice, report NCJ-127855.

U.S. Department of Justice, Bureau of Justice Statistics. (1990a). *Criminal victimization 1990.* Washington, DC: U.S. Department of Justice.

U.S. Department of Justice, Bureau of Justice Statistics. (1990b). *Criminal victimization in the United States, 1988.* Washington, DC: U.S. Department of Justice.

United States Bureau of the Census. (1985). *Projection of age demographics.* Washington, DC: U.S. Government Printing Office.

United States House of Representatives, Select Committee on Aging. (1981). *Elder abuse: An examination of a hidden problem.* Washington, DC: U.S. Government Printing Office.

United States House of Representatives, Select Committee on Aging. (1985). *Elder abuse: A national disgrace.* Washington, DC: U.S. Government Printing Office.

United States House of Representatives, Select Committee on Aging. (1990). *Elder abuse: A decade of shame and inaction.* Washington, DC: U.S. Government Printing Office.

Walker, S. (1989). *Sense and nonsense about crime: A policy guide (2ed).* Pacific Grove, California: Brooks/Cole.

Yin, P. (1985). *Victimization and the aged.* Springfield, Illinois: Charles C Thomas, Publisher.

Zimring, F.E. (1989). Toward a jurisprudence of family violence. In L. Ohlin & M. Tonry (Eds). *Family violence.* (pp. 547–569). Chicago: University of Chicago Press.

Chapter Six

ADULT PROTECTIVE SERVICES AND THE SOCIAL SERVICE SYSTEM

JEROME B. McKEAN AND DAVID L. WILSON[1]

INTRODUCTION

Among the most perplexing questions to confront Adult Protective Service (APS) practitioners is that of defining the desirable outcome of their intervention in a case of abuse or neglect. Although we shall see that drawing parallels between abuse and other forms of family violence can be misleading, APS practitioners share the common problem of other protective service workers: balancing the rights and the preferences of the victim, the appropriate disposition of the offender, and other desirable goals, such as the preservation of the victim's family and living arrangements. Often, these goals conflict. Often, it is difficult to determine the most desirable outcome of intervention.

APS and Social Services

In this chapter, we attempt to describe some of the ways in which *social services* can be of assistance in determining the least intrusive and most appropriate disposition for cases of abuse and neglect. By "social services," we mean services provided by helping professionals, such as social workers, nurses, counselors, educators, ministers, caseworkers, and therapists. Lay volunteers and "natural" caretakers—good-hearted friends and neighbors—may also provide social services.

Although the title of this chapter refers to the social service system, in many communities one of the chief problems is that nothing resembling a systematic approach to providing services to the elderly and other adults is in existence. Bergman (1989) argues that abuse and neglect cases require a comprehensive protective-service system that includes a variety of social services. He identifies three elements of a protective service system (1989, p. 97, numerals added):

(1) A coordinated, interdisciplinary service system to respond to both chronic and emergency cases.
(2) A set of core services (social, health, housing, mental health and legal services) available to utilize in these cases.
(3) A set of preplanned individual case responses or protocols to guide service providers in responding to emergency or chronic cases.

Bergman sets forth a lengthy list of core services which should be available. His list includes (1989, pp. 98–100) the protective-service worker, case-assessment capacity, core social services, core health service, core mental health services, guardianship services, legal services, emergency cash assistance, police services, emergency services (a 24-hour/7 day-per-week response capacity), emergency housing services, and crisis-intervention capacity.

This chapter focuses on the services identified by Bergman as core social, health, and mental health services. The list includes caseworkers, homemaker services, meals, chore services, friendly visitors, transportation, inpatient and outpatient care, physicians, visiting nurses, home health services, physical and speech therapists, ambulance services, psychiatric care, mental health counseling, and psychiatric social workers (Bergman, 1989, pp. 98–99). We shall refer to the listed services generically as "social services" and the helping professionals who provide the services as "social service professionals."

The services listed above can be a tremendous asset to efforts to protect adults from abuse and neglect. Helping professionals in these service areas can play an invaluable role in accomplishing several parts of the protective services mission. Specifically, they can assist in the *prevention* of abuse and neglect, the *identification* of abuse and neglect, the *assessment* of the victims and perpetrators of abuse and neglect and the *response* to abuse and neglect cases.

Most of this chapter is devoted to reviewing the practice-oriented literature and the results of original research by the authors to identify the roles that may be played by social service practitioners in accomplishing the protective services mission and the impediments to that role created by policy conflicts, weaknesses in the body of knowledge about elder abuse and neglect, lack of training and information exchange, lack of coordination among agencies and practitioners, and other problems.

THE RESEARCH LITERATURE

Filinson (1989, p. 19) accurately characterizes research on abuse and neglect as "sparse, methodologically weak, and theoretically insubstantial." Chapter 2 describes many of the problems in defining abuse and neglect, estimating their incidence and extent, and explaining their occurrence. These problems must be briefly considered here, for they pose great obstacles to coherent policy-making, identification of abuse and neglect by practitioners, and the assessment of abuse and neglect cases.

Defining Adult Abuse and Neglect

The definition of a phenomenon is central to its explanation, and both are central to its control. Definitions of abuse and neglect abound, and the abundance has confounded attempts to explain its occurrence or control it.

From the point of view of the APS worker, definition is of fundamental importance, for it indicates who is eligible for protective services, under what circumstances one is eligible, and what services need to be available, either from APS directly or from the broader network of social services. In short, definitions address who APS protects and what it protects them from.

Protection from What?

Attempts to define abuse and neglect, by researchers as well as by policy-makers and practitioners, almost always seem to have a strong normative element and to incorporate assumptions about the likely setting in which the events of interest occur and even the likely perpetrators (see Sprey and Matthews, 1989). Here we make a distinction between *maximizing definitions* and *minimizing definitions*. Maximizing definitions are those which attempt to define elder abuse and neglect as widely as possible; minimizing definitions define the terms as narrowly as possible.

Maximizing Definitions

Johnson (1986) notes that attention to elder abuse and neglect as distinct phenomenon is very recent, and much effort has been devoted to raising public consciousness of the existence of elder mistreatment and the plight of its victims. A less-kind observer (Callahan, 1982) has attributed rising interest to the efforts of social service professionals "looking for new markets."

Whatever the reason, many writers on the subject have sought to define elder abuse and neglect in very broad terms, and to include virtually every indignity that can be suffered by human beings under the rubric of abuse and neglect. Among the categories of mistreatment identified by Johnson (1986) as employed in current research on the issue are abuse, neglect, active neglect, passive neglect, physical abuse, physical neglect, psychological abuse, psychological neglect, verbal/ emotional abuse, material abuse, medical abuse, exploitation, violation of rights, sexual abuse, financial abuse, multiple abuse, abandonment, neglect of environment, societal abuse, misuse and abuse of drugs, self-abuse, and self-neglect. Not all these categories of mistreatment appear in all studies, and many of the researchers Johnson cites have sought to deliberately narrow their definitions of abuse and neglect to manageable limits. But the wide variety of interests reflected in the list above reflect an urge to use the definitions as a vehicle for including every form of elder mistreatment.

An example of the urge to maximize the number of events defined as abuse or neglect illustrates the point. A widely-cited report from the Subcommittee on Health and Long-Term Care of the House Special Committee on Aging (United States House of Representatives, 1985) includes the violations of rights in its definition of elder abuse, and enumerates thirteen specific "rights" that older Americans should enjoy. Included are the rights to "adequate and appropriate medical treatment," "privacy," "a clean, safe living environment," and the "right to be treated with courtesy, dignity and respect." It is little wonder that the Subcommittee found that "The horrifying conclusion to be drawn was that elder abuse . . . was everywhere (United States House of Representatives, 1985, p. 1)."

A similar urge to maximize the definitions of elder abuse and neglect may be found in articles by Griffin and Williams (1992), who seek to tie these concepts to racism, poverty, and the risk of exposure to personal violence, and by Blanton (1989), who argues that "Elder abuse cannot be properly defined without considering the corporate neglect and abuse practiced by social institutions (p. 34)."

Minimizing Definitions.

The objections to broad definitions of elder abuse and neglect are well stated by Crystal (1986), who expresses concern about "categorical" responses, such as elder abuse reporting laws, that seek to establish measures which are specific to elder abuse by law enforcement and social service agencies. Advocates of categorical responses adopt very broad definitions of elder abuse, such as those presented above. Crystal lists four problems with categorical responses (1986, p. 332):

> First, the nature and extent of the problem has not yet been clearly established, and there is no consensus or reliable knowledge base on the effectiveness of alternative approaches to resolving elder abuse when it occurs. Second, many of the responses that have been proposed or implemented in legislation are based on a false analogy to the child abuse problem. Third, categorical approaches by their nature tend to define the abuse element as the central problem to be addressed in what often turns out to be very complicated situations. Fourth, programs, policies, and legislation defined in terms of elder abuse establish a separate set of public responses, based on age, to problems that are shared with those of many nonelderly people.

Crystal (1986) argues that if abuse is narrowly defined to refer to "active harm" to an individual, then it is not clear that the elderly suffer the most frequently or severely from this form of harm and endangerment. Thus, focusing on abuse as the basis for responding to harm to the elderly may misdirect resources that may better be used to meet more pressing needs. Crystal cites his own research, which shows that abuse (narrowly defined) is encountered in a relatively small proportion of the cases processed by protective service workers (1986, p. 334).

Advocates of both maximizing and minimizing definitions of abuse and neglect seem to be pointing to issues that go far beyond the creation of nominal definitions for events harmful to persons, or the identification of such events in practice settings. Both strategies lead to the conclusion that the unmet needs of the elderly and, for that matter, the general adult population, are not clearly identified, nor are the situations in which the elderly experience acute and chronic problems divorced from the broader social context in which the problems arise.

Maximizing definitions may have the advantage of allowing the local protective service worker to use discretion in identifying cases of abuse and neglect and initiating casework where the practitioner thinks it is needed. It is in this spirit that Blanton argues that a broad definition allows one to address the needs of the elderly, "while at the same time addressing the politics of greed and self-serving power which deny [an elderly person] and us of the means of living with dignity (1989, p. 34)."

Advocates of minimizing definitions would reply that when such definitions are translated into statute, they artificially define persons over a certain age as more likely to be weak and helpless, allowing unnecessary intrusions into their lives while diverting resources from adults under the age limit who may be less competent and in greater danger. Crystal notes that such statutes may raise the visibility of elder abuse and neglect, but they do not raise the appropriations for dealing with the problems of adults in danger or in need of services (1986, p. 339). Broad definitions of elder abuse and neglect may increase the discretion of a protective service practitioner in some cases, but without a corresponding increase in resources, they limit the capacity to respond to the very complicated situations he or she often encounters in the field.

Johnson (1986) attempts to sort out some of these issues by identifying "mistreatment" as a generic term for both abuse and neglect, and equating mistreatment with unnecessary suffering. She notes that not all suffering is unnecessary: "... sometimes suffering must take place in order to preserve one's quality of life (1986, p. 29)." Suffering, unlike harm, has a subjective, or "qualitative," dimension that takes into account the alleged victim's perception of an event and should include such factors as level of severity, frequency, and scope (1986, p. 29).

Reporting Mistreatment

Two of the issues raised by Crystal (1986) have generated the most debate: the child abuse analogy in the definition of elder mistreatment, and legislation mandating the reporting of incidents of elder mistreatment as events distinct from other problems. Although the legal and legislative dimensions of the problem are described in detail elsewhere in this volume, provisions for mandatory reporting based on an analogy to child abuse have a direct and profound effect on the practices of social service professionals.

Elder abuse and neglect have a very short history as matters of legislative concern in the United States (Thobaben, 1989). The first Congressional hearings on the subject were held in Boston in 1979 (Benoit, 1992). Although the Select Committee on Aging of the U.S. House of Representatives has done much to keep elder abuse and neglect in the limelight, the federal role in confronting these problems has been limited by a lack of appropriations to fund policy and program initiatives (Wolf and Pillemer, 1989; Wolf, 1990; Benoit, 1992). Benoit (1992) notes that the first significant appropriation for elder abuse prevention activities did not occur until 1990. In the absence of federal leadership, the individual states have crafted a wide variety of legislative responses to the problems of elder mistreatment, usually with guidance from social workers in public agencies (Wolf and Pillemer, 1989). Shapiro (1992) reports that there are now forty-three states that mandate reporting for some list of health and social service professionals. The mandatory reporting requirement was often adapted from similar requirements found in statutes addressing child abuse (Wolf, 1991).

Critics of the child abuse analogy, both in statutory construction and in researchers' definitions of elder abuse and neglect, argue that it fosters a stereotype of the elderly as helpless and dependent. As Shapiro points out (1992, p. 26):

> Unlike children, most elderly Americans are financially independent (40 percent live on their own), financially secure (they have a median household net worth of $60,300, nearly twice the national average) and capable of taking care of themselves.

Aging itself is implicitly seen as a form of disability in the language of some statutes. For example, Crystal (1986, pp. 338–339) cites Florida's statute, which defines an aged person as one "suffering from the infirmities of aging as manifested by organic brain damage, advanced age, or other physical, mental, or emotional dysfunctions." Utech and Garrett attribute this view of aging to an infantalization process (1992, p. 424):

> American culture emphasizes independence, economic productivity, health, and physical strength, and the perceive loss of any of these qualities represents a threat to the values that are dominant in the culture. Fear and revulsion of growing old may cause Americans to internalize negative attitudes toward the aged and result in old-age stereotyping that disregards individual differences. Infantalization of the elderly may be the result of this.... Implicit in the infantalization is the perception that old people are senile ...

The imputation of disability or senility to the aged leads in turn to the treatment of the aged, in statutory language *and in social service practice,* as childlike.

Critics charge that this sort of stereotype informs mandatory reporting statutes. Wolf summarizes the additional problems that arise from mandatory reporting requirements (1991, p. 89):

Questions have been raised regarding the legal definitions of mistreatment which are so broad that they could be found unconstitutional, and the groups to be covered which frequently equate age with disability and dependency. Furthermore, it is said, that by defining the class of persons who are to report so broadly, the impact and enforcement of the laws may be diminished. In addition, many of the persons mandated to report are also subject to statutory privilege, making communication with their clients or patients confidential. The law presents these professionals with a dilemma: either to violate the law or break the trust of a client and possibly jeopardize a therapeutic relationship. Paradoxically, the law may keep the victims from seeking help for fear of being reported. Even when mandatory reporting exists in a state, professionals may be unfamiliar with the legislation or the symptoms to identify it [elder abuse].

Surveys of nurses and physicians in Alabama by Clark-Daniels, Daniels, and Baumhover (1989) illustrate the problems that mandatory reporting may pose for health professionals. As Wolf suggests, physicians showed little understanding of the mandatory reporting requirements of Alabama law. Nurses understood the requirements, but expressed negative attitudes toward the law, expressing fears that reporting incidents of abuse might result in lengthy court appearances or make the abuser angrier (Clark-Daniels, Daniels, and Baumhover, 1989, p. 68). Nurses also cited a lack of compliance with the mandates of the law for prompt investigation and intervention following reports to the Alabama Department of Health and Rehabilitation (DHR) (1989, p. 69). Clark-Daniels, Daniels, and Baumhover note that the level of services provided for victims of elder mistreatment in Alabama makes reporting cases problematic (1989, pp. 70–71):

> The nurses in the survey were uniform in their belief that social services for the elder abuse victims in Alabama are inadequate. This lack of services is particularly damaging, as it imposes a draconian choice on DHR workers: institutionalization or no intervention. In some cases institutionalization is not even an option.

A 1991 study of the effectiveness of mandatory reporting laws by the General Accounting Office (GAO) indicates that it is not necessarily the best way to identify cases of elder mistreatment. Interviews with experts and program administrators revealed that they identified public and professional awareness of the problem as more effective than such laws, as well as other factors (agencies' reputations for resolving cases, interagency coordination, legal authority for investigating cases, training agency staff, guaranteed confidentiality to reporters, hotline telephone numbers, and guaranteed immunity for reporters (General Accounting Office, 1991; Wolf, 1992).

A study comparing three model projects on elder abuse showed that mandatory reporting requirements did not increase the number of cases referred by physicians, lawyers or police, nor did it increase the number of substantiated cases of elder abuse reported to the agencies involved (Wolf, Godkin, and Pillemer, 1986). This study, and a study of the State of Washington's mandatory reporting statute by Fredriksen (1989) did show that mandatory reporting increased the number of unsubstantiated or inappropriate reports of elder abuse. The results raise the issue of whether mandatory reporting laws require agencies to divert resources to investigating unfounded reports that might be better used elsewhere.

Social Service Practitioners and the Identification of Mistreatment

Identification Instruments

Given the lack of consensus about definitions of elder abuse and neglect and legislative strategies for dealing with it, it is not surprising that the instruments used to identify elder mistreatment vary widely in the sorts of events that they count, the methods required to use them, and the stance toward elder mistreatment that they implicitly convey. Currently there is no nationally accepted model for identification instruments, although efforts are underway to develop possible models (Sengstock and Hwalek, 1987) and the American Medical Association has recently offered a standard instrument. Johnson (1989) reports that only seventeen states have uniform instruments in use statewide.

Sengstock and Hwalek (1987) have reviewed the identification instruments used in the early research on elder abuse and neglect and in field settings. Using six categories of abuse and neglect (physical abuse, physical neglect, psychological abuse, psychological neglect, material abuse, and violation of personal rights) as well as a category labeled "risk indicators" for items that might correlate with abuse, Sengstock and Hwalek (1987) found that over half the items in the instruments dealt with risk indicators. The emphasis in the remaining items was on physical abuse and neglect (Sengstock and Hwalek, 1987, p. 24). The authors note that risk indicators themselves do not explicitly identify abuse or neglect. We would add that the uncertainties surrounding the etiology of elder abuse and neglect make the selection of risk indicators problematic.

Sengstock and Hwalek (1987) note some additional problems with the instruments that they analyzed. They found that the measures depend largely on the victim's willingness to report abuse and neglect, require the service provider to have in-depth knowledge of each case, rely a great deal on the judgment of the service provider rather than guiding the provider in collecting information, and " . . . often contain an implicit censure of both caretaker and victim (Sengstock and Hwalek, 1987, p. 34)." "The victim is seen as a difficult patient: whining, dependent, incontinent; and the caretaker as rigid, authoritarian, and suspicious (p. 33)."

Johnson (1989) reviewed the statewide forms used in fifteen states to evaluate victims of elder abuse. Her review showed that most of the states included physical abuse, psychological abuse, sociological abuse (isolation, role confusion, misuse of living arrangements) and legal abuse (material abuse and theft) in their instruments. All the states included abuse and neglect imposed by others, but only two-thirds included items dealing with self-abuse and self-neglect. Two-thirds require the victim to exhibit some sort of mental or physical disability, and two-thirds require the victim be sixty years of age or older (Johnson, 1989, pp. 21–23).

Johnson reports that several items were not usually found in the statewide instruments. Most of the states asked no questions about the victims views or whether the victim understood the level of risk, possessed problemsolving skills, or is included in decisions having impact on him or her (Johnson, 1989, p. 23). Most did not specify that service providers could be precipitators of abuse, and the instruments in nine of the states implied " . . . that the precipitator/s are understood to be family members by the questions asked (Johnson, 1989, p. 25)." Only seven states used instruments that inventoried existing services used by the respondent and only six states have questions that call for a care plan for the respondent (Johnson, 1989, pp. 26–27). The purposes of the instruments were primarily screening (determining the presence or absence of a problem) and diagnostic (identifying the extent to which a problem exists) (Johnson, 1989, pp. 25–26).

In her analysis of her findings, Johnson notes that "Adult protective service workers almost by definition are in an adversarial relationship with the alleged victim/s and alleged precipitator/s (1989, p. 32)." She advocates a comprehensive perspective on unnecessary suffering that would broaden the investigative process to include service providers which the persons involved have voluntarily engaged in an effort to prevent suffering rather than to categorize and label cases as instances of abuse and neglect (1989, pp. 32–33). Johnson would prefer an emphasis on what the problem is rather than on who is responsible for it.

The Role of Social Service Professionals

As our discussion of mandatory reporting laws and identification instruments indicates, social service professionals may be unclear about the role they should play in reporting suspected incidents of mistreatment and hold negative attitudes toward reporting requirements and toward APS agencies. There seem to be a number of barriers to the *detection* of cases of elder mistreatment and to the *reporting* of cases to APS agencies.

Breckman and Adelman (1988) suggest that the *lack of a protocol* for dealing with cases of mistreatment may inhibit many practitioners. Because they are unclear about agency expectations and the consequences of their own involvement in a case, they feel "unprepared and overwhelmed" by elder abuse and neglect (Breckman and Adelman, 1988, p. 33). Breckman and Adelman report that social service professionals may be fearful that their elderly clients may suffer further harm if they intervene, may fear for their own safety, and may be concerned about their civil and criminal liability in reporting suspected cases. In light of this last concern we note that Thobaben's (1989) survey of state statutes on mandatory reporting found that three states that required reporting did not offer civil or criminal immunity (Delaware, Missouri, and South Dakota) and eight states did not provide for immunity from criminal liability (Louisiana, Maine, Maryland, Michigan, New York, Oregon, Utah, and Wisconsin).

Breckman and Adelman also cite *ageism* as a barrier to the detection of mistreatment. They note that service providers may prefer to discuss matters affecting an elderly person with the caretaker (who may be the perpetrator of abuse) rather than the affected person based on their perception that the elderly person is "too old" to comprehend the discussion (1988, pp. 33–34).

Lack of knowledge about elder mistreatment is another barrier mentioned by Breckman and Adelman (1988). Those who are unfamiliar with the dynamics of the problem may assume that any mistreatment will be apparent and that the victim will readily report any problem. "They are unaware that most elder abuse victims are too ashamed or humiliated to talk about their problem, might fear retaliation if they did summon help, and often minimize the seriousness of their situation (Breckman and Adelman, 1988, p. 34)."

A lack of knowledge of the problem obviously poses a fundamental barrier to detection. Peterson (1990) reports that a survey of members of the National Association of Social Workers showed that formal training in gerontology in preservice programs as well as in continuing professional education lags behind the needs in the practice of social work. The present authors can report that preservice and continuing education in elder abuse are not readily available to law enforcement personnel in most parts of the country. We have already noted the General Accounting Office (1991) study that indicated that researchers and program administrators prefer devoting resources to improving awareness and understanding of elder abuse and neglect to other methods of encouraging reporting. Blakely and Dolon (1991) found that direct service workers in Area Agencies on Aging suggested increased public awareness of the problem most frequently as a means for improving services.

The *isolation* of elderly victims of mistreatment poses yet another barrier to its detection (Breckman and Adelman, 1988). If the isolation is imposed by an abusive caregiver, the problem may be complicated by the caregiver's attempts to interpose himself or herself between the elderly person and a home visitor. An ageist preference to speak to a younger caregiver about the elderly person's problems may further increase the distance between the victim and needed resources. Breckman and Adelman suggest that professionals visiting the home should interview the elderly client privately, followed by a separate interview with any relatives present (1988, p. 35). A complete protocol for these interviews is provided by Quinn and Tomita (1986).

Even when social service professionals are trained to recognize and document incidents of mistreatment, they may hesitate to report the incidents in the belief that nothing will be done if they do. The study by Clark-Daniels, Daniels, and Baumhover (1989) described above reveals that nurses, who were more knowledgeable about elder abuse statutes, were also less willing to comply with them in the belief that their report of elder abuse would result in no action.

The perception that reporting elder abuse cases may prove fruitless can be complicated by the statutory limitations placed on APS agencies, and the lack of an umbrella agency to deal with cases of elder mistreatment. Weiner (1991) describes such a situation in New York, where Protective

Services for Adults (PSA) may only intervene in cases where the elderly person is incompetent. That requirement led to the rejection of over half the cases referred to Brooklyn Protective Services, and referrals back to the originating agency, which could not or would not provide the services needed (Weiner, 1991, p. 112):

> Unless there was a clear-cut case for legal interventions, many just waited for the case to resolve itself . . . (sometimes in the death or placement in a nursing home of the elderly person). In some cases, workers waited until enough evidence existed to have the person declared incompetent and again referred the case to PSA.

The findings cited above speak to the need for more responsive, better-coordinated delivery of services to the elderly and adult victims of abuse and neglect.

Ethical Issues in Reporting Mistreatment

Implicit in our discussion of barriers to the reporting of mistreatment has been the assumption that such events *should* be reported. But a number of ethical conflicts may arise for social service professionals confronted with this decision. Fulmer and O'Malley (1987) note that abuse statutes usually employ very broad definitions of abuse and neglect that may include cases which involve no intentional injury and may not warrant legal or criminal proceedings. The term, "abuse," carries with it a connotation of criminal wrongdoing that may harm the "perpetrator" as well as the victim. Fulmer and O'Malley recommend that the health professional consider the *purpose* of identification (estimating the prevalence of abuse and neglect versus triggering a response from the protective service system), the *effects of labeling* on the victim and the perpetrator, the principle of *primum non nocere* (first, do no harm), and the professional requirements of *confidentiality* in their relationship to the patient (1987, pp. 132–135).

Fulmer and O'Malley (1987) make it clear that it is *up to the health care professional* to decide if a suspected case of abuse and neglect should be reported. They express concern that reporting cases " . . . would trigger a criminal/legal response system designed to address a broad definition of abuse and neglect (1987, p. 134)." They cite a case in which an aging husband is unable to care for his wife after a severe stroke, resulting in her admission to the emergency room with dehydration and pyelonephritis (1987, p. 134):

There is a victim; however, there is no crime in the sense of intentional injury. The real question is whether reporting this case will help resolve the inadequate care. It is unlikely that any statute which defines this case as a crime could be applied beneficially. Indeed, it is likely that the husband would be labeled as a "wife neglecter." The ethical issue of whether to report a case such as this must rest with the caretaker's assessment of the risks and benefits that such a report may have on the elderly person. Inappropriately labeling a case of inadequate care as abuse and neglect may be hazardous to a patient's health.

Conflicts Between APS and Social Services

Fulmer and O'Malley's advice to health care professionals makes it clear that they regard them as far better equipped to determine the appropriate outcome for their elderly patients than protective service workers. The gist of their advice is that reporting suspected cases of abuse and neglect will place the cases in the hands of persons who cannot be completely trusted to act according to the ethical guidelines that they advocate.

As we have seen, the literature describes a number of unresolved policy and practice issues that may lead to conflicts between APS practitioners and other workers in the social services. It is clear that honest persons may differ over the best ways of addressing elder mistreatment, but when differences lead to turf battles, resentments, and the use of referrals as weapons for social and political policy battles, it seems likely that elderly victims of mistreatment will suffer the most. Similarly, failing to report cases of elder mistreatment to APS may deny the victim ready access to needed services and expose social service professionals to the risk of criminal liability.

Quinn and Tomita (1986) note that the APS worker is often mandated to investigate reports of abuse and neglect and cannot choose her cases. As Weiner's (1991) discussion (quoted above) suggests, other agencies may refer unwanted or intractable clients to APS as a last resort. The statutory mandates are often imposed on APS workers without their input and placed them in the spotlight as the "point men" for public criticism of treatment of the elderly and other adults in need of services.

APS workers are criticized for impersonal relationships with their clients when the problem may be excessive caseloads. They are criticized for abusing their authority to enter a client's home and remove the client for emergency medical care (Quinn and Tomita, 1986, p. 243). Emergency intervention of this sort is obviously a last resort, but no data exists of which we are aware that shows that emergency removal occurs with alarming frequency.

It is relevant to note that when responsibility for investigating mandatory reports of abuse and neglect is placed in an agency other than APS, as is the case in Rhode Island, similar criticisms arise. In Rhode Island, the Department of Elderly Affairs (DEA) receives reports of elder abuse. Wolf and Pillemer (1989) report that Elderly Affairs found itself inundated with reports, unable to afford extensive involvement in cases, and unable to provide needed services. As a result, cases were often referred to other agencies. Wolf and Pillemer quote a staff person from another agency as complaining that "when they weren't too busy, they wanted to be in charge of cases. When they got busy, they wanted to push cases over to community services" (1989, p. 136).

In their analysis of the Rhode Island case, Wolf and Pillemer argue that an "imbalanced exchange" existed between the Department of Elderly Affairs and other agencies, in which the former added to the burden of the latter without a concomitant addition to resources (1989, p. 136). We suspect that a similar problem exists in many states where reporting is mandated. Because APS is often the receiving agency for mandatory reports, it is likely to be perceived in much the same light as Rhode Island's DEA.

The perception of APS as a "do-nothing" agency may be excaberated by the inability of the APS practitioner to report on her actions to reporters of abuse and neglect due to the requirements of confidentiality. The reporter may therefore not be aware that the case has been referred to another agency or that the putative victim has refused any intervention (Quinn and Tomita, 1987, p. 244).

Perhaps the most damaging criticism of APS is that protective service practitioners are viewed as "trigger happy" when it comes to their willingness to "shove" the client into a nursing home (Quinn and Tomita, 1986, p. 243). We have already cited Clark-Daniels, Daniels, and Baumhover (1989) comment that often the APS worker may have no alternative to residential placement available.

Quinn and Tomita note that charges that APS may intervene too readily to institutionalize their clients are very controversial because premature institutionalization may result in "transfer trauma" and premature death (1986, p. 244). The identification of transfer trauma itself is problematic, and (assuming its existence is verified) the chain of responsibility for transfer trauma is far too complex to allow any particular culprit to be identified. But such stinging criticism exemplifies the worst sort of finger-pointing and blame-passing among agencies.

A non-representative survey of APS workers by Dolon and Blakely (1989) indicates that "changing the living situation of the victim" was viewed as the most effective method of intervention in abuse cases. Dolon and Blakely suggest that APS workers might regard this alternative as most effective because it can permanently prevent abuse from re-occurring (1989, p. 42). We note that "changing the living situation" is an ambiguous phrase, which may indicate the removal of the client *or the perpetrator* from the client's home. The same survey showed that the most common outcome of cases recalled by the respondents was "client safe and stable," followed by "client enters long-term care facilities" (Dolon and Blakely, 1989, p. 44).

Data from the Florida Department of Health and Rehabilitative Services (DHRS) (1992) do not seem to indicate an over-reliance on either judicial disposition of cases or residential placement. In 1991, 91 percent of Florida cases (N = 10,497) received a non-judicial disposition, and 45 percent of those cases received no ongoing services. The next three most common dispositions were voluntary protective services, referral to other Department of Health and Rehabilitative Services programs, and referral to non-DHRS programs (Florida Protective Service Systems, 1992, p. 26). Of the 970 cases receiving a judicial disposition, long-term residential placement was employed for 32.16 percent of the clients. The data is not cross-tabulated in a way that allows any evaluation of the appropriateness of these dispositions based on client characteristics. Although data from one state cannot be used for inferences about the other forty-nine, the Florida experience demonstrates that an APS referral does not automatically result in judicial disposition of a case or in residential placement.

We have already noted Johnson's observation that APS workers can find themselves in an adversarial relationship with both victims and perpetrators (1989, p. 32). The problem is only worsened when other social service professionals also see their relationship to APS as adversarial. Johnson's call for a "problem-centered" rather than a "parties-centered" approach to resolving cases of unnecessary suffering among the elderly (1989, p. 29) applies not only to the approach to alleged perpetrators and victims, but to the other service providers involved as well.

Quinn and Tomita (1986) suggest four principles that should guide adult protection practitioners (pp. 238–239, numerals added):

(1) When interests compete, the practitioner is charged with serving the adult client.
(2) When interests compete, the adult client is in charge of decision making until he delegates responsibility voluntarily to another or the court grants responsibility to another.
(3) When interests compete, freedom is more important than safety.
(4) In the ideal case, protection of adults seeks to achieve, simultaneously and in order of importance, freedom, safety, least disruption of life style, and least restrictive care alternative.

Although these principles may prove controversial in themselves, they provide a starting point for the clear articulation of the APS mission, both internally and externally. A clearly-stated mission for APS provides the best basis for building and sustaining cooperative relationships with other service agencies.

Coordinating Multi-Agency Efforts

As we have seen, efforts to prevent elder mistreatment probably require a coordinated effort among several agencies to create a protective service *system*. Although APS is an essential component of such a system, it is only one of the "frontline" agencies that may have responsibilities when a case of mistreatment is detected.

There are a number of methods for coordinating multi-agency efforts reported in the literature. The methods vary in the amount of additional funding required, the scope of involvement in elder mistreatment, and their relationship to APS. Since funding is often the critical factor in implementing coordination efforts, we have arranged the discussion beginning with the least expensive methods and moving to the most expensive.

Protective Service Committees

Bergman (1989) suggests that an effective protective service system begins with the creation of a committee composed of direct-service providers and supervisory staff from area social service, health care, mental health, housing, and legal service agencies (p. 97). He lists the following goals for the committee (p. 97, numerals added):

(1) Establish informal, and later, formal linkages between the agencies that will lead to the development of responses or protocols to respond to individual protective-service cases.

(2) Provide regular, monthly meetings to review how the current system is responding to known protective-services cases.

(3) Provide a vehicle for identifying problems or gaps in the existing response system and planning ways of overcoming these problems.

(4) Provide an educational forum for having special presentations on topics of interest to the members.

(5) Provide a place for frontline workers to get to know each other and provide mutual peer support, which is important for workers who handle protective-service cases.

Elder Abuse Task Forces

Amendments made in 1987 to the Older Americans Act of 1965 made the prevention of elder mistreatment a priority for government funding and directed State Offices on Aging to identify non-profit organizations involved in serving mistreated elders as well as determining the extent of unmet needs (Foelker, Holland, Marsh, & Simmons, 1990). The responsibility for this task often fell upon Area Agencies on Aging.

Foelker and his associates (1990) report that the Dallas Area Agency on Aging (DAAA) responded to this responsibility by creating a task force on elder abuse charged with documenting the extent of the problem, cataloging the services available, and initiating an educational program to increase the awareness of the community (p. 560). The task force consisted of representatives of APS and eleven other local programs.

Through its research, the task force documented a lack of public and professional awareness of the role of APS, gaps in service to victims of mistreatment, the role of neglect by formal caregivers, and the limitations that lack of funding and the constraints of the Texas APS statutes placed on the effectiveness of intervention efforts (Foelker, et al, 1990).

The task force became a permanent subcommittee of the advisory council for DAAA, and its effort led to reforms in the state statutes, increased funding for APS, and increased efforts to improve public awareness of elder mistreatment. As Foelker and his associates note, the amendments to the Older Americans Act " . . . can become a major policy and funding incentive for communities to address the problems of maltreated older persons (1990, p. 562)."

Multi-Disciplinary Teams (M–Teams)

Multi-disciplinary teams may be established by Area Agencies on Aging or by APS agencies. Hwalek, Williamson, and Stahl (1991) identify four types of multi-disciplinary teams (M-teams) that bring the skills of professionals from a variety of disciplines together to deal with cases of elder mistreatment (pp. 46–47):

Hospital-based M-teams may focus on assessment of suspected victims of mistreatment to determine whether a case should be reported to the appropriate state agency, or may additionally provide assistance in connecting the victim to community services.

Family-practice M-teams, headed by a family physician and including an APS practitioner, assess cases detected at the physician's office and work with the physician in dealing with the case.

Consortium M-teams are similar to Bergman's (1989) protective services committee. They are composed of agency representatives and meet to assist in the resolution of difficult cases.

Community-based M-teams assist APS practitioners with difficult cases, either through telephone assistance or regular meetings. The community-based team " . . . is formed by and for one agency serving elder abuse victims" (Hwalek, Williamson, and Stahl, 1991, p. 47) and the members are chosen for the knowledge and resources they can bring to bear on a case. Illinois has recently mandated that community-based M-teams be created in all agencies providing elder abuse services to service populations over 7,200 (Hwalek, Williamson, and Stahl, 1991, p. 61).

Members of community-based M-teams may be compensated for their participation or may participate voluntarily. In Illinois, the teams studied by Hwalek, Williamson and Stahl (1991) had representatives from mental health, medicine, law enforcement, the clergy, law, and the private financial sector, as well as a coordinator from the local elder abuse agency. The members of the team provided consultation on cases presented to them by elder abuse caseworkers and educational sessions.

Community Elder Abuse Programs

By far the most costly option for improving the response to elder mistreatment is the creation of specialized programs within existing agencies to deal specifically with this problem. In their evaluation of three model projects in Syracuse, New York, Rhode Island, and Worcester,

Massachusetts, Wolf and Pillemer (1989) argue that there is a need for such programs. They found that existing service programs could not address cases of elder mistreatment in all their complexity (Wolf & Pillemer, 1989, p. 148).

Based on their evaluation, Wolf and Pillemer recommend the Syracuse, New York, model project as most readily replicable at other sites. The Syracuse project adopted a case-coordination approach from a successful child-abuse program: a case coordinator establishes teams to handle elder mistreatment cases with representatives of relevant agencies (including APS). The team assesses each case and assists the victim in connecting with needed services (1989, pp. 116–117). In addition, the Syracuse project offered direct services, most notably the use of elder abuse aides who spent two to four hours a week in the client's home and functioned as friendly visitors, socializing agents, and advocates for their clients (1989, p. 118).

In Illinois, after the implementation and evaluation of four elder-abuse demonstration projects, the state Department of Aging has decided to create elder abuse intervention programs based on an "advocacy/voluntary reporting model" to coordinate with local Case Coordination Units that already provide case-management services to elderly persons (Hwalek, Hill, and Stahl, 1989). The intervention programs will provide intensive casework and develop a treatment plan either for the short-term or for long-term follow-up by the Case Coordination Units. The programs will also provide or purchase services such as emergency aid, respite care, legal assistance, and housing (Hwalek, Hill, and Stahl, 1989, pp. 202–205).

The research by Wolf and Pillemer (1989) and by the Illinois Department of Aging (1987) are the only efforts at systematic and comparative evaluation of elder mistreatment programs found by the authors in the literature. The results seem to us to be essentially similar: programs that provide a mix of advocacy and direct services, preferably *without* mandatory reporting requirements, have had the greatest success.

Wolf and Pillemer provide the following guidelines for a successful elder abuse program (1989, pp. 148):

1. A need exists for specific elder abuse programs.
2. An elder abuse project should be located in, or affiliated with, a high-profile community agency.
3. An elder abuse project should offer direct services.
4. Interagency coordination is critical to the success of a project.

5. The existence of mandatory reporting without sufficient appropriations can hinder elder abuse intervention.

Client and Community Services

The literature allows us to identify a number of services of potential benefit to the clients of APS and other elder abuse agencies as well as services that may assist in increasing public and professional awareness of elder mistreatment and preventing its occurrence.

Existing Services

Several studies attempt to ascertain the types of services needed by victims of elder mistreatment and the agencies providing needed services. All of the studies indicate that the type of services and service-providers needed vary with the type of mistreatment encountered.

Dolon and Blakely's (1989) non-representative survey of APS workers, discussed earlier, asked the respondents to rank the effectiveness of various interventions for abuse and neglect cases. The respondents ranked "changing living situation of victim" first in effectiveness for abuse victims, followed by "planning and arranging for appropriate services," "home visit," "case monitoring," "family crisis intervention," "legal intervention," "advocacy," "individual counseling for victim," and "instruction on self-care." For neglect victims, "planning and arranging appropriate services" was ranked first, followed by "home visit," and "changing living situation of victim." The remainder of the interventions were ranked in the same order as for abuse cases (Dolon and Blakely, 1989, p. 41). Social services, home health aides, agency home-makers, and visiting nurses were ranked as the top four resources with potential for reducing both elder abuse and neglect (Dolon and Blakely, 1989, p. 46).

In a similar study, Blakely and Dolon (1991) surveyed direct practice workers in Area Agencies on Aging. The respondents were asked to rate the amount of help provided by occupational groups in the treatment of elder abuse and neglect. For both forms of mistreatment, the respondents ranked social-service providers first, followed by visiting nurses, agency homemakers, health aides, and hospital social workers (Blakely and Dolon, 1991, p. 193). When asked to suggest methods for improving services to victims, a majority of respondents suggested increasing public awareness of elder abuse and neglect, improving cooperation among local agencies, and providing more services (Blakely and Dolon, 1991, p. 196).

A study of elder mistreatment *cases* in Illinois by Sengstock, Hwalek, and Petrone (1989) found that the number and type of services provided varied with the type of mistreatment. Case management services were provided the vast majority of all victim types. Legal services and crisis intervention services tended to be the least used sorts of services. Sengstock, Hwalek, and Petrone make three inferences from their analysis (1989):

> First, it appears that the workers tended to provide . . . the same type of services which are available to the frail elderly, whether or not they are victims of abuse or neglect (p. 52).
>
> . . . .
>
> A second major inference is that victims are more likely to receive a large number of services if the types of abuse or neglect from which they suffer is [sic] familiar in social work and home health care settings (p. 54).

The authors also note that in self-neglect cases, workers were able to assume control of the client's life and provide services with little opposition. Physical abuse cases required the worker to "compete for control" with others, leading to greater reluctance to get involved (Sengstock, Hwalek, and Petrone, 1989, p. 55).

In short, service providers tend to use the resources with which they are most familiar and to provide those resources more readily in cases where they feel knowledgeable and in control. Sengstock, Hwalek and Petrone (1989) recommend continuing professional education and greater advocacy on behalf of clients.

Services Related to Mistreatment

In addition to the services available to all qualified elderly persons, specific services for victims of elder mistreatment are identified by several writers.

We have already mentioned the use of elder abuse aides in the Syracuse, New York, project praised by Wolf and Pillemer (1989). They note that by offering a direct service such as this, the project was made more attractive to other agencies whose cooperation was needed, and allowed the project staff to monitor cases without constant involvement (p. 149).

Scogin, Beall, Bynum, Stephens, Grote, Baumhover and Bolland (1989) describe an Alabama program that trains caregivers "at-risk" for abuse in issues related to aging, problem-solving, stress management, and using community resources. They report that the training reduced the psychological stress of the participants as well as the perceived burden associated with caregiving. A similar program is described by Barusch and Spaid (1991).

Keigher (1991) suggests that more attention be paid to the role of informal care by non-relatives, including the co-residence of informal caregivers with the elderly. She argues that "natural" caregivers should be viewed by agencies as potentially valuable assets in serving the needs of their clients and "understood, respected, valued, and supported, rather than overlooked, disparaged, or suspected" (Keigher, 1991, p. 56). Griffin and Williams (1992) argue that public service providers should become much more aware and supportive of the informal and formal support networks found in African-American communities.

CONCLUSIONS

Defining and Identifying Mistreatment

Our review of the literature began with a discussion of the definitional confusion associated with abuse and neglect of the elderly and other adults. Our own informal survey[2] of administrators and supervisors in South Florida agencies involved in providing services to the elderly (conducted by Wilson) indicates that we are correct in thinking of this as a practice issue as well as a conceptual problem for researchers. Administrators we interviewed complain that legal definitions of abuse and neglect provide little guidance as to what events or behaviors should merit their attention.

The lack of definitional clarity is closely tied to the debate over mandatory reporting. Mandating the reporting of abuse and neglect clearly places enormous burdens on the agencies designated to receive the reports without adding anything to the resources available to deal with cases of mistreatment. But mandatory reporting is a fact of life in most jurisdictions.

From the practitioners viewpoint, the debates over definition and mandatory reporting point to a weakness in the literature. Frequently, writers on the subject of elder and adult mistreatment are far more concerned about what should be than what is. Given a statute on the books with vague definitions of abuse and neglect, and given a mandatory reporting requirement, the practitioner needs help in discovering the best ways to identify and assist victims of mistreatment. For example, our review turned up one article (Hwalek, 1989) that dealt directly with training APS practitioners in the assessment of reports of alleged mistreatment.

Although the literature on the identification of elder mistreatment is fairly extensive, it suffers from a lack of systematic evaluation. At this time, the literature offers only descriptive studies of identification instruments and discussions of the obstacles to recognition and reporting of mistreatment. Comparative analyses of the validity and reliability of identification instruments (Johnson, 1989) is in its infancy.

These issues are intertwined. Creating valid and reliable identification instruments depends on valid and reliable definitions of elder mistreatment, as well as methodologically sound research into the etiology of mistreatment to provide some empirical basis for the identification of risk factors associated with various forms of mistreatment.

The Role of APS Practitioners

The literature on obstacles to the identification of mistreatment, ethical issues in mistreatment, and conflicts between APS practitioners and others point to a neglected topic: the role of the APS practitioner. The functions of APS agencies vary widely from state to state, and the scope of the APS role in dealing with mistreatment varies as well (Quinn and Tomita, 1986).

The issues raised by Quinn and Tomita (1986), Johnson (1989), Breckman and Adelman (1988), Weiner (1991) and Fulmer and O'Malley (1987), among others, point to some degree of *role conflict* for APS workers, similar to that felt by others on the interface between social service, civil law, and criminal law such as probation officers and parole officers. Although often trained as social service providers, they may find themselves in an adversarial relationship with their clients (Johnson, 1989) and with other service workers (Fulmer and O'Malley, 1987). It is clear that Fulmer and O'Malley, for example, consider APS as an unpalatable last resort in dealing with cases of elder mistreatment.

The effects of this potential role conflict on recruitment, training, retention, and on attempts to coordinate efforts among social service agencies may be profound. The role of the APS worker thus deserves far more attention than it has received.

Our informal survey of agency administrators and supervisors made it clear that other aspects of the APS worker's role also deserve attention. They echoed the concern expressed by Sengstock and Hwalek (1987) that instruments and procedures for identifying victims of elder mistreatment are poorly defined. The respondents in our survey were also concerned about the lack of training in social work they found among workers, as well as the low pay and high caseloads.

We hope that researchers will devote a great deal more attention to some basic questions about APS. What are the formal and informal tasks performed by APS practitioners? How do they vary from state to state and among localities within states? How do statutory provisions and limitations on the discretion of APS agencies influence the performance of their tasks and their relationships with other agencies serving the elderly? How well-trained are APS practitioners in basic social work skills, and specifically in dealing with elder and adult mistreatment? Are APS workers trained in case management and the coordination of services with other agencies? Do APS agencies offer or purchase direct services?

Evaluating Outcomes

Perhaps the greatest problem with the practice-oriented research to date is that little attention has been paid to evaluating *outcomes* in serving victims of mistreatment. Other than surveys of the outcomes preferred by APS workers (Dolon and Blakely, 1989) and Area Agency on Aging workers (Blakely and Dolon, 1991), only one study describes actual case disposition and referral practices in detail (Sengstock, Hwalek, and Petrone, 1989).

In their study of three model elder abuse projects, Wolf and Pillemer (1989) report the only *evaluation* of a large number of case outcomes that we encountered. In examining changes in manifestations of abuse and neglect, the mental health of the victim, and the dependency of the victim, Wolf and Pillemer found that the projects in Syracuse, New York, and Worcester, Massachusetts—which emphasized direct provision of services and service-advocacy or service-brokering—were more effective than the Rhode Island Department of Elderly Affairs, which required mandatory reporting of cases of elder mistreatment (1989, pp. 89–92).

The majority of cases were *not* resolved at the time the evaluation ended at any of the three sites (Wolf and Pillemer, 1989, p. 92). Changes in the living arrangements of the victim were recorded in less than half the cases, with the *lowest* percentage of victims in unchanged living arrangements in Rhode Island, the site with mandatory reporting (Wolf and Pillemer, 1989, p. 93).

We believe that the time has come to make a systematic attempt to evaluate the types of services offered to various types of clients in light of the outcomes. This sort of research is especially germane to the contention that a program specifically designed to provide advocacy, brokering, and direct services for elderly victims of mistreatment is needed (Wolf and Pillemer, 1989). Wolf and Pillemer's findings should inspire further research to provide a comparison to the nature of outcomes in localities that rely on general services to the elderly.

Research on the provision of services in Illinois by Sengstock, Hwalek, and Petrone (1989) suggests that victims of some forms of mistreatment, such as self-neglect, may be better served by existing social services than others, such as victims of physical abuse and financial exploitation. This latter group may receive fewer, and less appropriate services simply because service providers tend to use the resources with which they are most familiar.

A similar problem may be indicated by Keigher's (1991) observation that agencies tend to view the potential value of natural caretakers, and Griffin and Williams (1992) plea that informal support networks in African-American communities be given greater recognition and support.

Taken together, the studies cited above suggest that APS and social service professionals tend to fall into a pattern found among many overworked service providers: referring clients to the most familiar and available services. The extensive and intensive involvement with clients needed to *create* support networks that include both informal and formal resources may be beyond their current capacities.

All this is conjecture, and points to the need for further research. What services are provided to various types of victims of elder mistreatment? How relevant are the services to their needs? How satisfied are clients with the services provided? Are informal service resources employed? Is the provision of services adequately coordinated among various agencies?

Connecting to Practitioners

In our review and critique of the research literature, we have tried to focus on topics of direct interest to practitioners. The agenda for further research that we have described reflects our belief that research to date has not been of great assistance to those who provide services to the victims of mistreatment.

We began this chapter by noting that defining the desirable outcome of intervention in a case of mistreatment is a difficult task. We have raised several questions requiring further research about the connections between the situations that bring clients to the attention of APS practitioners, the appropriate role for APS practitioners in addressing those situations, and the desirable outcomes for the clients.

The sort of research we have in mind does have value for the practitioner, for it is aimed at the discovery and communication of the lessons of practice and their implications for both practice and policy. Information alone cannot solve all the problems that practitioners confront, such as overwhelming caseloads and inadequate resources. It can provide a basis for ordering priorities and spending scarce dollars wisely.

To be used, the information gained from research must be known. The *dissemination* of knowledge is therefore crucial, but is all too often a low priority in busy agencies. All the respondents to Wilson's informal survey of administrators and supervisors in South Florida saw a need for increased in-service training, and an even greater need for training in stress-reduction and burnout-prevention. The respondents noted that very few of their direct service staff members had preservice training in social work, and many noted that the lack of grounding in basic social work techniques complicated the ability to make the "judgment calls" that are involved in case assessment.

While the respondents acknowledged the need for more training for their staff, they did not show a great awareness of developments in the field themselves. For example, only three of the seventeen administrators and supervisors interviewed by Wilson had heard of the term, "M-team," although all saw it as a good approach and wanted to know more about it. One of the top administrators for the Florida Department of Health and Rehabilitative Services in South Florida noted that his own training had simply not prepared him for the challenges of dealing with mistreated adults.

Peterson's (1990) survey of National Association of Social Work members, discussed earlier in this chapter, indicates that both preservice and inservice training of social workers who deal with the aging is not keeping up with the needs of practitioners. In addition to adding a gerontology component to preservice education programs, Peterson advocates the expansion of continuing education offerings in gerontology (1990, p. 415):

> This continuing education can be undertaken by national associations, schools of social work, or gerontology instructional programs, each with its own network and areas of specialization. The challenge, however, is to make it an education of high quality and to design a set of procedures so that current practitioners can complete a sequence of workshops rather than constantly repeat an introductory session on aging.

We would add that APS practitioners, who may not be trained as social workers nor belong to relevant professional associations, should be a special target for training programs dealing with the fundamentals of casework, crisis intervention, and case management as they apply to working with the elderly and with special populations of adults. It is important that such training be grounded in efforts to describe and analyze the tasks of APS workers and closely related to the conditions they face in the field.

The M-teams described earlier might provide a basis for connecting practitioners to those who have the knowledge that they need. An M-team coordinator is in a good position to identify training deficits among APS workers, and to engage the other members of her team in ways of overcoming those deficits.

We hope to see efforts to coordinate multi-agency efforts become widespread in APS practice. A multidisciplinary approach to the problem of mistreatment is clearly needed, not only to meet the needs of clients, but to overcome real and potential conflicts among the many social service professionals involved in identifying and dealing with mistreatment.

Wilson's South Florida survey reveals that administrators and supervisors are very concerned that direct service workers have a "helpless-hopeless" attitude toward their jobs. Although the respondents were impressed with the dedication and energy of direct service workers, they perceived many direct-service workers as overwhelmed by the magnitude and complexity of the problems they encounter.

On the basis of our review of the literature, we suspect that negative attitudes toward APS workers are common among social service professionals, especially in states where APS is the recipient of mandatory reports of abuse and neglect. If our suspicions are correct, a feeling of isolation and a pessimistic attitude about the chances of bringing cases to successful conclusions may be widespread among APS workers.

Our hope is that efforts at coordinating the response to the mistreatment of elders and other adults would aid in overcoming such attitudes and in connecting APS workers to the larger network of service providers in a more positive way. In turn, we believe, positive connections would serve to overcome some of the morale problems from which APS practitioners may suffer.

ENDNOTES

[1]The authors wish to thank Nancy Tagliaferri for her assistance in the preparation of this chapter.

[2]Wilson surveyed seventeen administrators and supervisors in agencies providing direct services to the elderly in Dade County, Broward County, and Palm Beach County, Florida. The surveys were conducted via telephone interviews lasting between 20 and 60 minutes and averaging about 40 minutes in length. The questions asked were open-ended and the respondents were encouraged to give their own observations on services for the elderly. The agencies represented included Adult Services, Protective Service Systems (the Florida APS agency), Adult Day Care, Domestic Assault and Victim Services, and Mental Health.

REFERENCES

Barusch, A.S. & Spaid, W.M. (1991). Reducing caregiver burden through short-term training: Evaluation findings from a caregiver support project. *Journal of Gerontological Social Work, 17,* 7–15.

Benoit, M.D. (1992). Elder abuse: A legislative update. *Journal of Elder Abuse and Neglect, 3,* 65–71.

Bergman, J.A. (1989). Responding to abuse and neglect cases: protective services versus crisis intervention. In R. Filinson & S.R. Ingman (Eds.), *Elder abuse: Practice and policy* (pp. 94–103). New York: Human Sciences Press.

Blakely, B.E. & Dolon, R. (1991). The relative contributions of occupation groups in the discovery and treatment of elder abuse and neglect. *Journal of Gerontological Social Work, 17,* 183–199.

Blanton, P.G. (1989). Zen and the art of adult protective services: In search of a unified view of elder abuse. *Journal of Elder Abuse and Neglect, 1,* 27–34.

Breckman, R.S. & Adelman, R.D. (1988). *Strategies for helping victims of elder mistreatment.* Beverly Hills, CA: Sage.

Callahan, J.J. (1982). Elder abuse programming: Will it help the elderly? *Urban and Social Change Review, 15,* 15–19.

Clark-Daniels, C., Daniels, R.S. & Baumhover, L.A. (1989). Physicians and nurses responses to abuse of the elderly: A comparative study of two surveys in Alabama. *Journal of Elder Abuse and Neglect, 1,* 57–71.

Crystal, S. (1986). Social policy and elder abuse. In K.A. Pillemer & R.F. Wolf (Eds.), *Elder abuse: Conflict in the family* (pp. 331–340). Dover, MA: Auburn House.

Dolan, R. & Blakely, B. (1989). Elder abuse and neglect: A study of adult protective service workers in the United States. *Journal of Elder Abuse and Neglect, 1,* 31–49.

Filinson, R. (1989). Introduction. In R. Filinson & S.R. Ingram (Eds.), *Elder abuse: Practice and policy* (pp. 17–34). New York: Human Sciences Press.

Filinson, R. & Ingman, S.R. (Eds.). (1989). *Elder abuse: Practice and policy.* New York: Human Sciences Press.

Florida Department of Health and Rehabilitative Services. (1992). *Florida Protective Service Systems, annual report, 1991, adult protective investigations.* Tallahassee, FL: author.

Foelker, G.A., Jr., Holland, J., Marsh, M., & Simmons, B.A. (1990). A community response to elder abuse. *The Gerontologist, 30,* 560–562.

Fredriksen, K.I. (1989). Adult protective services: Changes with the introduction of mandatory reporting. *Journal of Elder Abuse and Neglect, 1,* 59–70.

Fulmer, T.T. & O'Malley, T.A. (1987). *Inadequate care of the elderly: A health care perspective on abuse and neglect.* New York: Springer.

General Accounting Office (1991). *Elder abuse: Effectiveness of reporting laws and other factors.* Washington, DC: author.

Giordano, N.H. & Giordano, J.A. (1984). Elder abuse: A review of the literature. *Social Work, 29,* 232–236.

Griffin, L.W. & Williams, O.J. (1992). Abuse among the African-American elderly. *Journal of Family Violence, 7,* 19–35.

Hwalek, M. (1989). Proper documentation: A key topic in training programs for elder abuse workers. *Journal of Elder Abuse and Neglect, 1,* 17–29.

Hwalek, M., Hill, B., & Stahl, C. (1989). The Illinois plan for a statewide elder abuse program. In R. Filinson & S.R. Ingman (Eds.), *Elder abuse: Practice and policy* (pp. 196–207). New York: Human Sciences Press.

Hwalek, M., Williamson, D., & Stahl, C. (1991). Community-based M-team roles: A job analysis. *Journal of Elder Abuse and Neglect, 3,* 45–71.

Illinois Department of Aging (1987). *Elder abuse demonstration project. Third interim report to the Illinois General Assembly on Public Acts 83-1259 and 83-1432.* Springfield, IL: author.

Johnson, T. (1986). Critical issues in the definition of elder mistreatment. In K.A. Pillemer & R.S. Wolf (Eds.), *Elder abuse: Conflict in the family* (pp. 167–196). Dover, MA: Auburn House.

Johnson, T.F. (1989). Elder mistreatment identification instruments: Finding common ground. *Journal of Elder Abuse and Neglect, 1,* 15–36.

Keigher, S.M. (1991). Informal supportive housing for elders: A key resource for preventing self-neglect. *Journal of Elder Abuse and Neglect, 3,* 41–59.

Peterson, D.A. (1990). Personnel to serve the aging in the field of social work: Implications for educating professionals. *Social Work, 35,* 412–415.

Pillemer, K.A. & Wolf, R.S. (Eds.). (1986). *Elder abuse: Conflict in the family.* Dover, MA: Auburn House.

Quinn, M.J. & Tomita, S.K. (1986). *Elder Abuse and neglect: Causes, diagnosis, and intervention strategies.* New York: Springer.

Scogin, F., Beall, C., Bynum, J., Stephens, G., Grote, N.P., Baumhover, L.A. & Bolland, J. (1989). Training for abusive caregivers: An unconventional approach to an intervention dilemma. *Journal of Elder Abuse and Neglect, 1,* 73–86.

Sengstock, M.C., & Hwalek, M. (1987). A review and analysis of measures for the identification of elder abuse. *Journal of Gerontological Social Work, 10,* 21–36.

Sengstock, M.C., Hwalek, M., & Petrone, S. (1989). Services for aged abuse victims: Service types and related factors. *Journal of Elder Abuse and Neglect, 1,* 37–56.

Sengstock, M.C., McFarland, M.R., & Hwalek, M. (1990). Identification of elder abuse in institutional settings: Required changes in existing protocols. *Journal of Elder Abuse and Neglect, 2,* 31–49.

Shapiro, J.P. (1992, January 13). The elderly are not children. *U.S. News and World Report, 112,* 26, 28.

Sprey, J. & Matthews, S.H. (1989). The perils of drawing policy implications from research: The case of elder mistreatment. In R. Filinson & S.R. Ingman (Eds.), *Elder abuse: Practice and policy* (pp. 51–61). New York: Human Sciences Press.

Thobaben, M. (1989). State elder/adult abuse and protection laws. In R. Filinson & S.R. Ingman (Eds.), *Elder abuse: Practice and policy* (pp. 138–152). New York: Human Sciences Press.

United States House of Representatives, Select Committee on Aging, Subcommittee on Health and Long-Term Care. (1985). *Elder abuse: A national disgrace.* Washington, DC: U.S. Government Printing Office.

Utech, M.R. & Garrett, R.R. (1992). Elder and child abuse: conceptual and perceptual parallels. *Journal of Interpersonal Violence, 7,* 418–428.

Weiner, A. (1991). A community-based model for identification and prevention of elder abuse. *Journal of Gerontological Social Work, 16,* 107–119.

Wolf, R.S. (1990). Testimony on behalf of the National Committee for the Prevention of Elder Abuse before the U.S. House Select Committee on Aging, Subcommittee on Human Services. *Journal of Elder Abuse and Neglect, 2,* 137–150.

Wolf, R.S. (1991). Testimony on behalf of the National Committee for the Prevention of Elder Abuse before the U.S. House Select Committee on Aging, Subcommittee on Human Services. *Journal of Elder Abuse and Neglect, 3,* 87–99.

Wolf, R.S. (1992). Making an issue of elder abuse. *The Gerontologist, 32,* 427–429.

Wolf, R.S., Godkin, M.A., & Pillemer, K. (1984). *Elder abuse and neglect: Report from three model projects.* Worcester, MA: University of Massachusetts Medical Center.

Wolf, R.S. & Pillemer, K.A. (1989). *Helping elderly victims: The reality of elder abuse.* New York: Columbia University Press.

Chapter Seven

PROVIDING PROTECTIVE SERVICES TO SPECIAL POPULATIONS

SHIRLEY R. SALEM AND BEVERLY C. FAVRE

INTRODUCTION

Social policy for abused and neglected adults and elders has been developed by federal initiatives and state legislation within the last 20 years. These steps have fragmented the population to be served and the services to be provided. No single state or federal agency is responsible for all forms of abuse and neglect of adults/elders or for the provision of services to them. Protective services, including legal remedies, are fragmented between health care, mental health, social service, and legal systems. If protocols and services are to be linked to the needs of the mistreated or neglected, then specific subpopulations and their service requirements will need to be identified.

Elder abuse and domestic violence, especially spouse abuse, overlap to some degree in the nature of the abuse, services, and legal remedies. State and local statistics on reported cases indicate that the spouse was responsible for a small percent of elder abuse and neglect, while a random survey of the elderly living in the Boston Metropolitan area reported that spouses were responsible for 58 percent of the abuse (Pillemer and Finkelhor, 1988). Domestic violence legal remedies such as civil protection orders (Finn and Colson, 1990) are available for abused elders and adults living with other family members. Rosalie Wolf suggests that the spouse abuse model may be more appropriate than the child abuse model for adult protective services (1989, p. 119), including domestic violence services will help to clarify the assumptions concerning societal intervention and different approaches to the provision of the adult protective services.

Services for the abused/neglected elder are provided by a myriad of agencies/units. This array of services operate in different systems—social services, health care, civil and criminal courts, and volunteer services.

169

Table 1 provides a list of these services which are part of the aging network's continuum of care or are specifically associated with abuse and neglect cases. The entire catalogue of aging network programs (Gelfand, 1988) are deemed appropriate in abuse and neglect cases, especially since some were created to prevent elder neglect. Generally, medical care and limited in-home services such as home health care, meals-on-wheels or congregate meals, and homemaking assistance are considered to be widely available to elders. In order to service the needs of the abused or neglected adult/elder, coordination or team management is needed to ensure the delivery of services between these systems.

Adult protective services can in practice or by law have different responsibilities for the delivery of services to the abused and neglected. Adult protective services can directly provide services; contract and/or coordinate the delivery of services by others; or limit their authority to investigation of the reported abuse or neglect followed by referral to other professionals for case management and delivery of services (Burr, 1982; Wolf and Pillemer, 1989).

Services are provided to abused, neglected, and/or exploited adult "victims" at various points along the APS continuum: investigation; case assessment, APS plan; care management, service coordination, and referral. The delivery of services normally is associated with the end of the process. However, it is difficult to separate these stages in practice. For example, the initial assessment interview might involve a description of service options to the victim.

This analysis will focus on the following central issues: (1) identification of the special populations to be served and their characteristics; (2) the role of the polar values of self-determination vs societal intervention play in decisions to intervene and in the provision or services; (3) the array of resources and programs available for and needed by the abused and neglected elder/adult; and (4) gaps in their service delivery system.

RESEARCH LITERATURE

Abused and neglected elders or adults do not constitute a defined population. For research, legislative, and service purposes, the population tends to be defined by certain characteristics. These include: the age of the victim of the abuse or neglect; the degree and type of mental impairment or physical disability; the living arrangements of the adult

Table 1
List of Potential Services for Victims of Abuse and Neglect

A. Medical/Health Care
    1. Hospitalization or other emergency medical care
    2. Nursing home placement
    3. In-home medical services—home health aides or visiting nurses
B. Psychological and psychiatric services
C. Social Services
    1. Case Management—Coordination of services and monitoring
    2. Supervision and Reassurance
    3. Institutional placements
        a. Long-term care facilities
            1) Extended care facilities
            2) Skilled nursing facilities
            3) Intermediate care facilities
            4) Mental hospitals
        b. Long-term residential
            1) Board and care, personal care and domiciliary care homes
            2) Adult foster homes
        c. Short-term care facilities
            1) Emergency shelters/safe houses
    4. Counseling
        a. Family counseling
        b. Individual/group counseling for abused
        c. Individual/group counseling for abuser
    5. Nutrition programs
        a. Home-delivered meals (Meals-on-Wheels)
        b. Congregate meals in senior centers and other settings
    6. Homemaker and chore services
        a. Light household services, e.g. cleaning and laundry
        b. Help with home maintenance
    7. Socialization Programs
        a. Home visitor
        b. Adult day care
        c. Senior citizen centers or recreation activities
    8. Housing or relocation assistance
        a. Eviction of the abuser (e.g. protection order)
        b. Change in residence
    9. Transportation services
    10. Financial resources
        a. Representative payee
        b. Conservatorship
        c. Supplemental income
        d. Daily money management

Table 1 (Continued)

11. Mobilizing the family and social network of the abused/neglected person
    a. Family members
    b. Clergy
    c. Friends and neighbors
    d. Battered Women's Program
    e. Volunteer services
D. Legal Services
    1. Civil
        a. Temporary restraining orders or protection orders
        b. Guardianship orders
        c. Conservatorship
    2. Criminal — referral to police or district attorney's office for criminal prosecution
    3. Miscellaneous legal assistance — filing legal papers or correspondence
E. Services to the abuser or caregiver
    1. Respite care for the elder or adult
    2. Training in more effective care-giving behavior
    3. Counseling
    4. Adult day care centers as respite service
    5. Financial compensation for services

or elder (private residence, nursing home, board and care home, etc.); the types of abuse or neglect; the relationship of the victim to the caregiver/abuser, if any; the motives or intent of the person responsible for the neglect or abuse; the dependency and impairment of the caregiver, if any; and the resources of the victim and abuser. It may also include the degree of resistance or cooperation from the abused or neglected person and their family as well as the degree of social isolation. The incidence of abuse or neglect, the decision to make a mandatory or voluntary referral, the legal responsibility of APS agencies, the potential for legal actions, and eligibility as well as the need for services may vary with the definition of the population according to the preceding characteristics. Given that many cases are not referred (Pratt, Koval & Lloyd, 1983; Phillips and Rempusheski, 1986) or reported (U.S. House of Representatives, Committee on Aging, 1990) to adult protective service units, the characteristics of APS cases do not necessarily resemble those of the population of abused or neglected elders.

The variability in state legislation on adult/elder abuse and neglect makes it difficult to develop accurate national statistics on the population to be served or the incidence of reported abuse or neglect. Most state adult protective service (APS) units are responsible for reported abuse and neglect to elders over age 60 or 65 and to persons 18 years of age or older who are disabled, incapacitated, dependent, or impaired (Garfield, 1991; Thobaben, 1989). Elder victims constitute about 70 percent of the reported APS cases according to a House of Representatives survey (1990). Disabled adults seem to constitute the other main category of APS cases (Wolf, 1989, p. 119–120). The state legislative mandate normally does not extend in practice to institutional abuse or neglect. Patient/resident abuse and neglect in long-term care facilities are normally dealt with by ombudsman programs, medicaid fraud control units, and state attorneys general.

Whether or not the APS cases reflect the racial and cultural diversity of the elder population is unclear. One research study documented a predominantly white clientele in three northeastern states (e.g. 90% white in Wolf and Pillemer, 1989). National statistics on the race or ethnicity of APS cases are not available, however, some state statistics demonstrate more cultural diversity. The research and literature on elder abuse in minority communities is almost nonexistent (U.S. Senate, Special Committee on Aging, 1991, Section VI).

Research suggests the causes of elder/adult abuse and neglect cannot be explained by a single theory or set of factors, but may vary by the type of abuse or neglect. Wolf (1989; Wolf and Pillemer, 1989) identified three distinct profiles of elder abuse and neglect: physical or psychological abuse; self-neglect; and financial exploitation. Table 2 identifies these profiles which were developed as part of a widely reported study of three model elder abuse and neglect projects in Rhode Island, Massachusetts, and New York. While these profiles may not correspond to most recognized theories, they do provide an indication of the salient factors confronting practitioners in APS cases.

Building on these profiles, we can begin to develop a typology of the neglected and abused population. At a minimum, the special populations would include:

(1) self-neglect of elders/adults;
(2) elders/adults physically or psychologically abused:

   a) by spouses or dependent adult caregivers, which may be covered by both domestic violence and APS legislation;
   b) by elders/adults or neglected by non-dependent caregivers in the community;

(3) financial exploitation of elders.

Table 2
Profiles of Elder Mistreatment

Victim	Physical or Psychological Abuse	Self-Neglect	Financial Abuse
Age/Marital Status	Younger married	Not married	Older/not married
Physical/ Functional	More independent in IADL/ADL	Problems with management & transportation	Problems with IADL; need for supportive devices; dependent in ADL and companionship
Psychological/ Cognitive Status	Poor emotional health		Recent decline in mental health; problems with orientation, memory and giving consent
Social Network	Stable	Recent loss of supports	Loss of social supports
Perpetrator Lives with Victim	Lives with Abuser		
Perpetrator Depends on Victim	Dependent Abuser		

Source: Wolf, Rosalie and Pillemer, Karl A. (1989). *Helping Elderly Victims: The Reality of Elder Abuse.* New York: Columbia University Press.

Research in Illinois on the provision of services to abuse and neglect victims suggests that the service needs of these subpopulations do differ (Sengstock, Hwalek, and Petrone, 1989). Before turning to the provision of services to these subpopulations, it is necessary to examine some obstacles to successful intervention.

Victim or perpetrator resistance to intervention is the largest single barrier to the delivery of appropriate services. From 31.2 to 41.5 percent of APS workers in a 1987 survey indicated that victims or perpetrators "often" or "very often" refuse access or assessment (Dolon and Blakely, 1989). Wolf and Pillemer (1989) reported an even higher proportion of barriers to the delivery of services—67 to 74 percent of the victims and 83 to 90 percent of the perpetrators were not initially receptive to help. In the later study, APS workers were able to overcome this resistance in half the cases. To the extent that the resistance is based on the victim's fear, shame, and incompetence, research does not provide effective strategies to overcome these obstacles to treatment (Dolon and Blakely, 1989).

The lack of funding for services to abused and neglected elders has been a constant theme in U.S. House of Representative hearings, while research has documented that needed services are not available for APS cases. The key gaps in services are identified as: respite care, emergency shelters, financial management (assistance, advice, bill paying, etc.), and legal services (Anderson and Theiss, 1989; Fiegener, Fiegener and Meszaros, 1989; Wolf and Pillemer, 1989). In addition, support groups and counseling are needed by both victims and abusers/caregivers, but were not always available. Most states in a recent survey favored federal legislation and funding to establish: a temporary emergency shelter for victims; abuse prevention and treatment programs; and Medicare home and community-based care benefits, including respite care for informal caregivers (U.S. House of Representatives, Select Committee on Aging, 1990). In general, there are references to socialization programs as a service in the APS literature. The literature alludes to APS workers' perception that a full continuum of residential and care facilities are not available for the abused and neglected elderly, especially intermediate care such as adult foster care or board and care arrangements. However, no empirical research has examined this issue.

The limited research on services and their provision might be attributed to the assumption that the aging network provides a continuum of care for the elderly. Apart from medical care and limited in-home services (home health care, meals-on-wheels or congregate meals, and homemaking assistance), this assumption does not appear to be valid. This raises the question of whether the delivery of services is more a function of what is available than what is needed.

Some research suggests that elder victims referred to APS units might not be receiving even basic services of the aging network except for medical care. Wolf and Pillemer found that victims at the time of their referral were not participating in the programs of the aging network (1989, p. 87). This explains, in part, the research finding by Sengstock et al. (1989) that both substantiated and non-substantiated cases of abuse and neglect need multiple services, although the substantiated ones may require more services. Thus, adults and elders referred to adult protective services may have greater unmet needs than those who are involved in non-medical programs in the aging network.

In 1989, Mary C. Sengstock, Melanie Hwalek, and Sally Petrone stated that research had not been undertaken on the nature of the services provided to victims. Their study of 204 cases in Illinois is one of the few that looks at services with data on the characteristics of individual victims. As would be expected, case management was provided in almost all cases. The other services commonly provided were homemaking assistance (34.8%) and miscellaneous legal assistance (24.5%).

Self-neglect cases were found to require more and a different pattern of services than the other types of mistreatment. This was attributed to a APS worker judgement that "they are in need of supervision or care, since they are highly likely to receive supervision/reassurance or to be placed in an institution or under guardianship care. They are also more likely to receive in-home assistance (such as meals or homemaking aid) or to get medical care" (Sengstock, et al., 1989, p. 49). The researchers suggest that this was caused by worker familiarity with this type of case and their freedom of action in the absence of family members or an abuser. However, the variety of services could reflect different degrees of neglect in individual cases and the selection of services to correspond to those needs.

The physical abuse cases, in contrast, had the lowest number of services provided. None of the physical abuse cases received protection orders, court work, investigation, or crisis intervention (Sengstock, et al., 1989). This suggests that APS workers were not using the legal remedies for domestic violence (Buzawa and Buzawa, 1990; Finn and Colson, 1990).

For financial exploitation cases, it is hardly surprising that about half of the cases received miscellaneous legal assistance, since this might have involved theft, fraud, or coercion. However, the authors could not explain the higher than average provision of homemaking assistance (42%) or institutional placements (25%), except to speculate that the victims might have suffered from multiple forms of abuse (Sengstock, et al., 1989). Clearly, more information is needed on this subpopulation.

Coordination with the legal system in providing services to the abused and mistreated elders appears to be infrequent in some APS jurisdiction. In a study by Sengstock et al. (1989), services of the legal system (police visits, guardian orders, protection orders, court work, and investigation) constitute only about 4 percent of all services provided to the sample. Dolon and Blakely (1989) found that legal services ranked low as a community resource to reduce elder abuse and neglect. Lawyers ranked almost last among occupational groups in amount of help provided in the treatment of elder abuse and neglect (Blakely and Dolon, 1991, p. 193). APS workers are probably more knowledgeable about social services and the aging network programs than legal alternatives and procedures and, therefore, more likely to use them.

Changing the social/living situation of the victim was ranked as the most effective intervention strategy in abuse cases and the second most effective in neglect cases in a survey of APS workers (Dolon and Blakely, 1989). Wolf and Pillemer reported that: "While the underlying practice for all Model Projects was to try to keep the family unit intact, changes in the living situation were made in almost half the cases, either through departure of perpetrator or placement of the victim in a nursing home, hospital, or new living quarters" (1989, p. 96). The literature is replete with implicit and explicit criticisms of APS workers for relying too heavily on removing mistreated elders from their homes.

Not all cases can or will be successfully resolved according to an APS worker survey (Dolon and Blakely, 1989). In the Model Projects study in three areas, little or no success was achieved in resolving the cases for one-quarter to one-third of the cases, while the remaining cases were divided between those completely resolved and those with some progress toward resolution (Wolf and Pillemer, 1989). The unwillingness of the victim or perpetrator to cooperate continues to be the single most frequently cited cause of the failure to resolve cases of neglect and abuse, even though workers are sometimes able to overcome these obstacles.

The practitioner literature discusses proposed intervention strategies (Breckman and Adelman, 1988) and descriptions of innovative or specific programs, but it rarely focuses on specific services in abuse or neglect cases. In other words, the emphasis is on effective casework, not on the delivery of services. The tone of this literature is reflected in the next section on practice issues. It is informing workers about how to deal effectively with clients.

A scant amount of literature focuses on specific intervention or services for mistreated elders. There are some interesting discussions on the issues affecting a few specific interventions. For example, some interesting literature exists on guardianship orders (Morrissey, 1982; Schmidt, 1982; Iris, 1988; Quinn, 1989; Wilber, 1991). It includes descriptions of innovative programs such as an emergency shelter in Washington, D.C. (Cabness, 1989) and an adult foster care intervention (Foekler and Chapman, 1988). However, empirical data is rarely available to document the effectiveness of these interventions or innovative programs.

The literature does not provide a clear image of adult protective services, the specific interventions that are working or failing, or the role of APS workers. In part, this is because systematic evaluations of these treatment models or intervention strategies are not available. There is also a notable absence of descriptions of the APS organizations and their policies. The same applies to APS workers, although there are some articles on their role in APS cases.

Practitioners recognize that they need additional specialized training in the provision of services to abused and neglected elders (Dolon and Blakely, 1989; Fiegener, Fiegener, & Meszaros, 1989). Over 90 percent of APS workers in a 1987 survey indicated that more training opportunities could improve their provision of services to victims (Dolon & Blakely, 1989, p. 36). However, the training needs of APS workers have not been identified. Fiegener, Fiegener, and Meszaros (1989) conducted a survey of professionals in 16 types of agencies in 67 counties in Pennsylvania. Since over 50 percent of the respondents had not encountered a case of elder abuse within the past year, the specific training needs of these respondents might not correspond to those of APS workers. Given the absence of specifics in the practitioner literature, this perception of the need for further training is understandable.

APS workers might experience considerable frustration when dealing with elder abuse and neglect. Roughly half of the APS workers agreed that these cases are a source of frustration in a 1987 survey (Dolon and Blakely, 1989). If the victim or perpetrator refuse assistance, this might contribute to professional stress and burnout. The question is how to assist APS workers in dealing with and overcoming the stress involved in this work.

RECOMMENDATIONS FOR FUTURE RESEARCH

There is a great need for applied or policy research on adult protective services. Research on the service needs of abused and neglected are very limited and evaluations of the APS interventions with clients are nonexistent. This research is urgently needed to evaluate practice and policies. This will be difficult because it requires imaging what services could be delivered in addition to services which are currently available or funded. The research should collect data on individual clients and their needs to allow for analysis of service requirements of individuals and subpopulations within the APS clientele. Hopefully, this research will enable us to determine if service needs change over time in these cases. For example, is a nursing home placement a temporary measure to stabilize the victim or is it envisioned as a permanent placement? This research should help to identify gaps in the service delivery system.

Evaluations of the success of the APS interventions, specific programs, and services are almost non-existent. Proposed or current intervention strategies have not been evaluated. Research on what works or doesn't work will be fundamental to the development of policy and training. The lack of empirical evidence to support intervention strategies is a serious weakness in APS programs. Some imaginative research might attempt to draw upon the knowledge of APS workers in successful interventions to determine appropriate strategies for subpopulations.

In terms of empirical research, the incidence of abuse and neglect in the general population needs to be explored. An attempt should be made to ascertain whether the level of elder abuse and neglect in racial and cultural minorities corresponds or differs from the rest of the population. Estimates of elder abuse and neglect based on APS cases may only reflect those referred or reported cases. A fertile area of research could be a thorough comparison of elder abuse with research and theories on spouse and child abuse. For theory development, it is essential to determine whether the same causal factors are applicable to all three categories of abuse.

If APS workers are to become specialists in providing assessments and services to the abused and neglected elders/adults, then research must provide them with greater knowledge as a foundation for their decisions and interventions. While policy manuals might provide some assistance, APS workers face major ethical decisions with little guidance.

PRACTICE ISSUES:
LIMITATIONS ON INTERVENTION STRATEGIES

Intervention strategies need to weigh the polar values of self-determination for the abused or neglected vs state intervention for their protection. This potential conflict of values has a direct effect on the role of professionals in providing services. While APS agencies were modeled on child protective services with the implicit notions of *parens patriae* and state intervention in the best interest of the child, domestic violence statutes were based on models of marriage and divorce laws or on criminal law with a presumption of legal proceedings and victim complaints constituting consent to particular actions. In APS statutes, provisions regarding the "least restrictive alternative" for services and the elder right to refuse consent are compromises which fail to resolve the basic conflict in values or clearly define the role of APS workers. Domestic violence mandatory arrest provisions are a step in the direction of state intervention, but the dominant pattern in domestic violence legislation is to defer to the initiative and wishes of the abused adult.

This conflict in values is inherent in the role of APS workers. Are professionals to function as advocates for the abused or neglected adult in their choice of services (Staudt, 1985)? Or are they to serve the state's interest in protecting the adult or elder from abuse, neglect, or exploitation? Alternatively, are they to merely process these cases by providing whatever services are routinely available and thereby ignore the potential conflict of interest between the abused or the state?

The policies concerning protective services have not clearly defined certain practice issues. Domestic violence legislation generally assumes that the abuser will be removed from the residence (mandatory arrests, protection orders with provisions for the eviction of the abuser, etc.). The assumptions concerning elder mistreatment are less clear. Current public policy tends to provide services for elders and/or their families to enable continued residence in the community, while maintaining that a continuum of care should be provided for those unable to be cared for in family homes. When mistreatment or neglect occurs in the home, the question is whether to improve the caregiving in the home or to remove the elder to a facility. The discussion on elder abuse does not provide clear policy directions.

Services are provided to abused, neglected, and/or exploited adult "victims" at various points along the APS continuum: investigation; case assessment; APS plan; case management, service coordination, and referral. At each stage, APS workers encounter obstacles and decisions. During the investigation period, the interview is the vehicle through which service is provided. The goal during this contact is to gather data in order to make an assessment of the situation. Based on the findings of the investigation, an APS plan is prepared. Inherent in providing services to the "victim" is the ability of the workers to get the victim to cooperate. The workers must be able to build a relationship that makes the victim comfortable enough to want to tell the facts. This may not always be an easy task. The workers must be able to enter into a crisis situation and obtain the necessary information in a non-threatening way.

In order to be effective, workers need to be properly trained. The training should include how to interview the elderly and an understanding of the normal biological, psychological and social aging processes as well as the role of the workers as advocates for and empowerers of the elderly clients. There also is a need for the workers to understand how and where the "victims" fit in their surroundings, the relationship with the suspected abuser, the relationship with those factors in their social environment which impinge upon their "survival."

Of equal importance for the workers is an understanding of the meaning that the victims have attached to their environment, either if they live alone or in a family unit. Elderly victims living with their abusers often have many fears and feelings. They are embarrassed, humiliated, alienated, ashamed and fear retaliation (Costa, 1984; Fulmer and O'Malley, 1987; Jacobson, 1988; Breckman and Adelman, 1988). The workers must recognize that they are interviewing adults. This is an important statement because often workers take on a paternalistic and condescending approach towards the elderly or those who have less to exchange in a relationship. This paternalistic and condescending approach becomes the power tool for the worker.

During this investigation period, gaining access into the home can be an obstacle. There may be strong resistance to talking with a worker. As in any similar situation, defense mechanisms become paramount. Being prepared with creative strategies to gain access in order to obtain information is a must during this period because much of the worker's time and efforts may entail trying to deal with resistance and anger (Fulmer and O'Malley, 1987). Workers must become aware of the anger that will be directed towards them from the family member(s). It is suggested that frequently it is preferable to interview the family members first. This allows the worker to assess the family member's attitude and relationship with the victim. It also may serve as a way of gathering information of other available resources. The personal, situational, and environmental factors surrounding the victim and the household in which the victim resides are examined during the assessment period.

Abused elders might not acknowledge their abuse and, therefore, be unwilling to cooperate with the APS assessment or provision of services. For example, one study found that the majority of interviewed elder victims did not mention the abuse as one of their three most serious problems during the past month (Sengstock, Barrett, and Graham, 1984). Risa Breckman maintains that his lack of acknowledgment of the abuse characterizes the reluctance stage of the change process (Breckman and Adelman, 1988). Victims at this stage also exhibit extreme social isolation, self-blame, low self-acceptance, and ambivalence. She argues that intervention strategies must assist victims in overcoming this reluctance in order to progress to the recognition and rebuilding stages of the change process. In order to overcome this reluctance, Breckman and Adelman (1988) argue that:

> Victims in the reluctance stage, because of their denial, tend to minimize the seriousness of their situation. To address the victim denial directly, workers should arrange a 'keep-in-touch' method with them. The worker should ask the victim to call once a week so he or she can know if the problems at home have continued. If this is not acceptable, perhaps the worker could send a letter. If the victim agrees to call, ask what the back-up plan should be if the contact is not made. The worker might suggest that he or she will call the victim in this case. If the victim agrees, a decision must be made concerning what the worker should say in the event the victim does not answer the phone. This is necessary because victims often do not want family members to know they have established outside contact . . . The idea is to come up with a 'keep-in-touch' method that the victim finds acceptable (p. 110).

This strategy is more clearly designed to deal more with physical or psychological abuse than with financial exploitation or self-neglect. The degree and type of resistance in these two subpopulations has not been defined clearly in the literature.

Of interest in this discussion are the cases which involve major conflicting factors and issues. These are cases where the worker's conclusion verifies the abuse, neglect and/or exploitation of a mentally competent victim, but the victim does not appear to want the services identified by the APS plan. Refusal of victim to acknowledge the problem has been identified as one of the greatest barriers to providing services (Costa, 1984). The issue revolves around the right of the victim to be abused. It is during this investigation period that the worker's judgement becomes paramount. How much effort should the worker expend in order to come to the conclusion that the victim does not want any services, thus closing the case? How much effort does the worker expend in order to come to the conclusion that the victim should receive these services and negate the victim's choice of refusing them? Policies and guidelines cannot take into account each individual situation.

Implied in this is an ethical issue of autonomy or self-determination. Does the victim have a right to be left alone, a right to refuse service, the right to say no? Most workers would adamantly say "yes." Yet when they are confronted with the situation, the "yes" becomes weak. It becomes weak because the worker knows if something is not done, the abuse will reoccur, thus starting the process all over again. The question becomes how to stop the cycle without violating the client's rights.

Workers can be classified into two categories: bureaucratic-oriented workers and client-oriented workers. Services provided by the bureau-cratic oriented worker are prioritized based on the rules and regulations of the agency. The client-oriented worker is more alert to what the client says and needs. The latter type of worker may hear the victim say "no" but proceed to try and understand the meaning of the refusal in order to help the victims understand how their participation in this process will help them and not hurt them. The difference lies in the effort expended to look beyond the negative response of the victim rather than taking the "NO" at face value. The client centered worker with appropriate training would be more effective in encouraging the victim to cooperate.

Encouragement can be synonymous with influence. Workers can assume the position that protection of clients from harm is preferable to adher-ing to the victim's right to be abused. Workers have justified the use of influence strategies on moral grounds and have used subjective factors to justify their use (Abramson, 1991). Thus, the decision becomes societal intervention rather than self-determination. The workers act in *parens patriae*. This use of influence can also be viewed as violation of civil rights. The issue surrounding the use of influence is the question: Who benefits from this? Is it being done in the best interest of the victim or is it being done to make the worker feel "successful"? Can this be consid-ered an abuse of power by the workers? For some, the answer lies in whether the ends justify the means.

Another ethical issue emerges when the victim's mental competence is evaluated as it relates to the victim refusing services. Workers must be able to differentiate between behavior which does warrant action and behavior which does not warrant action. Because an elderly person is impaired, does not mean that (s)he is also incompetent. Again, the workers' judgment enters the process. In this type of situation, the principle of least restrictive alternative of care in the APS plan may involve the removal of the victim from his/her present environment and/or referral for a psychiatric evaluation as a preparatory step towards a competency hearing. In some situations this leads to a court appointed public guardian. The process leading to these types of decisions are also based on the judgment of the workers. Societal determination takes precedence over self determination.

The next phase of an investigation involves victims who are willing to receive services through the APS system. It is at this point that team intervention begins. The service component generally includes some combination of health, social, psychological, medical and legal assistance. The coordinating component is case management as identified in an APS plan. It is at this point that intervention can be made by members from several agencies. Case management refers to having professional social workers responsible for coordinating all services needed by the victim. Families should also be brought into the service. It has been suggested that there should be case management systems that will link elderly individuals and their families who are to benefit from the system with services appropriate to their needs (Tobin, 1985).

The victims who are receiving services during this phase of an APS system may be those who were categorized during the initial assessment phase as reluctant or resistant. However, the workers were able to help the victims see that their abusive, neglected or exploited state did not have to exist. Not only can intervention strategies vary but the strategies could be exercised passively or actively. Workers need to be creative in using various interventions with the victim; an eclectic approach should be the rule. Constraints have been identified which limit the alternatives workers perceive to be available. Among these constraints is the one related to the worker's perceived consequences of action as it relates to a reflection on his/her professional ability (Phillips and Rempusheski, 1986). It is at this point that the need to bring in community resources occurs (Burr, 1982; Foekler and Chapman, 1988). There is a continuous reevaluation of the plan in order to provide the most appropriate services to the victim. Of concern should be those personal factors which influence the mental state of the victim. Depression, isolation and feelings of helplessness and loneliness are likely to decrease actions to resolve the abuse or to break off relations with the abuser (Anetzberger, 1987; Pillemer and Prescott, 1989). Reducing isolation is important because if others are not around to help, self-neglect can be the outcome.

Limited resources are available for the abuse and neglected elders. Funds limit what is available and the extent of service. Creativity is a requirement when funding sources are limited. Agencies must not use limited funding as an excuse not to serve the disenfranchised population. Several programs exist for this population but the adequacy of them is almost impossible to determine. It can be said that any program which enables the elder to maintain independent living in the community and avoid abuse and exploitation is better than nothing.

The focus of services within the APS system is often of a reactive focus since most agencies become involved with the abused and neglected elder after data confirm abuse and neglect. Agencies should develop a proactive focus. Preventive approaches are imperative. Workers may not recognize cases of elder abuse due to their inability to help or through a lack of resources (Fulmer & O'Malley, 1987; Weiner, 1991). The current service delivery system is geared to provide limited, concrete services and lacks the extensive coordination and resources needed for cases of elder abuse and neglect.

A critical issue is the limited availability of resources for victims who are to be removed from their homes. There has been an intensive development of services for victims of family violence. Even though the number still is not enough, shelters for battered women do offer potential placements for female victims of elder abuse (Gelles, 1987). A community based health and social care system would establish the right of the frail elderly to choose to live in the least restrictive environment.

Home care can prevent institutionalization. Some in home services are offered through Medicare, Medicaid, Title XX of Social Security Act and Title III of the Older Americans Act. However, they are often inadequate in terms of being insufficient to meet the long-term care needs of the chronically ill elderly (Palley and Oktay, 1983).

The protection and provision of services for victims of elder abuse and neglect should be the joint responsibility of a network of community agencies. (Roberts, 1983; Burr, 1982; Gelles, 1987). These agencies could include all those responsible for the services in Table One. While there is some cooperation between those agencies in the aging network, there is little evidence to document a coordinated or team approach with agencies outside the network, such as police departments.

INTEGRATING RESEARCH AND PRACTICE

Most of the literature on APS units and the services to the abused and neglected APS cases is little more than descriptive research. As such, it is unlikely to serve as an adequate test of theories concerning the causes of abuse and neglect. On the other hand, we identified a modest amount of theory and research which could provide assistance to practitioners in their difficult effort to provide services to the abused and neglected elders and adults for whom they are responsible.

The research in this area has focused on the incidence of elderly abuse and neglect, the referral process, and the development of assessment instruments. There has been little attention to link these to the delivery of services at the end stages of the process. The research and practice tendency to treat assessment and the APS case plan as distinct stages in the process has impoverished our understanding of the link between needs and services.

The major studies on elder abuse and neglect were undertaken prior to the drug epidemic of the late 1980's and early 1990's. Therefore, the subpopulations were identified from data collected in the early 1980's. Given the impact of this drug epidemic on family life in general and crime in particular, the natural hypothesis would be that the nature of physical abuse and financial exploitation of elders might have changed. Within the inner city minority areas, there is a perception that grandchildren are abusing or financially exploiting their elder relatives in order to obtain money for drugs. Clearly, this is an area which should be explored in future research.

This may reflect a larger problem in the research literature, notably a lack of emphasis on the special needs of distinct populations. There is almost nothing published on the differences in elder abuse and neglect among racial or cultural minorities. Clearly, APS workers need to be sensitive to issues of cultural diversity. However, the elder abuse literature provides little guidance for working with diverse ethnic and cultural populations. Similarly, the incidence of elder abuse is estimated to be lower for rural states, but little analysis has focused on the causes or practice issues differentiating urban and rural areas.

There have been few attempts to identify subpopulations or to define appropriate treatment/service protocols for them. There is a dearth of empirical evidence to support the development of specific care plans for services or intervention strategies. Evaluations of specific intervention in cases are limited, at best. The same is true regarding APS workers and the stages of the process that they are responsible, especially in the provision of services. There is a void in the academic, policy research, and social work literature. While the literature suggests a higher degree of frustration and burnout among APS workers, neither this or proposed prevention strategies have been examined. While the focus has been on elder abuse and neglect, the literature does not seem to acknowledge the development of an APS system in spite of the profusion of legislation.

When APS workers express the need for training, their cry for help from the workers is reflective of the pitfalls in the program and the

overwhelming ethical issues that they confront. The statutory requirements reflect inconsistent demands and lack of direction for APS workers.
Neither the research nor the APS policy manuals provide guidance to
overcome this problem. Their search for direction is further complicated by the lack of empirical basis for the assertions concerning proposed intervention strategies. At the same time, the literature seems to
reflect implicit or explicit criticisms of the APS workers without an
expressed understanding of the rationale for their actions. Creativity is
crying to be heard.

REFERENCES

Abramson, M. (1991). Ethical assessment of the use of influence in adult protective
services. *Journal of Gerontological Social Work, 16,* 125–135.

Anderson, J.M., & Theiss, J.T. (1987). *Survey of key informants on elder abuse and
neglect: A report to the Texas Senate Select Subcommittee on Elder Abuse,* Austin, TX.

Anetzberger, G.J. (1987). *The etiology of elder abuse by adult offspring.* Springfield:
Charles C Thomas.

Blakely, B. and Dolon, R. (1991). Area agencies on aging and prevention of elder
abuse: The results of a national study. *Journal of Elder Abuse and Neglect, 3,*(2),
21–40.

Breckman, R.S. and Adelman, R.D. (1988). *Strategies for helping victims of elder
mistreatment.* Newbury Park: Sage.

Burr, J.J. (1992). *Protective services for adults.* Washington, D.C.: U.S. Department of
Health and Human Services.

Buzawa, E.S. and Buzawa, C.G. (1990). *Domestic Violence: The criminal justice response.*
Newbury Park: Sage.

Cabness, J. (1989). The emergency shelter: A model for building the self-esteem of
abused elders. *Journal of Elder Abuse & Neglect, 1,*(2), 71–82.

Costa, J.J. (1984). *Abuse of the elderly: A guide to resources and services.* Lexington:
Lexington Books.

Dolon, R. & Blakely, B. (1989). Elder abuse and neglect: A study of adult protective
services workers in the United States. *Journal of Elder Abuse & Neglect, 1,*(3), 31–48.

Fiegener, J.J., Fiegener, M., & Meszaros, J. (1989). Policy Implications of a statewide
survey on elder abuse. *Journal of Elder Abuse & Neglect, 1,*(2), 39–58.

Finn, P. & Colson, S. (1990). *Civil protection orders: Legislation, current practice, and
enforcement,* Washington, D.C.: National Institute of Justice.

Foekler, G.A. Jr. & Chapman, D. (1988). Adult foster care: A case study in protective
service intervention. *Adult Foster Care Journal, 2,*(2), 89–99.

Fulmer, T. & O'Malley, T. (1987). *Inadequate care of the elderly.* New York: Springer.

Garfield, A.S. (1991). Elder abuse and the States' adult protective services response:
Time for change in California. *Hastings Law Journal, 42,*(3), 859–937.

Gelfand, D.E. (1988). *The aging network: Programs and services,* (3rd. ed.). New York: Springer.

Gelles, R. (1987). *Family violence.* Newbury Park: Sage.

Iris, M.A. (1988). Guardianship and the elderly: A multi-perspective view of the decision making process. *The Gerontologist, 28,* 39–45.

Jacobsen, J. (1988). *Help I'm parenting my parents.* Indianapolis: Benchmark.

Morrissey, M. (1982). Guardians ad item: An educational program in Virginia. *The Gerontologist, 22,*(3), 301–304.

Palley, H. & Oktay, J. (1983). *The chronically limited elderly.* New York: Haworth.

Phillips, L.R. & Rempusheski, V.F. (1986). Making decisions about elder abuse. *Social Casework, 67,*(3), 131–140.

Pillemer, K. & Finkelhor, D. (1988). The prevalence of elder abuse. A random sample survey. *The Gerontologist, 28,*(1), 51–57.

Pillemer, K. & Prescott, D. (1989). Psychological effects of elder abuse: A research note. *Journal of Elder Abuse & Neglect, 1,*(1), 65–73.

Pratt, C.C., Koval, J., & Lloyd, S. (1983). Social workers' responses to abuse of the elderly. *Social Casework, 64,*(3), 147–153.

Quinn, M.J. (1989). Probate conservatorship and guardianships: Assessment and curative aspects. *Journal of Elder Abuse & Neglect, 1,*(1), 91–101.

Roberts, A.R. (1983). *Helping crime victims: Research, policy and practices.* Newbury Park: Sage.

Schmidt, W. (1982). Issues in public guardianship. *Urban & Social Change Review, 15,*(1), 21–26.

Sengstock, M.C., Barrett, S., & Graham, R. (1984). Abused elders: victims of villains or of circumstances? *Journal of Gerontological Social Work, 8,* 101–108.

Sengstock, M.C., Hwalek, M., & Petrone, S. (1989). Services for aged abuse victims: Service types and related factors. *Journal of Elder Abuse & Neglect, 1,*(4), 37–56.

Staudt, M. (1985). The social worker as an advocate in adult protective services. *Social Work, 30,*(3), 204–208.

Thobaben, M. (1989). State elder/adult abuse and protection laws. In R. Filinson & S.R. Ingman (Eds.), *Elder Abuse: Practice and Policy.* New York: Human Sciences Press.

Tobin, S.S. (1985). The function, form and future of formal services. In C. Galtz, G. Niederehe, & N. Wilson (Eds.), *Aging 2000: Our health care destiny.* New York: Springer.

Weiner, A. (1991). A community-based education model for identification and prevention of elder abuse. *Journal of Gerontological Social Work, 16,* 107–119.

Wilber, K. (1991). Alternatives to conservatorship: The role of daily money management services. *The Gerontologist, 31,*(2), 150–155.

Wolf, R.S. & Pillemer, K.A. (1989). *Helping elderly victims: The reality of elder abuse.* New York: Columbia University Press.

Wolf, R.S. (1989). *Elder abuse: An assessment of the federal response.* Prepared statement. In U.S. House of Representatives, Select Committee on Aging. Washington, D.C.: U.S. Government Printing Office.

U.S. House of Representatives, Select Committee on Aging (1990). *Elder abuse: A*

Decade of shame and Inaction. Washington, D.C.: U.S. Government Printing Office.

U.S. Senate, Special Committee on Aging (1991). *An advocate's guide to laws and programs addressing elder abuse: An information paper.* Washington, D.C.: U.S. Government Printing Office.

Chapter Eight

STAFF BURNOUT IN ADULT PROTECTIVE SERVICES WORK

TIMOTHY F. WYNKOOP AND LAWRENCE H. GERSTEIN

INTRODUCTION

You are driving home from work one evening. Your eye sight becomes blurry and you notice a strange, warm sensation on your cheeks. Your upper lip is tickled and you sense the taste of salt. You realize that you are crying. This is not you. You believe in controlling your emotions. You have to be, in control to present a professional facade to the public.

It was your duty, recently, to remove an aged and demented female from the home of a caregiver (i.e., a daughter). The new placement was the county hospital. The client had severe bed sores. In the buttocks area, the sores were so large and deep that you could actually see skeletal matter. When you summoned an ambulance and had the client removed from the home the family became angry. To justify their neglect, they accused you of being Gestapo, and insulted you personally.

You felt somewhat satisfied about the case. It was a successful removal, and an appropriate placement, for now. You were able to make your case that the client was incompetent. A temporary guardian was appointed, and a more permanent placement was to be made.

You received news this afternoon that your client had just died. She had suffered too much infection and dehydration in the neglect process to recover. She was too weak. You wonder what this is all about. You try to fight back the tears.

You are the entire staff for a seven county APS operation. Your budget is under $32,000 per year. Your local prosecutor is supportive, and underwrites part of your operation by providing office space, furniture, and use of a county car. However, because you have no secretarial help,

191

you must do all of your own paperwork and nuisance duties yourself. You feel squeezed. With almost 500 cases reported to your office annually, even without performing your own secretarial duties, there would not be enough time to provide adequate coverage. When you are on the road at one end of your catchment area, you are paged to respond to an emergency at the other end, some two hours away. You wonder if there is any end in sight. You realize that the legislature is unlikely to appropriate more funds to lighten the load. The only end in sight becomes your retirement from Adult Protective Services (APS).

You are on your way to investigate a report that you had received from a local social services agency. An older adult was living in deplorable conditions. You park in front of the house. It is in disrepair. As you step out of your vehicle, you are met with an offensive odor. The odor grows stronger as you approach the house. You knock at the door. An elder male answers. As he opens the door, the stench makes you feel as though you might vomit. You smell urine and see a half dozen cats and squalor. You explain who you are and why you are there. He appears oriented and coherent. You question the way he lives. He tells you to mind your own business. You know that he would not be judged incompetent in a court of law, and, therefore, he can choose to live in this manner if he desires. Nonetheless, it drains you emotionally to have to leave without helping this person.

You present your findings to the referring social worker who begins to berate you, the performance of your duties, and your personal character. You try to aid the worker in her endeavor by suggesting that she contact the local health department, who may be able to threaten condemnation of the premises if they are not cleaned. You try to explain that legally your hands are tied. She tells you that you are the cause of her client's continued suffering. She wonders why you are drawing a pay check. The director of the social work agency complains of your incompetence to your supervisor. A headache will be your partner for the evening. You are frustrated. Not only did you suffer abuse from the referred client, but also from another professional. You wonder why professionals cannot be on the same side in such matters.

These are but a few examples in the lives of the APS workers whom we interviewed in preparation for writing this chapter. There are many more. In speaking with APS workers, we discovered that this line of work is a breeding ground for stress. In fact, if one were to create a situation to produce burnout in humans, APS would be a good model to follow. In our investigation we found high APS staff to report ratios, challenging clientele, community constrictions, low remuneration commensurate with responsibility, and unpredictable work hours. This type of stress, if left unchallenged, can lead to feelings of helplessness and despair that can result in a state of coping known as burnout.

When preparing to write this chapter, we found a dearth of literature specific to stress and/or burnout among APS workers. This situation is likely the result of a dearth of professional literature pertinent to APS. Because of this, we will discuss the literature on burnout, relating it to APS by the use of examples.

The chapter begins with a discussion of the definition of burnout. It then proceeds with a section on stress, a concept that forms the basis for burnout. Also included will be discussions on career and supervision theory that we will apply to APS. New models of stress/burnout will be presented along with remediation and prevention programs targeted to stress in APS work.

BURNOUT AND STRESS

Burnout

Burnout has been defined a variety of ways in the literature. It has been characterized as "a state of fatigue or frustration" (Freudenberger & Richelson, 1980, p. 13), occupational tedium (Pines & Kafry, 1978), a "loss of idealism, energy, purpose, and concern" (Edelwich & Brodsky, 1980, p. 14), "feelings of physical depletion, helplessness, and hopelessness" (Pines & Aronson, 1981, p. 15), a progression through stages of enthusiasm, stagnation, frustration, and apathy (Edelwich & Brodsky, 1980), as a state of physical, emotional, and mental exhaustion (Pines & Aronson, 1988), and as job dissatisfaction (Harrison, 1980). As can be seen in these definitions, there are similarities and differences in how this phenomenon has been defined. The common denominator is that burnout is unpleasant and unproductive. Even authors who have written about it in different terms, and at different times (Edelwich & Brodsky, 1980; Pines & Aronson, 1981) have focussed on the loss of energy, motivation, and concern for clientele. For the majority of authors, burnout is a "process, not an event" (Farber, 1983, p. 3; see also Golembiewski, Munzenrider & Stevenson, 1986; Golembiewski & Roundtree, 1986).

Several adjectives have been used to describe individuals who are burned out, including cynical, pessimistic, discouraged, negative, irritable, lacking in motivation, exhausted, angry, rigid, and blaming (of clientele for one's own problems). These qualities are a change from the eager, idealistic professional that once existed.

Maslach (1982) defined burnout as a syndrome characterized by the elements of "emotional exhaustion, depersonalization, and reduced personal accomplishment" (Maslach, 1982, p. 3; see also Maslach & Jackson, 1981). According to Maslach (1982), it is the direct result of a maladaptive reaction to chronic stress caused by human interaction. Emotional exhaustion is described as "feeling drained and used up" (Maslach, 1982, p. 3) in the helper's encounters with others. Depersonalization is a defensive response to one's own emotional reaction to others where feelings of compassion and/or empathy are repressed. It implies an emotional distance from others (typically clientele). Feelings of reduced personal accomplishment stem from the apathy and guilt that often accompany the first two elements. It implies a sense of failure at being a caring, helping human being. According to Maslach (1982), it is this shift in one's attitudes toward others, from positive to negative, that characterizes the syndrome in the afflicted professional. It is distinguished from other forms of job stress in that it is the prolonged contact with people and their problems, not other stressors, that is the cause.

Cherniss (1980a) defined burnout as "a process in which the professional's attitudes and behavior change in negative ways in response to job strain" (p. 5). He later reiterated that "burnout involves a change in attitude and behavior in response to a demanding, frustrating, unrewarding work experience" (Cherniss, 1980a, p. 6). Cherniss (1980b) presented a unique perspective on burnout as being a means of coping with stress. It is seen as an intrapsychic orientation to the problem of chronic stress as opposed to a problem solving, or environmental manipulation approach. According to Cherniss (1980b), organizational characteristics of "high ambiguity, conflict, and helplessness" (p. 48) are the elements that may guide the worker to choose an intrapsychic coping strategy (i.e., burnout) instead of taking a more active stance. In this light, the characteristics of burnout (e.g., emotional detachment) may be the most efficient way for the worker to deal with a situation over which he/she has little control.

Stress

To understand burnout, we must first comprehend its antecedent: Stress. Burnout is distinguished as being different from stress (Farber, 1983; Maslach, 1982), but resulting from chronic (Maslach, 1982) and "unmediated" (Farber, 1983, p. 14) stress (Cherniss, 1980a, b; Farber, 1982; Kahn, 1978; Maslach, 1976, 1982). The stress from which burnout results is related to a person-environment interaction (McMichael, 1978). It is also viewed predominantely as a consequence of prolonged, stressful interpersonal contact (Maslach, 1982; Pines & Aronson, 1988). In such contact the human services professional is at risk for the stress that may lead to burnout. He/she is seen as engaging repeatedly in giving (i.e., helping) relationships where little is expected in return (Pines & Kafry, 1978). In these situations, the primary "tool" (Farber, 1983, p. 13) is the worker him/herself, which lends to feelings of vulnerability and being used up at times.

In the workplace, stress is often perceived as a negative phenomenon. The literature on the subject, however, indicates that this is not entirely true. A stressful situation is seen as one in which the environment "taxes or exceeds" the abilities of the individual (Monet & Lazarus, 1977, p. 3). On the surface, this definition appears negatively loaded. This is not entirely true.

Experts on stress and stress management suggest that there are two types of stress: Distress and eustress (Selye, 1976, 1979). Distress carries with it the negative connotations that most of us associate with stress. It is the type of stress that we often associate with anxiety, fear, irritability, headaches, etc. Eustress, on the other hand, is considered positive. It is that limited amount of discomfort that motivates us to take action to achieve something of value. For example, if you want a good grade on an examination, you will be motivated to study. Without eustress, we would not have the motivation to act in our own best interest on a daily basis. There are some authors who contend that too little stress on the job can also contribute to burnout (e.g., Pines & Kafry, 1978).

Stress is not only a subjective emotional reaction, but it is also a physiological reaction (Farmer, Monahan, & Hekeler, 1984). In response to a perceived threat, the sympathetic branch of the autonomic nervous system (ANS) is activated (see Gleitman, 1986 for a discussion on the

ANS), and the individual is placed in a state of general arousal. This is termed as the General Adaptative Syndrome (GAS; Froehlich, 1978; Selye, 1976, 1979). Blood flow to the extremities is restricted to allow a buildup in the main trunk of the body in an effort to protect internal organs. The result is increased blood pressure. Adrenaline is secreted, heart rate and respiration are increased, and the senses are heightened. Common nomenclature for this condition is the *fight or flight* response (Whittlesey, 1986; Farmer et al, 1984; Tache & Selye, 1978). In short, the individual is being readied for self-preservation (i.e., to engage in a self-defensive act; to either fight off an aggressor, or to flee from the situation). This is a similar reaction to that experienced by those individuals in danger of physical threat, such as in a war. When there is physical threat, this response is adaptive. When an individual cognitively equates a non-physically threatening situation with a physically threatening situation, the response is maladaptive. The difference is between a real and a falsely perceived threat to the self.

In professions with stressors similar to APS (e.g., law enforcement, corrections, child protective services) the distinction between reality and faulty perceptions can become blurred. The APS worker may encounter real threats by angered family members, etc. Even if the APS worker is not the focus of danger, his/her clientele typically are at risk.

Not only can stress be classified along positive and negative dimensions (eustress and distress respectively), but it can also be classified as being either acute or chronic. This distinction has to do with the length of time that the stress is experienced. Acute stress is short lived, and typically related to specific psychosocial stressors. Chronic stress is long lived. While it may be related to a long term stressor (such as physical illness), it is most often seen as a maladaptive generalized reaction. For the APS worker, chronic stress may result from any number of stressors in connection with work. The stressors become associated with the work environment such that the entire work environment elicits the reaction (i.e., it becomes generalized). Eventually, even the thought of the job may elicit discomfort.

The notion of personal perception implies that the experience of stress is comprised of a combination of environmental and internal (i.e., within the self) influences. The degree to which each element influences the experience will vary from situation to situation. The concept is one of an individual/environment continuum.

According to Farmer et al. (1984), there are six elements common to stress. The reader will notice that the six elements can be conceptualized along the internal/external continuum. They are:

1. Environmental demands alone can be stress producers.
2. Inner emotional conflicts alone can be stress producers.
3. Environmental and inner demands can combine to produce stress when either one alone might not.
4. All people have adaptive resources.
5. Adaptive resources exist on several different levels.
6. Stress involves situations in which our adaptive mechanisms are over-burdened (Farmer et al., 1984, p. 13).

We included this list of concepts because it is fairly comprehensive and will aid in the reader's understanding of stress. Items 1–3 are fairly self-explanatory, and move from external to internal causes of stress. Items 4–6 are comprised of internal causes, and may require explanation.

The idea that individuals possess adaptive resources (Item 4) may be initially misleading. At issue is not how adequate the resources are to alleviate the experience of stress; rather, that everyone has some capacity to deal with some level of stress. According to Monet and Lazarus (1977), it is only when we exceed these resources that we experience stress (Item 6). These resources can exist in several areas (Item 5), and individuals will vary in their resources across areas. Some may be more physiologically able to withstand stress. Others may be able to modify their self-talk. Yet others may have more resources in the area of social support. The list of resources can be quite lengthy.

Another misconception might be that the list by Farmer et al. (1984) pertains only to negative stress (or distress). While positive stress (or eustress) may be different than distress, it still implies an extension of environmental demands over resources. For example, we would likely not study for an examination if we were confident in our knowledge in the particular area.

Multiple Stage Model of Emotions and Behavior

Because various persons react differently to similar, or same situations, it is logical to assume that there is something different about them. Some researchers have examined personality traits as related to stress (e.g., Gann, 1979; Heckman, 1980). The Type A personality has been described as being susceptible to stress (Friedman & Rosenman, 1974). Those lacking in a trait known as hardiness (comprised of the elements of interpersonal relatedness, self-efficacy, and interest/caring) also have been found to be at higher risk for stress (Kobasa & Maddi, 1981).

What appears to make stress so subjective is personal perception. It is no secret that what is stressful for one individual may not be so stressful for the next person (Farmer et al., 1984; Maslach, 1982). One APS worker may perceive the mound of paperwork (with the concomitant deadline) on the desk as a source of stress, while another may prefer this type of work to being away from the office.

Related to the concept of personal perception is anticipatory stress. Consider the feeling in the pit of your stomach when, as an APS worker, you are driving alone to a home where you are to investigate allegations of violence toward an invalid older person by an adult son. You do not know what awaits you there. Will he confront you verbally? Perhaps physically? To understand further how these internal moderators effect emotional and behavioral outcomes, a discussion of cognitive/behavioral models follows.

Cognitive/behavioral models of emotions and behaviors provide us with a heuristic as to how emotions and behaviors are moderated. In general, the cognitive/behavioral models view emotions and behaviors as the result of thoughts. How an individual perceives his/her particular situation is seen as the key element in how he/she reacts to it (Lazarus, 1981; Mason, 1975). There are several ABC-type models that claim to explain cognitive and behavioral outcomes. There is the ABC model of behaviorism: Antecedents, Behavior, and Consequences (Watson & Tharp, 1992). There is the ABC model of Rational Emotive Therapy (RET): Antecedents, Beliefs, and Consequences (emotional and behavioral) (Ellis, 1973). Rational Behavior Therapy (RBT; Maultsby, 1980, 1984) also has its own, though expanded ABC version: Activating Events, Perceptions, Self-Talk, Emotions, and Behavioral Consequences.

It is our opinion that a combined model better explains the mechanisms, and moderating influences, of human emotions and overt behavior. Such a model takes into account what we know about behavioral and cognitive (beyond, but including, conscious self-talk; Meichenbaum, 1977, 1985) principles. The result is a six stage model, which we believe best accounts for the complexity of human behavior (including emotional behavior):

1. **Antecedents.** These are antecedents in the classical conditioning sense (Pavlov, 1927; Thorndike, 1911). They can also be viewed as discriminative stimuli in the operant paradigm (Skinner, 1953). In addition

to being environmental, they can be internal stimuli (i.e., cognitive, biological).

2. Cognitive Screening. In this stage, if the orienting response is triggered, then schemata are activated to process the incoming information (see the Cognitive Processing model of Meichenbaum, 1977, 1985). This is a largely automatic, or out of awareness process. This process allows us to make sense, in an efficient manner, of our world on a moment by moment basis. If the activated schema (or schemata) is distorted in some way (e.g., a negative stereotype of the self or others), then the incoming information will be distorted proportionately. This is where Ellis's (1973) Beliefs, and Maultsby's (1980, 1984) attitudes (i.e., deeply rooted cognitions) would fit.

3. Self-Talk. This refers to the conscious, sub-vocal voice with which we speak to ourselves. Self-talk is much more amenable to change than are schemata, and can provide a mediating function for distorted schemata, or stereotypes (Devine, 1989). This is the same as Maultsby's (1980, 1984) Self-Talk, and it is the focus for Ellis (1973) in the modification of irrational beliefs.

4. Emotions. In this model, emotions are seen as the direct result of cognitive attributions (i.e., schemata, self-talk) to environmental antecedents. This explanation is similar to the emotional consequences of Ellis (1973) and Maultsby (1984), but it is also flexible enough to incorporate the cognitive attributions of physiological arousal elicited by environmental influences (Schacter & Singer, 1962). Cognitions can also be the cause of emotions in the absence of environmental antecedents (Watson & Tharp, 1992).

5. Behavior. All three ABC models previously discussed allow for overt behavior. Behavior is typically thought of as being overt, but it can also be covert (i.e., cognitive, or sub-vocal, speech behavior) (Watson & Tharp, 1992).

6. Consequences. This is consequences in the operant conditioning sense (Skinner, 1953). They can, however, be overt or covert (e.g., a good feeling) (Bajtelsmit & Gershman, 1976; Watson & Rayner, 1920; Watson & Tharp, 1992).

An example may help to explain how the model applies to APS workers. An APS worker is requested to investigate allegations of the sexual abuse of a developmentally disabled adult (Antecedent). Previous investigations of a similar nature have not been fruitful for this worker. There are personal emotional issues in sexual abuse to contend with, and the success rate in victim placement and perpetrator prosecution in such cases is difficult due to the limited credibility of the victim. The worker has developed a stereotype of such situations as being defeating (Cognitive Screening). He/she filters information through this attitude, thinking in self-defeating ways (i.e., Self-Talk). He/she begins to feel negative or despondent (Emotion). To counter these feelings, the worker suppresses them, distancing him/herself emotionally (a covert behavior). When he/she arrives on site, the emotional distancing is evident in a cold demeanor toward the client (overt Behavior). The worker believes that the client has been abused; however, the client is an unreliable source of information and there is not enough evidence to warrant removal or placement. As a result, the worker is punished emotionally for responding to the complaint (a Consequence), thus reinforcing his/her stereotype of such investigations. If this scenario occurs enough, and in several areas without intervention, burnout may result.

While such stage models are interesting and manageable heuristics, they are not representative of all human behavior. Human behavior is not limited to the linear progression that the model appears to propose. There will be times when an individual in a particular situation may appear to skip a step(s) (e.g., the behavior is elicited from environmental stressors without being cognitively processed). There also will be times when an individual may get stuck in a feedback loop (e.g., an angered individual generates negative self-talk as a result of being angry, which generates more anger, which generates more self-talk, and so on, until the individual may act out their anger overtly).

Additional Mediating Concepts

In the stages of Cognitive Screening and Self-Talk, there are three mediators that have been highly researched and merit discussion: Locus of control, self-efficacy, and learned helplessness.

Locus of control (Rotter, 1966; Rotter, Chance, & Phares, 1972) refers to the degree to which individuals perceive personal control over their behavior. It can best be described as a continuum of attributions from internal to external. Most persons fall somewhere in between the two extremes. Those who are oriented in the internal direction view themselves and their behavior as having an impact on the environment. Those whose orientation leans toward an external locus of control perceive outcomes of events in their lives as being controlled by environmental dictates. In other words, they view their own behavior as having little impact on (or themselves as having little control over), outcomes in their lives.

Locus of control has been given some attention in the literature on stress and burnout (Cherniss, 1980b; Quick & Quick, 1984). Research findings suggest that those with an internal locus of control are more stress resistant than those with an external locus of control (Anderson, 1977).

A related concept is that of self-efficacy (Bandura, 1986, 1992). Self-efficacy refers to a belief in one's own competence in a particular area (i.e., to have an impact on the environment). It is typically developed and strengthened via a series of successes in a particular area. It also can be weakened by a series of failures. These assumptions have been supported by research in a variety of areas (see Watson & Tharp, 1992, for a review), including physiological reactions to stress (Bandura, Taylor, Williams, Mefford, & Barchas, 1985). Self-efficacy has received limited attention in the literature on burnout (primarily in the area of hardiness and resistance to stress).

As a segue back into the literature specific to burnout, we discuss the issue of learned helplessness (Seligman, 1975). Learned helplessness refers to "an acquired sense that one can no longer control one's environment so that one gives up trying" (Gleitman, 1986, p. 114). Learned helplessness is a key element in psychogenic depression (Seligman, Klein, & Miller, 1976). Studies have displayed that when animals (i.e., dogs) are repeatedly exposed to mild electrical shocks that are beyond their control, and when they later are given the opportunity for control (e.g., via escape from the area), they typically will not exercise this option, but will instead lay on an electrical grid and continue to be shocked (Maier, Seligman, & Solomon, 1969; Seligman & Maier, 1967).

There are parallels to APS work. Consider, for example, the emotional consequences to the APS worker of the high number of cases that cannot be resolved to the worker's satisfaction (due to factors beyond his/her control). An interesting caveat is that in those situations in which two animals are being shocked and one of the animals is able to discontinue the shock for both of them, and does this consistently, the other animal without this control will not exercise their control when it is offered, but will instead accept the shocks as administered. There is a lesson in APS management to be learned here. Overbearing supervisors who choke their supervisees autonomy and ability to make decisions relevant to their own cases (even if highly supportive), run the risk of depleting the motivation of their work force. Oddly, as important as we believe learned helplessness to be to the concept of job stress and burnout it is noticeably absent in the major literature on the subject. The concept does appear in the literature to some extent, but it is not identified as such.

RESEARCH FINDINGS

Thus far we have discussed definitions of burnout and stress, and we have examined stress at length. It would be beneficial to now examine the etiology of burnout (i.e., what causes it). Such a discussion would, of necessity, include some of the mediating variables provided by the cognitive/behavioral models previously mentioned.

Conceptual Models

Maslach (1982) allowed for personality variables in the causation of stress and burnout, though to a lesser degree than environmental variables. Though environmental press could include a variety of stressors, it is prolonged client contact (generating forms of interpersonal stress) that is the primary cause. In our opinion, APS client contact would be inclusive of the identified victim, perpetrator(s), family members, other professionals, etc. It is most likely that, iven the numbers of persons involved in any APS case, the potential for interpersonal conflict on a case by case basis is very high (it is difficult to please everyone). Maslach (1982) also considered the overall job setting as a source of stress. Factors of job site stress would include work overload (e.g., large caseloads), organizational rules that diminish the professional's autonomy in decision making and practice, negative relationships with colleagues, and poor supervision (e.g., unsupportive, overbearing, reliance on negative feedback).

According to Whitehead (1989), the model of burnout proposed by Cherniss (1980b) is inclusive of Maslach's (1982) model and is, therefore, more comprehensive. Cherniss (1980a,b) writes in terms of organizational structure, and how this structure impacts the worker's internal process. Stressful organizational structure is conceptualized as being comprised of role structure, power structure, and normative structure. The human services organizational role structure refers to the manner in which job duties are assigned to workers.

In Cherniss's (1980b) conceptualization, role structure can be subdivided into role conflict and role ambiguity. Role ambiguity is said to exist when not enough information is provided for the worker to know the boundaries of his/her duties, or to know just what those duties are. This can lead to a state of uneasiness and confusion. Role conflict occurs when the worker perceives that he/she is being required to do too much (i.e., role overload), receiving inconsistent messages about job duties from management (i.e., intersender conflict), or when there are incongruencies between the worker's values, drives, or abilities and the dictates of the job (i.e., person-role conflict). The role structure of an organization can also have an impact on the motivation of its workers. Items such as variety of duties, continuing education, and feedback from supervisors can all be ways that the worker can recognize growth and diversity instead of stagnation (Cherniss, 1980b; Whitehead, 1989).

The power structure of the organization refers to the way in which decisions are made. Can the worker make decisions relevant to his/her caseload? Do workers have a voice in organizational matters? At issue here is worker autonomy within the parameters of the organization (recall that autonomy is antithetical to the concept of learned helplessness discussed previously).

The normative structure of the organization refers to the aims, philosophy, and standards (or norms). In other words, it refers to the "whole" of the organization. Pertinent issues would be treatment and research philosophies, the value of employee welfare, and standards that promote employee growth and autonomy (Cherniss, 1980a,b; Whitehead, 1989).

Cherniss (1980b) also placed emphasis on personality variables. He proposed that introverts, and those with a high external locus of control are at high risk for burnout. He also took into account career aspirations and the worker's life outside of work as potential exacerbators or inhibitors to stress (i.e., stress suffered from work).

Although models of burnout, in general, have been researched, the research has tended to test only specific propositions of theories (Whitehead, 1989). Demographic variables that have received attention have been age, gender, ethnicity, education, and marital status. An inverse relationship between age and burnout has been a consistent finding in the research (e.g., Byrne, 1991; van der Ploeg, van Leeuwen, & Kwee, 1990; Maslach, 1982). Being married also seems to provide a buffer against burnout (Maslach, 1982; Revicki & May, 1989), and having children enhances this effect (Maslach, Jackson, & Barad, 1982). There exists the possibility of confounds in this research, however, due to the fact that the older and/or married workers studied were those who had survived burnout (while their burnt-out colleagues may have already left the field).

Gender has been found to be relatively uncorrelated to burnout status (Byrne, 1991; Maslach, 1982; Shinn, Rosario, Morch, & Chestnut, 1984). Ethnicity has been difficult to examine due to the limited numbers of persons of color in the helping professions (Maslach, 1982). What has been found, however, is that, using Caucasians as a baseline, Asian Americans have similar rates of burnout, while Blacks have lower rates (Maslach, 1982).

Regarding education, there are some interesting findings. According to Maslach (1982), those workers with some college, but not a four year degree, experience burnout to a lesser degree than do those without any college education or with a bachelor's degree and/or graduate training.

Several Personality correlates have been examined. These include locus of control, Type A personality, hardiness, and personal perception. Those with an internal locus of control (i.e., believing that their actions will have an impact on their situation) have been found to be more resistant to stressful situations than those with an external locus of control (Anderson, 1977; Ashford, 1988; Bulman & Wortman, 1977; Johnson & Sarason, 1978; Lefcourt, 1980; Storms & Spector, 1987). The traits associated with Type A personalities (e.g., high drive) have been found to lend themselves to stress and burnout (Friedman & Rosenman, 1974; Hinkle, 1974; Holahan & Moos, 1985; Matthews, 1982). The qualities of hardiness (i.e., commitment, control, and challenge) have been found to aid in resistance to stress (Kobasa, 1979; Kobasa, Maddi, & Kahn, 1982; Kobasa & Puccetti, 1983). Personal perceptions, or cognitive appraisals, have been discussed as mediators between environmental stressors and behavioral outcomes (Kobasa & Puccetti, 1983; Lazarus, 1966; Meichenbaum, 1985; Miles & Perreault, 1976).

The mediating effects of role conflict and role ambiguity also have been researched (Crane & Iwanicki, 1986; Kahn et al., 1964; Miles & Perreault, 1976; Schwab, Jackson, & Schuler, 1986). In addition, the effects of supervision (Berkeley Planning Associates, 1977; Revicki & May, 1989; Ross, Altmaier, & Russell, 1989), ability for support from co-workers (Ashford, 1988; House, 1981; Revicki & May, 1989; Ross et al., 1989), and type of clientele served (Byrne, 1991) have been displayed to moderate the effects of stressful situations. Decision making capacity (Karasek, 1979), participative decision making (Schaubroeck, Cotton, & Jennings, 1989), and job demands (Dompierre & Lavoie, 1987) also have been researched with results being in the predicted (i.e., common sense) directions.

Structural Equation Modeling

Perhaps the most comprehensive means at present to research the causes and mediators of stress and burnout is a technique known as structural equation modeling (Pedhazur & Schmelkin, 1992). In this process, the researcher typically proposes a model of stress or burnout beginning with its antecedents and ending with its results. Typically, there are several variables involved. These can include multiple antecedents, mediating variables, and/or outcomes. A sample is identified (e.g., teachers, police), and measures (e.g., tests, interviews) administered. Then, the data are analyzed in terms of correlations, and directions of correlations (i.e., positive or negative) between the items in the original model. If some of the correlations do not support the proposed model, the model is adjusted accordingly. This has been a description of a confirmatory process. In some instances, however, the researcher will not propose a model, but will let his/her data generate the model (i.e., an exploratory process). There have been a few well conducted studies on burnout using structural equation modeling. We will discuss their findings.

Several studies have examined the influence of role conflict and role ambiguity on outcomes such as job tension, job satisfaction, and turnover. Job turnover has been the focus of much attention, likely due to its economical impact on industry. Bedeian and Armenakis (1981) proposed and tested a model in which both role conflict and ambiguity interacted to have an impact (i.e., a positive correlation with) turnover. They also proposed mediators of job tension (positively correlated with role conflicts and ambiguity, and turnover) and job satisfaction (negatively correlated with all of the other elements). In short, the model proposed that when role conflict and role ambiguity were high, job tension would rise which would decrease job satisfaction and increase employee turnover. In addition, Bedeian and Armenakis (1981) confirmed that role conflict and role ambiguity could exert unmediated effects directly on job satisfaction and/or turnover. Kemery et al. (1985) replicated these findings in three of four samples. The model has, however, been criticized as being incomplete (i.e., not taking other mediators or outcomes into account) (Schaubroeck et al., 1989).

Other researchers have investigated the mediating effect of commitment on turnover rates (e.g., Mobley, Horner, & Hollingsworth, 1978;

Stevens, Beyer, & Trice, 1978). There are differences of opinion as to where in the process commitment serves a mediating effect (Farrell & Rusbult, 1981; Morris & Sherman, 1981; Steers, 1977; Steers & Mowday, 1981). The research, reanalyzed *in toto* supports the idea that job commitment is mediated by job satisfaction (Williams & Hazer, 1986), meaning that a worker will need to be satisfied with his/her job before he/she can be expected to be committed to it. There has been additional support for the mediating effect of job satisfaction on the relationship between role conflict and role ambiguity, and job commitment in other studies (e.g., Oliver & Brief, 1977; Wunder, Dougherty, & Welsh, 1982). This research has been criticized, however, for not examining direct paths bypassing the satisfaction variable (Schaubroeck et al., 1989), which would have the effect of inflating the other item coefficients (i.e., making their relationships appear larger than they really are).

Schaubroeck, Cotton, and Jennings (1989) replicated the Bedeian and Armenakis (1981) and Kemery et al. (1985) studies in their examination of an expanded model. The results were supportive of the inclusion of job tension, satisfaction, and commitment as mediators in job turnover. In addition, job satisfaction had two paths to turnover: One mediated by commitment, and the other direct. Role ambiguity was demonstrated to have direct influences on job tension, satisfaction, and commitment, while role conflict had direct effects on job tension and satisfaction.

Schaubroeck et al. (1989) also studied the antecedent effects of participation, role overload, and social support on role conflict and ambiguity. The connections between job satisfaction, commitment, and turnover remained clear. The connection between job tension and satisfaction, however, was tenuous. When the three antecedents were included, however, this connection was reestablished. The inclusion of the three antecedents had significant impacts on the (now mediating) influences of role conflict and ambiguity. Employee participation in management had a direct positive effect on job satisfaction and a direct negative impact on role ambiguity (i.e., the more that employees perceived their influence in management decisions, the less their roles appeared ambiguous to them). Role overload (i.e., high volume of work) had direct positive effects on role conflict, role ambiguity, and job tension (i.e., the higher the work volume, to levels beyond reason, the higher the conflict, ambiguity, and tension). Social support, from both work colleagues and superiors, had direct negative effects on role conflict and role ambiguity (i.e., the more the perceived support, the less that conflict and ambiguity was experienced), and a direct positive impact on job satisfaction (i.e., the more that social support was experienced, the more that satisfaction was experienced). The interaction between role conflict and role ambiguity was weakened, as well as their direct influences on other mediators, with the inclusion of the three antecedents in the model.

Whitehead (1989) conducted two analyses using criminal justice professionals (i.e., probation and corrections officers) to test selected propositions of Maslach's (1982) and Cherniss' (1980a, b) mediating factors of burnout. Using a sample of probation officers, Whitehead (1989) tested the effects of age, amount of client contact, participation in decision making, role conflict, and job satisfaction on the three components of burnout (i.e., emotional exhaustion, depersonalization, personal accomplishment; see Maslach, 1982). The findings were somewhat surprising. Age was negatively correlated with burnout in general. Client contact was positively correlated with personal achievement, and unrelated to either emotional exhaustion or depersonalization (contrary to the main proposition of Maslach, 1982). Participation in decision making was positively correlated with job satisfaction, but only marginally related to burnout via personal accomplishment (contrary to Cherniss, 1980b). Role conflict was positively related to emotional exhaustion and depersonalization. Job satisfaction was negatively related to emotional exhaustion and depersonalization, while being positively related to personal achievement.

In a study using correctional personnel, Whitehead (1989) examined the same variables discussed in the previous study. In addition, the variables of administrative support and perceived stress were also examined. For the replicated variables, the pattern of inter-item correlations were similar. Administrative support was negatively related to emotional exhaustion and depersonalization (i.e., the more support the employees perceived, the less that burnout was experienced). An opposite pattern emerged for stress (i.e., the higher the stress, the more that burnout was experienced) (see also Lindquist & Whitehead, 1986, and Whitehead & Lindquist, 1986, for additional support).

In their work with nurses, Revicki and May (1989) proposed and confirmed a causal model to examine the relationships of organizational climate, supervisor behavior, and work group relations to role ambiguity, job satisfaction, occupational stress, and depression. Organizational climate (i.e., the constraints placed on line staff and mid-level management by upper-level management) was found to directly influence supervisor behavior, job satisfaction, occupational stress, and work group relations (all in the positive direction, except for occupational stress). Supervisor behavior and work group relations were directly and positively related. In addition, these variables had direct (inverse) influences on role conflict (which mediated their effects on job satisfaction and occupational stress). There was a direct and positive relationship between occupational stress and depression. A serendipitous finding was an inverse relationship between marriage and depression (i.e., those who were married suffered less depression).

Problems with Structural Equation Modeling

Though the process of structural equation modeling appears intuitively to be in a position to answer all of our causal questions on burnout, it does pose some problems. First, in a confirmatory analysis, the type of data collected is driven by the conceptual model of the researcher, leading to a theoretical bias, or self-containment problems (Duncan, 1975). Second, while it may make intuitive sense, then, to remove this bias by conducting an exploratory analysis, this type of analysis is also lacking. A rhetorical question is in order. Without a theory to guide the research, how does the researcher know what type of instruments or samples to choose, or what variables to include in the structural equation? The choice of sample and instruments will impact the resulting model.

Thirdly, structural equation modeling, as with any other research or statistical technique, is subject to confounds and artifact. For example, the issue of employee involvement in management was left unsettled in the studies discussed in the previous section. Schaubroeck et al.'s (1989) study provided support for the inclusion of "participation" (p. 41) in the causal model, while Whitehead's (1989) studies did not. Granted, there were differences in the models (i.e., different variables including different outcomes); however, the concept of employee involvement makes so much sense in the alleviation of stress (via feelings of influence and role definition, etc.), that one might suspect that the lack of support in Whitehead's (1989) studies may well have been the result of confounds in the data. Indeed, there has been other research to support the benefits of employee participation in alleviation of role conflict and role ambiguity (e.g., Jackson, 1983). Perhaps employee participation is different (or perceived differently) in corrections than it is in civilian federal and state (non-correctional) employment. Perhaps the definitions of the researchers differed (i.e., they may have been measuring different constructs). In addition, the constructs were measured differently, using different instruments (again challenging construct validity). It is most likely that further research will need to be conducted to reach a definitive conclusion.

The fourth problem that we will discuss in relation to structural equation modeling is the complexity of the models generated. In our quest for knowledge, we sometimes seek more detail than is warranted in the application of our research results to practice. An ideal model of human behavior is one that is specific enough to guide the agent of change in helping others, yet general enough to be applicable across a variety of situations (notice that we did not say all situations). Many structural equation models incorporate too many variables to be useful to the clinician or consultant in raw form. In the application of a model to real life, there can be dozens of inter-variable connections. A shift in just one variable can (and typically does) modify the impact of all of the other variables. In this respect, the more detailed the model, the more situation (and temporally) specific it becomes. The goal in model building for practical application is flexibility and generalizability (i.e., qualities that will allow use of the model at the local level).

An Interactional Model of Stress/Burnout

To this end, we considered qualitatively (Heppner, Kivighan, & Wampold, 1992) the generalities of the models previously presented. Their reduced elements appear to lend themselves well to a four stage interactive model of stress. The model is a modification of a model proposed by Gerstein & Russell (1990) in their work examining the stress encountered by medical students during training. The current model is proposed as a basis for practice and research on stress that is more specific to APS.

1. **Internal/External Variables.** The model takes into account not only the external (e.g., clientele, conflict) and internal (e.g., perceptions, cognitions) aspects of stress, but also the belief that these elements interact with each other to produce the conditions necessary for perceived stress. This interaction is best seen as lying on a continuum with high external/low internal interaction on one end and low external/high internal interaction on the other. The contribution that external and internal events contribute to the stressful situation will differ from situation to situation, and from person to person. The model takes into account the often synergistic interaction between the person and the

environment in the stress reaction (e.g., sometimes the individual can increase the stress level of the environment via his/her self-talk and/or other behavior).

2. **Emotional Response(s).** Emotional reactions occur in response to the interaction between the external and internal variables. They can be characterized as being positive, neutral, or negative. They will have an impact on the individual's behavioral response (next category). The emotional response may also impact the individual's cognitions of the event (i.e., a feedback loop), with the consequence of modifying the amount of perceived stress (i.e., an internal variable relating to the stressful situation). This will, in turn, re-impact the way in which the individual feels about the situation and so on.

3. **Behavioral Response(s).** Behavioral responses may be internal (e.g., self-talk) or overt (e.g., jogging). There may be more than one behavioral response for an individual situation. The individual's behavioral response(s) may also serve to impact upon the stressful situation through a feedback loop, modifying it somewhat. The tendency in the literature is to categorize responses as either adaptive or maladaptive. In our estimation, behavioral responses fall along a continuum from adaptive (e.g., accurate self-talk, exercise) to maladaptive (e.g., substance abuse, abuse of spouse or children). For example, substance abuse may be regarded as a maladaptive coping mechanism by most. Few, however, would argue that there does not exist a qualitative difference between the person who uses alcohol daily and the person who uses it on a once-a-month basis. To place both persons in the same boat is to lose sight of their differences. While an individual may use alcohol once a month, he/she may also jog, eat right, and enjoy fulfilling interpersonal and familial relationships. Our continuum perspective would alleviate the necessity of pegging such a person as coping maladaptively.

4. **Consequences.** According to our model, the behavioral response will either be reinforced (i.e., rewarded) or punished. Consequences will also have an impact on the initial stressful situation (again by a feedback loop). For example, if an apology is the behavioral response to an accusation that another individual had been wronged in some way, the situation would likely be defused.

An example of the application of the model may help to clarify its use. An individual is told by his/her supervisor (i.e., and external stressful event) that he/she is too rude to clientele, tending to express inappropriate anger toward them. The worker's self-talk is to the effect that the supervisor does not know what she is talking about (i.e., an internal variable), and immediately becomes angry at the supervisor (i.e., an emotional response). This may, in turn, make the situation seem worse to the worker than what it really is (i.e., feedback loop from the emotional response to the internal stressful variable), heightening the emotional response (i.e., the worker's anger increases). The worker remains in this feedback loop long enough to become angry enough to act irrationally toward the supervisor, cursing at her and telling her to mind her own business (i.e., a behavioral response). This response has the effect (via feedback to the stressor) which heightens the stressful impact of the situation. The worker is instructed to go to the supervisor's office and cool off (i.e., a consequence). The worker refuses, and leaves the work site (i.e., another behavioral response occasioned by the feedback loops heightening the stress of the situation). The worker is then discharged by the agency for insubordination (i.e., the final consequence).

We believe this model to be sufficiently specific to explain the mechanisms of stress/burnout reactions, while at the same time being general enough to be applied across situations. It is also flexible enough to allow for individual variability. Additionally, the model is brief enough to be of practical use.

Such a conceptualization of human behavior in stressful situations is consistent with the work of others (i.e., Beehr & Newman, 1978; Meier, 1983). In fact, Beehr and Newman's (1978) proposition is strikingly similar. They posit that stress is the result of a combination of environmental factors, personal factors, and an interaction between the two. In an examination of this type of a model with correctional staff, Gerstein, Topp, and Correll (1987) found general support for this paradigm. However, the environmental factors accounted for the vast majority of variance in the data. This leads us back to the propositions by Cherniss (1980a, b) and Maslach (1982), that although intrapsychic variables may mediate the stress response, it is the environment that is the key element.

APPLYING THE RESEARCH TO APS

Thus far, we have discussed theory and research not directly related to APS. In this section, we translate the research on stress and burnout to the APS situation. The reader is cautioned, that even though many of the studies cited previously can be generalized to APS, there may be instances where this may not be so.

Clientele

According to Maslach (1982), prolonged stressful client contact (in the human services) is the primary cause of burnout. The research has not consistently supported this proposition (e.g., Beck & Garguilo, 1983; Bensky et al., 1980; Olson & Matuskey, 1982; Whitehead, 1989). To the contrary, there are indications that the red tape and paperwork that prevent the concerned professional from spending needed time with clientele can be quite stress provoking (Herrick, Takagi, Coleman, & Morgan, 1983).

There is little doubt that the clientele of APS can be difficult. To be an APS client, one needs to be limited in some way—to be able to be victimized without reasonable volitional recourse. In addition, in cases of abuse, there is an abuser that often must be confronted by the worker. Frequently, there are unpopular decisions to be made. These could include removal of an abused or neglected client from the home of angry family members, determining that a victim does not meet criteria for APS intervention, or having to walk away from a case where victimization is occurring, but the competent client refuses services. There are also chronic cases (i.e., the clients that keep cropping up) that require assistance.

Cases can be dangerous as well. When making home visits, almost anything can happen. An angry client or family member can pose the threat of bodily harm to the APS worker.

Role Structure

While APS clientele may be difficult, it was our impression (in speaking with APS personnel) that the clientele were not the focus of their stressful concerns. It appeared that the APS worker expected the client to have problems, otherwise an intervention would not be required. The workers with whom we spoke seemed to be more concerned with having to leave cases without investigating them because of the lack of staff, amount of paperwork, and/or the amount of down time on the road (especially those responsible for multiple counties). These concerns would appear to be role structure issues. It struck us as odd that state legislators would not take notice of the huge referral to staff ratios that we encountered (an average of almost 450:1 annually).

Role Conflict/Ambiguity

The high number of referrals and the dual nature of APS positions is a situation ripe for role conflict and role ambiguity. On the one hand, the APS worker is to be an investigator/law enforcement officer (in some instances even armed). On the other hand, the APS worker makes placements and files reports, functioning as a social worker. In addition to these potentially conflicting roles, the worker's personal feelings of wanting to cease the victimization or to improve a client's quality of life complicates the situation, as does the public relations position that the APS worker fills (i.e., as a field representative of the local prosecutor— typically, an elected official). Such conflict in roles may foster role ambiguity if not addressed by management.

Community expectations can also serve to exacerbate the amount of role conflict experienced by the APS worker. For example, the APS workers that we interviewed relayed conflicts with law enforcement and social service agencies in the performance of their duties. It is sometimes difficult to get police and/or prosecutors to respond to certain cases (i.e., cases that may be personally and emotionally important to the individual APS worker). At the same time, social service agencies become frustrated with the legal limits to APS, sometimes taking this frustration out on the APS worker. This can have the effect of polarizing the APS worker, who is neither solely social worker nor solely law enforcement officer, but is at the same time both. We hypothesize that when confronted, or resisted, by social service providers, the APS worker is thrust into the position of law enforcement officer, and vice versa. In the social psychological literature, such shifts in attitudes are caused by environmental influences, and operate out of conscious awareness (Johnson, 1980). This situational shift can be quite confusing to the worker. In addition to conflicts with other agencies, there are conflicts with the community in general (e.g., dissatisfied family members, neighbors, the press).

Power Structure

With regard to power structure (Cherniss, 1980a, b), APS offices will likely vary. It makes sense, knowing what the literature has to say on employee participation in decision making, that APS staff be allowed as much autonomy as possible. This is especially true in light of the number of variables over which APS workers have little, or no control.

Normative Structure

The normative structure (Cherniss, 1980a, b) of APS will dictate how clients are treated, how families are handled, how the APS worker interacts with other agencies, and how the worker presents him/herself to the community. It will determine worker ethics, and it will establish accountability. In addition, the normative structure will determine how employee stress and burnout are handled. It is our impression that APS offices vary greatly in their values, dictated by the local community, other agencies, and management.

CAREER THEORY, STRESS, AND BURNOUT IN APS

As a segue into the solution portion of this chapter, we provide a brief discussion of how career theory is linked with stressful employment. Career theory is often overlooked in the literature on burnout, or given only token mention (an exception to this is Cherniss, 1980a, b). As with the literature on stress and burnout in general, the literature on career theory has not been written specifically for APS. It is, nonetheless, highly relevant to APS.

According to at least one theory of career development, a state of discorrespondence between the needs of the worker and the reinforcement capabilities of the work site can cause worker stress and/or dissatisfaction (Lofquist & Dawis, 1969). This theory of "work adjustment" (Osipow, 1983, p. 119) also considers the abilities of the worker to meet the needs of the work environment. In effect, the needs of the worker and the needs of the employer (i.e., the work site) must be reciprocally met (i.e., a state of correspondance between employer and employee) for the worker and employer to be satisfied with the employment arrangement over the long term.

This theory offers four dynamics to explain the resolution between the needs of the worker and the employer (Osipow, 1983). All four can be characteristic of the employee, employer, or both. The first two can be subsumed under the rubric of activeness: Reactive and active. If either party is not getting their needs met in the employment arrangement, then either party can decide to take a proactive or reactive stance in the resolution of such discorrespondence. Of course, taking a proactive stance implies anticipated concerns and preventative actions which is typically a more desirable means of problem solving. Taking a reactive stance implies that a problem already exists, and that there needs to be some sort of reaction to the demands of the other party.

Next, is the dynamic of flexibility. How flexible (on a continuum of flexibility to rigidity) is the employer/employee in which needs are to be met, and in the way they are to be met? There are typically multiple ways to complete a job task, or, as in APS, several ways to handle a case. The flexibility of the parties in determining the appropriate means to achieve the task will affect each party's evaluation of the outcome (and the subsequent experience of correspondence, or mutual satisfaction). The last dynamic refers to the speed at which each party can meet the needs, or adjust to meet the needs, of the other (the authors refer to this dynamic as celerity) (Osipow, 1983).

The work adjustment theory of Lofquist and Dawis (1969) also can be used to explain the inverse relationship between age and burnout noted earlier (e.g., Maslach, 1982). According to the theory, younger workers would not have differentiated their needs yet, or crystallized their direction in life. In effect, younger workers are less mature and less stable than their older counterparts. Hence, they may be more susceptible to stressful job requirements. Such is likely to be the case in APS-type work. The younger worker is likely to be more susceptible to the effects of role ambiguity, role conflict, and the high volume and the type of problems encountered, than would be the more mature and seasoned worker.

Not only does the domain of career theory address work satisfaction, but it addresses life satisfaction as well (Lofquist & Dawis, 1969; Osipow, 1983; Sharf, 1992; Super, 1990). Employee needs that are not met at work can be fulfilled off the job. The needs of the worker (including APS workers) will not only vary from person to person, but will also vary from time to time in the same person's life. According to Super (1990), individuals have several different areas of need that continue to varying degrees throughout the life development cycle. These areas include: Worker, homemaker, citizen, leisure, student, and child (Sharf, 1992; Super, 1990). As can be seen, work is but one area among several. Employee needs that are not satisfied at work do have the potential of being met in other areas (e.g., hobbies, volunteer work, interpersonal relationships). Indeed, many of the personal prescriptions for stress reduction (on the part of the individual) in the literature have included off-the-job activities.

Lofquist and Dawis (1969), as well as other career theorists (Osipow, 1983; Sharf, 1992), propose (or admit) that there comes a point where a stressed, or dissatisfied worker must consider finding new employment. The consensus among the major career theorists appears to be that not everyone is cut out for all types of employment (Holland, 1973; Krumboltz, 1979; Lofquist & Dawis, 1969; Roe, 1956; Super, 1990). This is likely to be true for work similar to that of APS. To leave such employment is not to admit defeat, but is rather an attempt to find a good match between one's own traits/needs and the environment of the workplace. In this respect, there are those who view burnout as an adaptive reaction, a signal to the worker that it is time to move on, particularly when client services are suffering (Daley, 1979; see also Jackson, Schwab, & Schuler, 1986).

COPING WITH STRESS AND BURNOUT

The most efficient way to cope with burnout is to prevent it. This, however, is not always possible. Given the person-to-person variability in the subjective experience of stress discussed earlier, what is preventative for one person could be burnout promoting for another. This is not to say that we should not try. Rather, we should be aware that there are exceptions to each case, and that flexibility in approaches to the problem is the key to success. This section will approach the issue of coping in a way that is consistent with the models presented earlier (i.e., internal/external, or worker/organizational factors). We begin with a discussion of worker issues, and then continue with a discussion on organizational changes that may limit workers' experience of stress and burnout.

Before we proceed, we offer a simplified description of burnout. In much simpler terms, burnout is but a special case of induced (or exogenous) depression. The elements described by Maslach (1982) are reminiscent of what has been written on depression. Emotional exhaustion (Maslach, 1982) is a hallmark of depression (APA, 1987). In addition, depression connotes pessimism, or negative attitudes toward others (i.e., depersonalization), and feelings of worthlessness (i.e., lack of personal accomplishment). This is predicated upon the fact that the concept of learned helplessness (Seligman, 1975) underlies the phenomenon of burnout, and is known to be a factor in depression (Gleitman, 1986). Therefore, our approach to the treatment or prevention of burnout will be very similar to that of working with depression.

Personal Issues

First, it is important that the individual realize that it is permissible to experience burnout. It has been demonstrated that workers can, and do, move in and out of the elements of burnout during their work lives (Schwab, Jackson, & Schuler, 1986). In this sense, it is not abnormal to have periods of work related depression, and the cynicism that accompanies it.

When does burnout become a problem? The literature on the subject does not readily address this. Once we equate the problem with depression, however, we do have criteria that we can use. The DSM–III–R (APA, 1987) indicates that depression (or any other psychological concern) is problematic when it interferes with the individual's "social or occupational functioning" (APA, 1987, p. 221). One can begin to see the value of objective and accurate supervisory feedback to the worker in determining the effect of worker mood and attitude on job performance.

As we saw in the multiple stage model of emotions and behavior, there are several stages where the worker experiencing stress can intervene on his/her own behalf. The first would be in the area of self-talk, challenging one's perceptions, or expectations of the work setting (see Meichenbaum, 1985). For APS workers this could include restructuring the way in which the worker perceives clientele. For example, if the APS worker has unrealistic expectations of the client and/or familial appreciation for interventions, then he/she may become confused and disappointed when the expectations are not met. The worker can inoculate him/herself against such emotional consequences by modifying expectancies to include the fact that clients and/or their caregivers are not highly functioning individuals and, therefore, cannot always be expected to react in an appropriate manner (or even in their own best interest). This is unfortunate, but true.

Similar changes in expectancies toward other community agencies (e.g., police, social services, community mental health) may also help the APS worker in lessening the experience of emotional defeat. It is likely that workers in these other agencies are required to operate within their own parameters, suffering their own sources of stress and burnout, and cannot be expected to respond in a manner that the APS worker would always like. We are not implying that the APS worker settle for mediocracy. What we are suggesting, is that if the APS worker harbors unrealistic expectations of clientele and/or other agencies, and these expectations are not met, negative stereotypes can be generated. Workers can then be heard to say "why bother calling the so-and-so agency, they won't do anything anyway," or, "these types of reports are useless, the client isn't going to cooperate anyway." Indeed, there may be, and usually is, partial truth to these, and similar, statements. The danger exists when such perceptions are generalized and lead to frustration and other emotions. In addition, there is the danger that such perceptions will limit output and increase client neglect, which will lead to guilt on the part of the worker.

The point that we are emphasizing, is that it is not only the APS worker that is having difficulties. Those with whom the APS worker comes into contact are experiencing difficulties as well (e.g., clients, superiors, social workers). It is the perceptions and expectations that are of concern to us as mental health professionals.

Cognitive (or self-talk) issues are relevant to the resolution of role ambiguity and role conflict. For example, two APS workers in the same job situation may have quite different perceptions. Clarification of roles within the organization may be an active way in which workers can resolve such concerns.

In the multiple stage model, emotions are easiest to access via the self-talk process. There are, however, other ways. The most notable is through the use of some form of relaxation training or meditation. In fact, many stress management programs incorporate these tasks (e.g., Whittlesey, 1986; Farmer et al., 1984). The relaxation response is helpful to learn. It can be cued during breaks throughout a stressful day to limit the additive effects of stress. The reader is referred to the references on the subject, or to professionals in the area of stress management, for further, more comprehensive information.

The behavior stage would also be an efficient place for the APS worker to intervene in job-related stress. Taking an active (Lofquist & Dawis, 1969) stance to modify the job environment would be an option for the APS worker (see Gerstein & Shullman, 1992). The APS personnel with whom we spoke appeared to be open to learning a better way to operate. The field worker is in a unique position to see where improvements can be made and then to convey this to his/her superior(s). The first rule, is to do a good job.

Leisure activities, play, and exercise can be ways to relieve accumulated anger and frustration (i.e., stress). These are also ways to meet other needs in life away from the job (Super, 1990). In fact, most stress management programs include some form of physical activity (exercise at a minimum) as well. There does arise a concern, however, in those APS positions where the worker's private time is interfered with in some way (e.g., working late, on-call duty).

In summary, there do appear to be measures that the individual APS worker can take to lessen the impact of job-related stress in his/her life (thereby reducing the chances of burnout). The worker can exercise influence over his/her self-talk, emotions, and behavior. Rewarding oneself for a job well done during work hours is one way that reinforcement can be provided. Leaving the job at the office can prove helpful to interpersonal relationships outside of work. Exercise and leisure activities may also be beneficial. The APS worker would do well to be jealous with his/her time away from work, not volunteering for after-hours duties (beyond what is customary) and by taking the phone off of the hook when not on duty (be warned that the superior may not appreciate this). Lastly, finding a job that meets one's needs, perhaps leaving APS work, may be the appropriate course of action for some.

Organizational Response to Burnout

Just as there are several strategies that APS workers can implement to limit the amount of stress experienced, so too there are measures that can be taken at the institutional level. As mentioned previously, it is believed that the organizational contribution to stress and burnout, and, hence, its control, far exceeds the individual's contribution or control (Cherniss, 1980a, b; Maslach, 1982; Whitehead, 1989).

Sauter, Murphy, and Hurrell (1990) suggested seven areas that employers can, and should, address to limit stress on the part of their employees: "Work load and work pace, work schedule, work roles, job future, social environment, job content, and participation and control" (p. 1151). Some of these may or may not be applicable to the local APS office, depending upon the size of the office (i.e., number of staff). The benefit to APS, as with other agencies/employers, would be seen in less employee illness, sick leave taken, increased performance, and lower employee turnover.

Work load and work pace seems pertinent to APS. Some authors (e.g., Maslach, 1982; Sauter et al., 1990) appear to be concerned as much with underwork as with overwork. Underwork did not appear relevant to those APS workers with whom we spoke. The staff to case (or referral) ratios that we encountered in conversation with APS staff appeared unmanageable. Given the limited budgets of APS offices, staff increases are unlikely. Therefore, creative means to lighten the load will need to be examined. The information that we received during our interviews led us to believe that many referrals were of a protective nature to the worker who make them (i.e., meant to protect them from liability), wasting much APS time and energy. Brainstorming for solutions might include some community public relations in which those agencies that supply the largest numbers of referrals are educated on what constitutes an appropriate referral.

The work schedule should allow not only time away from work, but also time away from the threat of work. The nature of APS work demands flexibility in work hours. A burned out worker is of limited value to the community that he/she serves. Emergencies occur 24 hours per day. A plausible solution would be to rotate after-hours duty (regardless of who's clients surface). For offices with limited staff, perhaps other agencies could be relied upon to handle after-hours emergencies. Similar arrangements could also be made with APS workers from adjacent counties. Carrying a pager or breaking out in a cold sweat when the phone rings is no way to spend one's time away from the job. The time away from the job is best spent replenishing emotional reservoirs.

Work roles would subsume role conflict and ambiguity discussed previously (Cherniss, 1980a, b). In positions where almost every case brings with it a unique set of circumstances, the more specific that the organization is with its parameters of operation, the easier (i.e., the less stressful) it is for the employee to make decisions. The APS worker is the agent of APS. It is, therefore, incumbent upon APS to define employee role parameters (for employee health as well as liability—another stressful item). We are careful to use the term parameter to connote that while the organization needs to define employee roles and functions, employees need to have latitude in operation (for efficiency, sense of control, and reduced stress).

APS programs have not impressed us as being large enough to spend much time discussing employee advancement. In fact, APS appears to be more of a job than a career. Some employees may use APS as an entry level position in government service. Others may transfer in for higher pay (in rare instances), or to escape other positions. This is not to say, however, that an employee's job future should not be addressed. The organization should be honest with its employees about what the future is likely to hold for them in APS. Briefing job candidates about their job future, even if bleak, can help to avoid problems in the long run.

The social environment of the workplace can also be instrumental in limiting stress (Gerstein & Shullman, 1992). In our estimation, two factors are relevant here. These are interpersonal relationships with one's fellow employees, and supervision.

APS workers are exposed to many, and varied external stressors on the job. In such situations it is important that there be a degree of internal cohesion. The unit supervisor can be an asset in facilitating such cohesion. The first author of this chapter spent considerable time employed as an emergency services worker with a community mental health agency. The unit consisted of five workers and a supervisor. Similar to APS, there was much in the way of environmental press: Involuntary/angry/threatening clients and families, conflicts with medical staff in local emergency rooms, conflicts with law enforcement regarding the disposition of cases, conflicts with inpatient psychiatric facilities that did not want to take psychotic patients, and being in a high profile position (i.e., the agency's representatives to the community). Our supervisor was very supportive and was successful at developing a sense of camaraderie. Emotional relief after a frustrating encounter was often found by bending the ear of the supervisor, or the ear(s) of a co-worker(s). In addition, most of us met daily to discuss the job. The constant exchange of support and ideas also allowed for a certain amount of employee participation and control (the last item of Sauter et al., 1990) in the operation of the unit. It was a difficult situation made better by the qualities of the supervisor. Those APS workers in one-person offices may need to form other professional connections, or support systems, to use in this regard.

The second element of the social environment is supervision as related to the level of employee experience. There is a large base of research to support the common sense idea that beginning human services workers have different supervisory needs than more experienced workers (e.g., Stoltenberg, 1981; Olk & Friedlander, 1992). In general, the beginning employee will need (and likely want) more direction and advice than the more seasoned employee (Worthington & Roehlke, 1979; Wiley & Ray, 1986; Worthington, 1987). Even seasoned professionals may require increased supervision and direction when changing their circumstances (e.g., job setting, clientele) (Worthington, 1984). Such directive supervision can also aid in diffusing role conflict and ambiguity issues of the new employee. The key, however, is for the supervisor to encourage autonomy on the part of the worker, and to know when to back off (Stoltenberg, 1984).

Job content refers to the activity of the worker. Given the nature of APS (i.e., large work loads, low numbers of staff), there may not be much that a local office can do in this regard. If the number of staff is high enough, workers may be able to establish specified work assignments (i.e., made up of particular categories of cases, administrative or appearance duties, paperwork) and rotate through these activities (i.e., taking a break from what one would consider to be the more stressful assignments).

In summary, there are several approaches that an organization can pursue to limit the amount of stress experienced by its workers. Some of these may be applicable to APS, while others might not. The determining factor seems to be the size of the local APS office/unit. It is our understanding that it is not uncommon, particularly in rural areas, for the entire APS staff to be comprised of one person. In such cases, that one individual needs to be creative, reaching out to others in the physical environment (perhaps other civil servants officed nearby) to form a social network of support. Creative solutions are required for APS to meet the psychological needs of its workers.

CONCLUSION

As stated in the beginning of the chapter, there is a derth of research relevant to stress and/or burnout in APS work. In a real sense, this area is wide open for research. Opportunities abound. We wonder, however, about the practical applications of such work. It is reasonable to conclude that, given the volume of clientele, amount of conflict, and limited resources, APS work is a breeding ground for stress and burnout. It is most likely that research will only serve to confirm this.

It is our belief that research with sociopolitical aims would have the broadest impact on APS staff stress. A major concern in the alleviation of APS stress would be the increase of staff and resources. Therefore, program evaluation research that could be presented to state legislators in an effort to convince them to increase funding would have the greatest impact on APS stress and burnout. Such research must focus attention on the community need for APS services, the benefit that APS has already provided to the community, the unreasonable caseloads of APS workers (including the number of cases that go under-investigated because of this), and how additional programs would improve services to the community.

It is unlikely that APS could conduct such research on its own. In our estimation, APS, at the state or national levels, would do well to form alliances with human services organizations or university departments (e.g., criminal justice, social work, sociology, psychology) that could provide such support. In the academic arena, such research could be underwritten by research grants or, as is the case with much research, by the university itself (by allowing its staff the liberty to engage in the research of their choice).

The road is rough for APS (i.e., under-budgeted, understaffed, and overworked). It is unlikely that little will change until legislators become willing to loosen the purse strings. The bright spot in all of this, is the dedication that APS workers bring with them to their duties, and their own abilities to effectively cope with burnout. State and local governments would do well to realize this dedication and the service that APS provides, and to reward them appropriately.

REFERENCES

American Psychiatric Association. (1987). *Diagnostic and statistical manual of mental disorders* (3rd ed., rev.). Washington, DC: Author.

Anderson, C. R. (1977). Locus of control, coping behaviors, and performance in a stress setting: A longitudinal study. *Journal of Applied Psychology, 62,* 446–451.

Ashford, S. J. (1988). Individual strategies for coping with stress during organizational transitions. *The Journal of Applied Behavioral Science, 24*(1), 19–36.

Bajtelsmit, J. W. & Gershman, L. (1976). Covert positive reinforcement: Efficacy and conceptualization. *Journal of Behavioral Therapy and Experimental Psychiatry, 7,* 207–212.

Bandura, A. (1986). *Social foundations of thought and action: A social-cognitive theory.* Englewood Cliffs, NJ: Prentice-Hall.

Bandura, A. (1992). Exercise of personal agency through the self-efficacy mechanism. In R. Schwarzer (Ed.), *Self-efficacy: Thought control of action* (pp. 3–38). Washington, D.C.: Hemisphere Publishing.

Bandura, A., Taylor, C. B., Williams, S. L., Mefford, I. N., & Barchas, J. D. (1985). Catecholamine secretion as a function of perceived coping self-efficacy. *Journal of Consulting and Clinical Psychology, 53,* 406–414.

Bedeian, A. G. & Armenakis, A. A. (1981). A path analysis study of the consequences of role conflict and role ambiguity. *Academy of Management Journal, 24,* 417–424.

Beck, C. L. & Garguilo, R. M. (1983). Burnout in teachers of retarded and nonretarded children. *Journal of Educational Research, 76,* 169–173.

Beehr, T. A. & Newman, J. E. (1978). Job stress, employee health, and organizational effectiveness: A facet analysis, model, and literature review. *Personnel Psychology, 31,* 665–699.

Bensky, J. M., Shaw, S. F., Gouse, A. S., Bates, H., Dixon, B., & Beane, W. E. (1980).

Public Law 94-142 and stress: A problem for educators. *Exceptional Children, 47,* 24–29.

Berkeley Planning Associates. (1977). *Evaluation of child abuse and neglect demonstration projects 1974–1977: Vol. 9. Project management and worker burnout: Final report.* Springfield, VA: National Technical Information Service (NCHSR 78-72).

Bulman, R. J. & Wortman, C. B. (1977). Attribution of blame and coping in the "real world": Severe accident victims react to their lot. *Journal of Personality and Social Psychology, 35,* 351–363.

Byrne, B. M. (1991). Burnout: Investigating the impact of background variables for elementary, intermediate, secondary, and university educators. *Teaching and Teacher Education, 7*(2), 197–209.

Cherniss, C. (1980a). *Professional burnout in human services organizations.* New York: Preager.

Cherniss, C. (1980b). *Staff burnout: Job stress in the human services.* Beverly Hills: Sage.

Crane, S. J. & Iwanicki, E. F. (1986). Perceived role conflict, role ambiguity, and burnout among special education teachers. *RASE-Remedial and Special Education, 7*(2), 24–31.

Daley, M. R. (1979). Burnout: Smoldering problem in protective services. *Social Work,* 375–379.

Devine, P. G. (1989). Stereotypes and prejudice: The automatic and controlled components. *Journal of Personality and Social Psychology, 56,* 5–18.

Dompierre, J. & Lavoie, F. (1987, January). *Empirical examination of an occupational stress model.* Paper presented at Division 27 of the APA annual meeting, New York.

Duncan, O. D. (1975). *Introduction to structural equation models.* New York: Academic Press.

Edelwich, J. & Brodsky, A. (1980). *Burnout: Stages of disillusionment in the helping professions.* New York: Human Sciences Press.

Ellis, A. (1973). *Humanistic psychotherapy.* New York: McGraw-Hill.

Farber, B. A. (1983). Introduction: A critical perspective on burnout. In B.A. Farber (Ed.), *Stress and burnout in the human service professions* (pp. 1–20). New York: Pergamon.

Farber, B. A. (1982). *Stress and burnout: Implications for teacher motivation.* Paper presented at the Annual Meeting of the American Educational Research Association, New York.

Farmer, R. E., Monahan, L. H., & Hekeler, R. W. (1984). *Stress management for human services.* Beverly Hills: Sage.

Farrell, D. & Rusbult, C. E. (1981). Exchange variables as predictors of job satisfaction, job commitment, and turnover: The impact of rewards, costs, alternatives, and investments. *Organizational Behavior and Human Performance, 27,* 79–95.

Freudenberger, H. J. & Richelson, G. (1980). *Burnout: The high cost of high achievement.* Garden City, NY: Anchor Press.

Friedman, M. & Rosenman, R. (1974). *Type A behavior and your heart.* Greenwich, CT: Fawcett.

Froehlich, W. D. (1978). Stress, anxiety, and the control of attention: A psychophysiological approach. In C.D. Spielberger & I.G. Sarason (Eds.), *Stress and anxiety* (vol. 5, pp. 99–130). New York: John Wiley.

Gann, M. L. (1979). *The role of personality factors and job characteristics in burnout: A study of social service workers.* Unpublished doctoral dissertation, University of California, Berkeley.

Gerstein, L. H. & Russell, N. (1990). The experience of medical school: A major life crisis. *College Student Journal, 24*(2), 128–138.

Gerstein, L. H. & Shullman, S. L. (1992). Counseling psychology and the work place: The emergence of organizational counseling psychology. In S. D. Brown & R. W. Lent (Eds.), *Handbook of Counseling Psychology* (2nd ed., pp. 581–625). New York: John Wiley.

Gerstein, L. H., Topp, C. G., & Correll, G. (1987). The role of the environment and person when predicting burnout among correctional personnel. *Criminal Justice and Behavior, 14*(3), 352–369.

Gleitman, H. (1986). *Psychology* (2nd ed). New York: W. W. Norton.

Golembiewski, R. T., Munzenrider, R. F., & Stevenson, J. G. (1986). *Stress in organizations: Toward a phase model of burnout.* New York: Preager.

Golembiewski, R. T. & Roundtree, B. H. (1986). Phases of burnout and properties of working environments: Replicating and extending a pattern of covariants. *Organization Development Journal, 7*(7), 25–30.

Harrison, W. D. (1980). Role strain and burnout in child-protective service workers. *Social Services Review, 54,* 31–44.

Heckman, S. J. (1980). *Effects of work setting, theoretical orientation, and personality on psychotherapist burnout.* Unpublished doctoral dissertation, California School of Professional Psychology, Berkeley.

Heppner, P. P., Kivlighan, D. M., & Wampold, B. E. (1992). *Research design in counseling.* Pacific Grove, CA: Brooks/Cole.

Herrick, J., Takagi, C. Y., Coleman, R., & Morgan, L. J. (1983). Social workers who left the profession: An exploratory study. *Journal of Sociology and Social Welfare, 10*(1), 78–94.

Hinkle, L. E. (1974). The effect of exposure to culture change, social change, and changes in interpersonal relationships on health. In B.S. Dohrenwend & B.P. Dohrenwend (Eds.), *Stressful life events: Their nature and effects* (pp. 9–44). New York: John Wiley.

Holahan, C. J. & Moos, R. H. (1985). Life stress and health: Personality, coping, and family support in stress resistance. *Journal of Personality and Social Psychology, 49*(3), 739–747.

Holland, J. L. (1973). *Making vocational choices: A theory of careers.* Englewood Cliffs, NJ: Prentice-Hall.

House, J. S. (1981). *Work stress and social support.* Reading, MA: Addison-Wesley.

Jackson, S. E. (1983). Participation in decision making as a strategy for reducing job-related strain. *Journal of Applied Psychology, 68*(1), 3–19.

Jackson, S. E., Schwab, R. L. & Schuler, R. S. (1986). Toward an understanding of the burnout phenomenon. *Journal of Applied Psychology, 71*(4), 630–640.

Johnson, D. W. (1980). Attitude modification methods. In F. H. Kanfer & A. P.

Goldstein (Eds.), *Helping people change: A textbook of methods* (2nd ed., pp. 58–96). New York: Pergamon.

Johnson, J. H. & Sarason, I. G. (1978). Life stress, depression, and anxiety: Internal-external control as a moderator variable. *Journal of Psychosomatic Research, 22,* 205–208.

Kahn, R. L. (1978). Job burnout: Prevention and remedies. *Public Welfare, 36,* 61–63.

Karasek, R. A. (1979). Job demands, job decision latitude, and mental strain: Implications for job redesign. *Administrative Science Quarterly, 24,* 285–308.

Kemery, E. R., Bedeian, A. G., Mossholder, K. W., & Touliatos, J. (1985). Outcomes of role stress: A multisample constructive replication. *Academy of Management Journal, 28,* 363–375.

Kobasa, S. C. (1979). Stressful life events, Personality, and health: An inquiry into hardiness. *Journal of Personality and Social Psychology, 37*(1), 1–11.

Kobasa, S. & Maddi, S. (1981). Personality and constitution as mediators in the stress-illness relationship. *Journal of Health and Social Behavior, 22,* 365–378.

Kobasa, S. C., Maddi, S. R., & Kahn, S. (1982). Hardiness and health: A prospective study. *Journal of Personality and Social Psychology, 42*(1), 168–177.

Kobasa, S. C. & Puccetti, M. C. (1983). Personality and social resources in stress resistance. *Journal of Personality and Social Psychology, 45*(4), 839–850.

Krumboltz, J. D. (1979). A social learning theory of career decision making. In A. M. Mitchell, G. B. Jones, & J. D. Krumboltz (Eds.), *Social learning and career decision making* (pp. 19–49). Cranston, RI: Carroll.

Lazarus, R. S. *Psychological stress and the coping process.* New York: McGraw-Hill.

Lazarus, R. (1981). The stress and coping paradigm. In C. Eisdorfer, D. Cohen, A. Kleinman, & P. Maxim (Eds.), *Models for clinical psychopathology* (pp. 177–214). Englewood Cliffs, NJ: Prentice-Hall.

Lefcourt, H. M. (1980). Locus of control and coping with life's events. In E. Staub (Ed.), *Personality: Basic aspects and current research* (pp. 200–235). Englewood Cliffs, NJ: Prentice-Hall.

Lindquist, C. A. & Whitehead, J. T. (1986). Burnout, job stress and job satisfaction among Southern correctional officers: Perceptions and causal factors. *Journal of Offender Services, Counseling and Rehabilitation, 10*(4), 5–26.

Lofquist, L. H. & Dawis, R. V. (1969). *Adjustment to work.* Englewood Cliffs, NJ: Prentice-Hall.

Maier, S. F., Seligman, M. E. P., & Solomon, R. L. (1969). Pavlovian fear conditioning and learned helplessness: Effects on escape and avoidance behavior of (a) the CS–US contingency and (b) the independence of the US and voluntary responding. In B. A. Campbell & R. M. Church (Eds.), *Punishment and aversive behavior* (pp. 299–342). New York: Appleton-Century-Crofts.

Maslach, C. (1982). *Burnout: The cost of caring.* Englewood Cliffs, NJ: Prentice-Hall.

Maslach, C. (1976). Burned out. *Human Behavior, 5*(9), 16–22.

Maslach, C. & Jackson, S. E. (1981). The measurement of experienced burnout. *Journal of Occupational Behavior, 2,* 99–113.

Maslach, C. & Jackson, S. E. (1982). *Maslach Burnout Inventory.* Palo Alto, CA: Consulting Psychologist Press.

Maslach, C., Jackson, S. E., & Barad, C. B. (1982). *Patterns of burnout among a national sample of public contact workers.* Unpublished manuscript.

Mason, J. (1975). An historical view of the stress field. *Journal of Human Stress, 1,* 6–12.

Matthews, K. A. (1982). Psychological perspectives on the Type A behavior pattern. *Psychological Bulletin, 91,* 293–323.

Maultsby, M. C. (1980). *Your guide to emotional well being: The handbook of rational self counseling.* Lexington, KY: Rational Self-Help Aids.

Maultsby, M. C. (1984). *Rational behavior therapy.* Englewood Cliffs, NJ: Prentice-Hall.

McMichael, A. (1978). Personality, behavior, and situational modifiers of work stressors. In C. L. Cooper & R. Payne (Eds.), *Stress at work* (pp. 127–147). New York: Wiley.

Meichenbaum, D. (1977). *Cognitive-behavior modification: An integrative approach.* New York: Plenum.

Meichenbaum, D. (1985). *Stress inoculation training.* New York: Pergamon.

Meier, S. T. (1983). Toward a theory of burnout. *Human Relations, 36*(10), 899–910.

Miles, R. H. & Perreault, W. D. (1976). Organizational role conflict: Its antecedents and consequences. *Organizational Behavior and Human Performance, 17,* 19–44.

Mobley, W. H., Horner, S. O., & Hollingsworth, A. T. (1978). An evaluation of the precursors of hospital employee turnover. *Journal of Applied Psychology, 63,* 408–414.

Monet, A. & Lazarus, R. S. (1977). *Stress and coping.* New York: Columbia University Press.

Morris, J. H. & Sherman, J. D. (1981). Generalizability of an organizational commitment model. *Academy of Management Journal, 24,* 512–526.

Oliver, R. L. & Brief, A. P. (1977). Determinants and consequences of role conflict and ambiguity among retail sales managers. *Journal Of Retailing, 53*(4), 47–58.

Olk, M. E. & Friedlander, M. L. (1992). Trainees' experiences of role conflict and role ambiguity in supervisory relationships. *Journal of Counseling Psychology, 39*(3), 389–397.

Olson, J. & Matuskey, P. V. (1982). Causes of burnout in SLD teachers. *Journal of Learning Disabilities, 15,* 97–99.

Osipow, S. H. (1983). *Theories of career development* (3rd ed.). Englewood Cliffs, NJ: Prentice-Hall.

Pavlov, I. (1927). *Conditioned reflexes.* Oxford, England: Oxford University Press.

Pedhazur, E. J. & Schmelkin, L. P. (1992). *Measurement, design, and analysis: An integrated approach.* Hillsdale, NJ: Lawrence Erlbaum.

Pines, A. & Aronson, E. (1981). *Burnout: From tedium to personal growth.* New York: Free Press.

Pines, A. & Aronson, E. (1988). *Career burnout: Causes and cures.* New York: Free Press.

Pines, A. & Kafry, D. (1978). Occupational tedium in the social services. *Social Work, 23,* 499–507.

Quick, J. C. & Quick, J. D. (1984). *Organizational stress and preventative management.* New York: McGraw-Hill.

Revicki, D. A. & May, H. J. (1989). Organizational characteristics, occupational stress, and mental health in nurses. *Behavioral Medicine, 15*(1), 30–36.

Roe, A. (1956). *The psychology of occupations.* New York: Wiley.

Ross, R. R., Altmaier, E. M., & Russell, D. W. (1989). Job stress, social support, and burnout among counseling center staff. *Journal of Counseling Psychology, 36*(4), 464–470.

Rotter, J. B. (1966). Generalized expectancies for internal versus external control of reinforcement. *Psychological Monographs, 80*(1).

Rotter, J. B., Chance, J. E., & Phares, E. J. (1972). *Applications of social learning theory of personality.* New York: Holt, Rinehart, and Winston.

Sauter, S. L., Murphy, L. R., & Hurrell, J. J. (1990). Prevention of work-related psychological disorders: A national strategy proposed by the National Institute for Occupational Safety and Health (NIOSH). *American Psychologist, 45*(10), 1146–1158.

Schacter, S. & Singer, J. (1962). Cognitive, social and psychological determinants of emotional states. *Psychological Review, 69,* 379–399.

Schaubroeck, J., Cotton, J. L., & Jennings, K. R. (1989). Antecedents and consequences of role stress: A covariance structure analysis. *Journal of Organizational Behavior, 10,* 35–58.

Schwab, R. L., Jackson, S. E., & Schuler, R. S. (1986). Educator burnout: Sources and consequences. *Educational Research Quarterly, 10*(3), 14–30.

Seligman, M. E. P. (1975). *Helplessness: On depression, development and death.* San Francisco: Freeman.

Seligman, M. E. P., Klein, D. C., & Miller, W. R. (1976). Depression. In H. Leitenberg (Ed.), *Handbook of behavior modification and behavior therapy.* Englewood Cliffs, NJ: Prentice-Hall.

Seligman, M. E. P. & Maier, S. F. (1967). Failure to escape traumatic shock. *Journal of Experimental Psychology, 74,* 1–9.

Selye, H. (1979). The stress concept and some of its implications. In V. Hamilton & D.M. Warburton (Eds.), *Human stress and cognition.* New York: John Wiley.

Selye, H. (1976). *The stress of life.* New York: McGraw-Hill.

Sharf, R. S. (1992). *Applying career development theory to counseling.* Pacific Grove, CA: Brooks/Cole.

Shinn, M., Rosario, M., Morch, H., & Chestnut, D. E. (1984). Coping with job stress and burnout in the human services. *Journal of Personality and Social Psychology, 46*(4), 864–876.

Skinner, B. F. (1953). *Science and human behavior.* New York: Macmillan.

Steers, R. M. (1977). Antecedents and outcomes of organizational commitment. *Administrative Science Quarterly, 22,* 46–56.

Steers, R. M. & Mowday, R. T. (1981). Employee turnover and post-decision accommodation processes. *Research in Organizational Behavior, 3.*

Stevens, J. M., Beyer, J. M., & Trice, H. M. (1978). Assessing personal, role, and organizational predictors of managerial commitment. *Academy of Management Journal, 21,* 380–396.

Stoltenberg, C. (1981). Approaching supervision from a developmental perspective: The counselor complexity model. *Journal of Counseling Psychology, 28*(1), 59–65.

Storms, P. L. & Spector, P. E. (1987). Relationships of organizational frustration with reported behavioral reactions: The moderating effect of locus of control. *Journal of Occupational Psychology, 60,* 227–234.

Super, D. E. (1990). A life-span, life-space approach to career development. In D. Brown & L. Brooks (Eds.), *Career choice and development: Applying contemporary theories to practice* (2nd ed., pp. 197–261). San Francisco: Jossey-Bass.

Tache, J. & Selye, H. (1978). On stress and coping mechanisms. In C.D. Spielberger & I.G. Sarason (Eds.), *Stress and anxiety* (vol. 5, pp. 3–24). New York: John Wiley & Sons.

Thorndike, E. L. (1911). *Animal intelligence: Experimental studies.* New York: Macmillan.

van der Ploeg, H. M., van Leeuwen, J. J., & Kwee, M. G. T. (1990). Burnout among Dutch psychotherapists. *Psychological Reports, 67,* 107–112.

Watson, J. B. & Rayner, R. (1920). Conditioned emotional reactions. *Journal of Experimental Psychology, 3,* 1–14.

Watson, D. L. & Tharp, R. G. (1992). *Self-directed behavior: Self-modification for personal adjustment* (6th ed.). Pacific Grove, CA: Brooks/Cole.

Whitehead, J. T. (1989). *Burnout in probations and corrections.* New York: Preager.

Whitehead, J. T. & Lindquist, C. A. (1986). Job stress and burnout among probation/parole officers: Perceptions and causal factors. *International Journal of Offender Therapy and Comparative Criminology, 29,* 109–119.

Whittlesey, M. (1986). *Stress.* Springhouse, PA: Springhouse Corporation.

Wiley, M. O. & Ray, P. B. (1986). Counseling supervision by developmental level. *Journal of Counseling Psychology, 33,* 439–445.

Williams, L. L. & Hazer, J. T. (1986). Antecedents and consequences of satisfaction and commitment in turnover models: A reanalysis using latent variable structural equation methods. *Journal of Applied Psychology, 71,* 219–231.

Worthington, E. L. (1984). Empirical investigation of supervision of counselors as they gain experience. *Journal of Counseling Psychology, 31*(1), 63–75.

Worthington, E. L. (1987). Changes in supervision as counselors and supervisors gain experience: A review. *Professional Psychology: Research and Practice, 18*(3), 189–208.

Worthington, E. L. & Roehlke, H. J. (1979). Effective supervision as perceived by beginning counselors-in-training. *Journal of Counseling Psychology, 26*(1), 64–73.

Wunder, R.S., Dougherty, T. W., & Welsh, M. A. (1982). A causal model of role stress and employee turnover. *42nd Annual Proceedings of the Academy of Management,* New York, pp. 297–301.

AUTHOR INDEX

SUBJECT INDEX

239